MW00813516

# TABLE OF CONTENTS

# Top 20 Test Taking Tips

1. Carefully follow all the test registration procedures
2. Know the test directions, duration, topics, question types, how many questions
3. Setup a flexible study schedule at least 3-4 weeks before test day
4. Study during the time of day you are most alert, relaxed, and stress free
5. Maximize your learning style; visual learner use visual study aids, auditory learner use auditory study aids
6. Focus on your weakest knowledge base
7. Find a study partner to review with and help clarify questions
8. Practice, practice, practice
9. Get a good night's sleep; don't try to cram the night before the test
10. Eat a well balanced meal
11. Know the exact physical location of the testing site; drive the route to the site prior to test day
12. Bring a set of ear plugs; the testing center could be noisy
13. Wear comfortable, loose fitting, layered clothing to the testing center; prepare for it to be either cold or hot during the test
14. Bring at least 2 current forms of ID to the testing center
15. Arrive to the test early; be prepared to wait and be patient
16. Eliminate the obviously wrong answer choices, then guess the first remaining choice
17. Pace yourself; don't rush, but keep working and move on if you get stuck
18. Maintain a positive attitude even if the test is going poorly
19. Keep your first answer unless you are positive it is wrong
20. Check your work, don't make a careless mistake

# Understanding Students with Learning Disabilities

**Learning disabilities**

<u>Basics</u>
People with learning disabilities frequently are very intelligent and have strong leadership skills. They often show amazing abilities in creative areas like art and music or are athletically gifted. They simply process information differently than others do. Learning disabilities tend to run in families. Basic reading and language difficulties are the most common issues encountered. People with learning disabilities are never "cured," but learn ways to cope with and work around whatever problems they have and many function very well in later life, especially if they receive help in the early years. Having parents and teachers who recognize and support their strengths, help them overcome or deal with their weaknesses and encourage them to develop their talents offer the best opportunities for these students to succeed. Albert Einstein, Walt Disney, George Patton, Nelson Rockefeller, Whoopi Goldberg and Charles Schwab all had learning problems, yet accomplished a great deal.

<u>Types</u>
- Dyslexia is a chronic neurological disorder in which a person has trouble learning to read and spell. He sees letters and words in reverse order (backwards); his handwriting is frequently illegible.
- Dyscalculia is a brain disorder that causes impairment in the ability to solve arithmetic problems and difficulty understanding mathematical concepts.
- Dysgraphia is a disorder that makes it difficult to form letters and numbers. A person suffering from this problem finds it almost impossible to write within a defined space.
- Auditory and Visual Processing Disorders cover a range of sensory problems in which a person, even though his hearing and vision are normal, has difficulty understanding language.
- Nonverbal Learning Disabilities are neurological disorders in the right side of the brain that cause problems with processing spatial, intuitive, organizational, evaluational and holistic functions.

<u>Causes</u>
Learning disabilities are complex and, at this time, not very well-understood. Scientists think the causes may be as complicated as the problems themselves and may be different for each person. For example, research has shown that the brains of people with a reading disability do function differently than readers who don't have reading problems. Because children who have these factors in their history have developed problems, learning disabilities may be caused by one or more of the following: heredity (runs in families), teratogenic elements (develops in the womb because the mother is addicted to alcohol or cocaine or has ingested lead), medical reasons (premature birth, diabetes, meningitis) and societal influences (malnutrition, poor prenatal healthcare). Since the causes cannot yet be pinpointed, it is more important to focus on determining the child's problems and developing educational tools in order to help him maximize his strengths and minimize his weaknesses so that he can function in the world.

<u>Signs</u>
It is normal for adolescents to occasionally exhibit some warning signs of a learning disability and not have a problem. However, if several signs are observed over a period of time, it is wise to take a closer look and have the student tested to determine if he has a learning disability. Common characteristics include:

- A poor speller who frequently spells the same word differently in the same writing assignment.
- A child who avoids reading and writing tasks, has trouble with essay questions on tests and whose handwriting is nearly illegible when he does write.
- A child who has trouble remembering facts, dates and assignments and difficulty summarizing data.
- A child who works slowly, misreads and misinterprets information and has a hard time understanding and retaining abstract concepts.
- A child who either pays too little or too much attention to details.
- A child who has difficulty adjusting to new people, new situations and new settings.

<u>Telling behavior</u>
Since teachers have regular contact with students and can usually be objective, they are in a unique position to observe students' behavior. Making note of awkward interactions with peers, difficulty with normal classroom requirements and frustrated attempts to master tasks is an excellent way to spot potential problems and bring them to the attention of parents and administrators. The signs listed are not diagnostic tools and should be weighed against the student's age and behavior of his peers. They should be considered hints rather than markers.

- Trouble understanding what he reads and remembering newly learned data.
- Difficulty getting and staying organized, following clearly defined directions and remembering and honoring deadlines.
- Problems using basic reading, writing, spelling and math skills.
- Making inappropriate comments and difficulty interacting with peers and teachers.
- Problems expressing thoughts and an inability to use proper grammar in speaking and writing.

<u>Disabilities confused with learning disabilities</u>
Even though some students suffer from other issues (see below) and these problems may also be present, they should not be confused with or considered to be learning disabilities. They include intellectual disabilities, autism, deafness, blindness and behavior problems. They are separate and distinct issues and should be dealt with accordingly. Attention disorders such as Attention Deficit/Hyperactive Disorder (ADHA) and learning disabilities, although they frequently occur in the same student, are not the same problem and should not be treated as such. Lack of educational opportunities, changing schools a lot and attendance and truancy issues should not be classified as learning disabilities. Students who recently immigrated to this country or are just learning English should not be considered learning disabled until they are given ample time to learn the language and acquire the necessary social and communicational skills. Once language proficiency is acquired, if symptoms persist, an accurate diagnosis can be made.

**Professionals from whom to seek treatment**

- Audiologist — measures hearing capability and offers auditory training.
- Educational Consultant — provides educational evaluations; may have experience as a special education teacher.
- Educational Therapist — develops programs that address learning and behavior problems.
- Neurologist — a medical doctor who specializes in the brain and its functions.
- Occupational Therapist — helps improve motor and sensory skills.

- Pediatrician is a medical doctor who specializes in the growth and development of children from birth to about eighteen (18) years of age.
- Psychiatrist — a medical doctor who specializes in behavioral and emotional problems.
- Psychologist — a clinician who provides treatment for mental and emotional issues.
- School Psychologist — primarily concerned with educational issues that affect students' mental and emotional health.
- Speech and Language Therapist — helps with language and speech problems.

## Response-To-Intervention (RTI) approach

Many educators believe it is in the best interest of students with learning disabilities to remain, if possible, in a general education classroom rather than be placed in a special education setting. Proponents believe that as long as the necessary instructional tools are provided and progress is monitored, this scenario addresses the special needs of the students and helps them succeed without being placed in a special education environment.

Using the response-to-intervention (RTI) approach, students receive the special education services that they need in a general classroom setting. Instructional tools are developed to address the student's particular issues and the effectiveness of the tools is monitored. If the student learns and shows progress, he stays in the general education classroom. If he does not thrive, however, and fails to achieve planned mandated milestones, a request for special education services is initiated. Both provide the appropriate environment for the student to succeed.

Support is available to teachers with students who have learning disabilities, especially when the student is in a regular classroom rather than a special education setting but varies depending upon individual state mandates and the particular school district's resources. Once a student with a learning disability has been identified, however, there are two ways a teacher can be helped. In a collaborative consultation, the general education teacher works with a special education teacher outside of the classroom to plan any necessary physical accommodations, develop lessons and activities and devise instructional tools to help the student. In a co-teaching situation, the two teachers make the same decisions as above but share instructional responsibilities in the same classroom. In both situations, the teachers involved should respect each other's talents and contributions and work together to address and meet the needs of the student with learning disabilities.

## Brain functions

In order to truly understand learning disabilities and their many manifestations, it is helpful to understand how the brain functions. It is important to note that the different professions which deal with students who have learning disabilities may use the same or similar words but apply different meanings as the terms relate to their area of expertise. There are four basic steps the brain must take for learning to happen. Each is important; if one is missing or does not work properly, learning may be delayed, difficult or disabled. The first step is to get the data from the senses, such as from the eyes and ears, into the brain (input). The brain then must make sense of the data received (integration). Once received, the data must be stored and kept ready to be retrieved (memory). When needed, the brain must make sense of the data and send the message to the nerves and muscles (output). The process is thus input, integration, memory and output.

## Identifying students with learning disabilities

Language used by The Department of Education may be more specific about response-to-intervention approaches but the Individuals with Disabilities Education Act (IDEA) does not specify which methods schools must use to identify students with learning disabilities. Two RTI methods commonly used are the Problem Solving Approach and the Standard Protocol Approach. The *Problem Solving Approach* identifies student difficulties by collecting and reporting data in observable, measurable terms. Problems are analyzed and a plan is developed, implemented and observed. Its effectiveness is evaluated, modifications made when indicated and referral to special education classes made when needed. In the *Standard Protocol Approach,* teachers identify students struggling with subject material. Students receive some type of help for a specific length of time while progress is monitored. If no progress is seen after the initial time is over, the same help is extended for additional time and progress is again monitored. Students who don't show progress are referred for special education testing and placement.

## Various types of disabilities

### Visual

Children with visual perception disabilities have trouble organizing position and shape. They may see letters, words and numbers in reverse (dyslexia). Capital "E" might look like capital "W" or he may see "dog" as "god." Some children have a problem focusing on the main figure in a scene. For example, he may have trouble finding the pencil among the books and papers on his desk. When reading, he may jump over or completely miss words or skip entire lines of text. Judging distance and depth and understanding his position in space are other visual perception problems. He may have trouble with the concepts of left and right and up and down. He may have a problem getting the message from his eyes to his hands or feet. This may show itself when he tries to catch a ball, jump rope, put a puzzle together or hammer a nail into an object.

### Input

The brain receives information as impulses primarily from the eyes (visual input) and the ears (auditory input). This process is called perception. If there are problems with or interruptions in the process, they have nothing to do with vision or hearing issues such as nearsightedness, farsightedness or hearing problems; perception takes place in the brain, not the eyes and ears. Visual perception disability is difficulty with processing impulses transmitted from the eyes. Auditory perception disability is difficulty with processing impulses transmitted from the ears. Children can have one or both of these disabilities. Some children have problems when required to use both processes simultaneously. For example: reading the written word while listening to someone read aloud or watching the teacher write on the board and listening to a lecture at the same time. Both of these common classroom occurrences can cause problems for a student with visual and/or auditory perception problems.

Input problems with the other senses, i.e., touch, smell and taste, are not very well understood and there is not much research data available. Scientists do know that some people do not like to be touched which would influence tactile sensations and make some learning experiences (working with clay, finger painting, sewing, weaving, dealing with live animals, etc.) difficult or impossible. Children who are clumsy, bump into things and can't do simple physical activities (jumping rope, catching a ball) may have trouble with the messages sent to the brain from certain nerve endings in the muscles. More study is needed to identify the causes of these disabilities so that treatment and/or training can be developed to help people trying to overcome or learn to function with or around these challenges.

## Auditory perception

A child with auditory perception disabilities sometimes has a problem distinguishing words that sound alike, i.e. flower and flour. He may hear a word that wasn't said which prompts him to answer incorrectly. For example: "How are you?" might be answered with "I'm fourteen." He heard "old" instead of or along with "are." He might have a problem picking an individual voice out of a crowd. Instructions in a noisy classroom may be missed completely because he cannot separate the sounds in the room. He is not ignoring the message; he does not hear it. Some children can't process sound as fast as others can. Given a series of commands without a stop in between each one may cause him to miss half of that which is said. This is called auditory lag. If instructions are given slowly, with a brief break in between each, his hearing perception can catch up with the sounds.

## Sequencing disabilities

There are multiple indications that a student might have problems with the sequencing step that integrates data in the brain. When telling a story, he might recount the end, the beginning and the middle in that order. He knows the pertinent information but the story does not make sense because he tells it in the wrong order. Using the correct letters to spell a word but putting them in the wrong sequence, i.e. spelling cat "a-c-t," might also be a sign. He might have difficulty taking information out of the order in which it was learned. He may know all the months of the year but if asked what month comes after September, he has to start at January and repeat the list until he gets to the month in question. He might have difficulty reading numbers. He might see "16" as "61." Playing baseball, he might hit the ball and run to third base instead of first.

## Integration disability

After information comes into and is registered in the brain, to be useful the data must be understood. This process is accomplished through two steps: sequencing and abstraction. Sequencing means to put data symbols into the correct order and from that unique order, determine the meaning of the information received. For example, the brain receives the symbols c-a-t. The brain must then decide how to put the symbols together sensibly for use. Is it c-a-t? Is it t-a-c? Is it a-t-c? Is it a-c-t? Once the brain determines the correct order of the symbols, it must figure out the meaning of the symbol because a word has both a general meaning and a specific meaning. "A" cat is different from "my" cat. The ability to understand the difference in the subtle meanings of the same word is called abstract thinking (abstraction).

## Memory problems

Short term memory is the ability to retain data for as long as the person is focused on the particular information. For example, calling directory assistance and retaining the number long enough to dial it or remembering a short list of items to pick up at the store would be considered short-term memory. Long term memory stores learned data until the information is needed and retrieved. A phone number used all the time is recalled quickly; putting a name to the face at the tenth class reunion might take longer. Examples of student short term memory issues include knowing the history dates the night before but not remembering them the next morning; understanding a concept in class but being unable to recall anything about the topic when trying to do homework that night.

NOTE: if someone has a long term memory disability, he would be diagnosed with some type of intellectual disability because he would be unable to function in daily life without assistance.

## Abstract thinking

Abstract thinking is the ability to figure out the subtle differences in the meaning of words and use the words appropriately in writing and conversation. Most learning disabled children don't have a serious issue with this step in brain integration but many do have some problems with abstract thinking. Elementary school children may be able to talk about a particular firefighter they know in their family or neighborhood. However, if asked about the responsibilities of firefighters in general, they won't be able to answer the question because they can't make the connection between the specific and the general. Students in middle and high school may not understand jokes, sarcasm and irony. Since this type of wit is based on word play, it only confuses an adolescent who is unable to think in the abstract.

Motor disabilities

When information comes out of the brain via muscle activity like writing, drawing and gesturing, it is called motor output. Gross motor output uses large muscle groups. Signs of a gross motor disability include difficulty running, swimming or climbing, bumping into walls and furniture, stumbling, falling and being generally clumsy. Fine motor output involves integrating many muscles to perform an action. When a child cannot get several muscle groups to work together, he has a fine motor disability. The most noticeable fine motor problem is difficulty writing, which results in writing slowly and poor, sometimes illegible, handwriting. The shape, size and position of the letters and the spacing between them are all out of kilter no matter how hard the student tries. When the brain processes or records vision perceptions incorrectly and the message sent to the muscles required to perform an activity requiring eye-hand coordination goes awry, the person has a visual motor disability.

Language disabilities

When the brain sends information via words, the result is language output. Communication involves both spontaneous language and demand language. The speaker initiates spontaneous language. He chooses the topic, has time to organize his thoughts and put together the words he wants to use before he speaks. Demand language is when another person begins the dialogue and requires a response. The listener is expected to collect his thoughts, find the correct words and answer appropriately in a split second. A child with a language disability has no problem with spontaneous language. He may never be quiet in class and when he voluntarily answers a question, he may sound quite normal. But when called on by the teacher to answer a question, he may respond with "Huh?" or "What?" or simply not answer at all. The child who was chattering just a moment earlier may be completely unable to respond. The inconsistency can be startling.

Attention Deficit Hyperactivity Disorder

Attention Deficit Hyperactivity Disorder – ADHD – is a behavioral problem involving inattention, hyperactivity and impulsivity that affects all areas of life: home, school, work and social relationships. While some children with ADHD also have various learning disabilities, ADHD is not classified as a learning disability. Scientists, citing recent research, are making a case for ADHD to be included on the list because the disorder directly impacts functions needed to learn. However, it currently is not included as a learning disability.

The American Psychiatric Association estimates that in a group of one hundred (100) children, between three (3) and seven (7) are affected with one or more characteristics of ADHD. The disorder is usually diagnosed in childhood and frequently continues into adolescence and adulthood. Children with the problem can sometimes be helped with medication and behavior modification and may eventually learn to cope with and work around the problems caused by the disorder. The main characteristics of Attention Deficit Hyperactivity Disorder – ADHD – are inattention, hyperactivity and impulsivity. At times everyone can be absent-minded, fidgety or impulsive so why are some children diagnosed with ADHD while similar behavior in others are considered normal? The difference is the degree of the behavior: when, where, how much and how often. In people with ADHD, these behavior patterns are the rule, not the exception.

ADHD symptoms vary. Individuals will have problems in different areas. Some are hyperactive; some are under-active. Some children may be unable to pay attention for more than a minute or two but have few problems with impulsive behavior. Some children may only have minor problems with paying attention but are unable to curb impulsive actions. Some may have problems in all three areas. ADHD is a complex behavior disorder and therefore the symptoms of each child, adolescent and adult should be dealt with according to his particular issues.

Children with Attention Deficit Hyperactivity Disorder – ADHD – who have particular problems paying attention make careless mistakes and when they do turn in assignments, the results are messy and incomplete. Social situations are difficult because they don't listen well, and therefore they lose track of conversations. They are not very good at following directions or rules, which affects their ability to play games and participate in classroom activities. At times most children display one or more of the following behaviors. It is cause for concern and further action when the behaviors are frequent, consistent and interfere with the ability to participate in routine activities. Some symptoms include when the child:
- Does not seem to be listening when spoken to directly.
- Does not pay attention to details or follow instructions and loses tools (pencils, notebook, assignments) necessary to complete required tasks.
- Is frequently forgetful and has difficulty organizing assignments and other activities.
- Is easily distracted and has problems keeping attention focused on the current task.

The American Heritage College Dictionary defines attention as "the ability or power to concentrate mentally; a close observing or listening." Paying attention is a process that requires a person to focus his concentration in the moment (initiate), keep his focus for as long as necessary (sustain), avoid distractions that take his focus away (inhibit), and move his focus as required (shift). Children with Attention Deficit Hyperactive Disorder – ADHD – are capable of paying attention. Their issues are with what they focus on, how long they focus and what is going on around them. In order to help a child with ADHD, it is necessary to determine where his ability to pay attention breaks down. There are three common problem areas:
- Inability to sustain attention, especially to tedious or repetitive tasks.
- Inability to resist distractions, especially when he finds something more interesting to focus on.
- Inability to pay close enough attention, especially to instructions, details and organization.

Hyperactivity
The American Heritage College Dictionary defines hyperactive as "behavior characterized by constant, excessive activity." Research shows that of the three main characteristics (attention problems, hyperactivity, impulsivity) of Attention Deficit Hyperactive Disorder – ADHD – hyperactivity is the most visible. It even affects the person during sleep. Age influences the signs of hyperactivity. In the pre-school child, ADHD is motor driven; he is always on the go. In elementary school, these children squirm and fidget and have trouble staying in their seats. Adolescents (and adults) are very restless and have difficulty with sedentary activities. Signs seen in all ages include:
- Loud, incessant talking; interrupting other people.
- Hands and/or feet in constant motion.
- Difficulty paying attention and participating in quiet activities.
- Often running or climbing in inappropriate settings; this drive is manifested as restlessness in adolescents (and adults).

Intellectual disabilities
The American Heritage College Dictionary defines intellectual disabilities as "subnormal intellectual development or functioning due to congenital causes, brain injury, or disease and characterized by any of various deficiencies, ranging from impaired learning ability to social and vocational inadequacy." This means people who are diagnosed as intellectually disabled have difficulty communicating and acquiring the skills needed to function independently in the world. Intellectual disabilities cannot be cured but

people who are mentally challenged can learn to do many things; it simply takes them longer. There are many causes for intellectual disabilities. The following are the most common:

- Genetic Conditions: abnormal genes or errors when genes combine.
- Problems During Pregnancy: improper brain development because cells divide incorrectly; the mother is alcoholic, contracts rubella or doesn't get adequate prenatal care.
- Complications At Birth: the baby doesn't receive enough oxygen.
- Health Problems After Birth: measles, meningitis, malnutrition; exposure to lead, mercury or other poisons.

A caring, supportive teacher can make an enormous difference in the life of a student with intellectual disabilities. These students can learn; it simply takes patience and repetition, getting their attention and keeping them interested in the subject. Discover his strengths, weaknesses and interests. Develop plans and activities that emphasize the strengths, improve the weak areas and pique his curiosity. Create opportunities for him to succeed. Demonstrate rather than just explain. Use pictures and hands-on materials and give concrete examples that relate to his life and experiences. Break tasks into small steps, explain each step individually, help when needed and give immediate feedback. Make sure he is involved in all classroom situations and encourage him to interact with the other students in group activities and in extracurricular clubs. All of these actions help the student grow mentally and emotionally while learning life skills necessary to function independently in the world.

Intellectual disabilities affect the brain's ability to learn, think, solve problems and generally make sense of the world. A child may have trouble learning daily living skills like dressing and feeding himself and taking care of personal hygiene needs. He may have a difficult time following and participating in conversations, understanding simple directions and communicating with people outside of his immediate circle. His social skills may be inadequate or almost non-existent, which makes it difficult for him to function outside of a protected environment. He may have trouble processing information and thinking logically. He may be unable to see or predict the consequences of his actions. Intellectual disabilities may not be recognized until the child starts school and is unable to function and learn at the same level as his peers. The U.S. Department of Education estimates that about one (1) in four (4) special education students have some form of intellectual disabilities.

## Developmental psychology

Developmental psychology is the scientific study of the emotional and behavioral growth of human beings from birth to death. This branch of psychology studies the development of motor and language skills, problem-solving abilities, conceptual and moral understanding, and the formation of a unique identity. A major research focus is how children are different from adults: are they qualitatively different or do they merely lack experience because they haven't lived as long? Also, do human beings accumulate knowledge or move from one way of thinking to another as they age? As questioned in the nature versus nurture debate, are babies born with certain information imprinted in their brains, or do they learn how to figure things out as they learn life lessons? The broad science of developmental psychology encompasses many fields including: educational psychology, child psychopathology, social psychology, cognitive psychology, and comparative psychology among others.

## Erik Erickson's eight stages of psychosocial development

Erik Erickson's eight stages of psychosocial development are widely accepted and have greatly influenced later theories of psychological development. Erickson believed each stage was crucial to healthy development. He believed great emotional harm would occur and hinder children's success throughout life if they were not allowed to move through the stages at their own pace, without being and not be rushed or pushed.

In brief, here are Erickson's eight stages of development with the major task of each one:
1. Infancy, birth to twelve months: trust versus mistrust.
2. Younger Years, one to three years: autonomy versus shame and doubt.
3. Early Childhood, three to five years: initiative versus guilt.
4. Middle Childhood, six to ten years: industry versus inferiority.
5. Adolescence, eleven to eighteen years: identity versus role confusion.
6. Early Adulthood, eighteen to thirty-four years: intimacy versus isolation.
7. Middle Adulthood, thirty-five to sixty years: generativity versus stagnation.
8. Later Adulthood, sixty years to death: ego integrity versus despair.

## Jean Paiget's stages of cognitive development

Based on the observation that unlike adults, young children keep making the same mistakes, Paiget's theory of cognitive development examines the premise that children's thought processes are innately different from those of adults. His theory maintains that the validity of new information is confirmed from knowledge previously learned. He believes there is a chronological order to the way children structure data; that is, they use old knowledge to test new information against its usefulness in the real world.  The ages in Paiget's developmental stages are approximate because studies show a huge variation between individual children, and therefore age should not be used as a rigid criterion. The stages are:
1. Sensorimotor – birth to two years: children learn through their senses.
2. Preoperational – two to seven years: children acquire motor skills.
3. Concrete Operational – seven to eleven years: children learn to apply logic to situations.
4. Formal Operational – eleven years forward: children develop abstract reasoning ability.

## Adolescence and puberty

According to <u>The American Heritage College Dictionary</u>, adolescence is "the period of development from the onset of puberty to maturity." Psychologists consider adolescence the transition from childhood to adulthood, spanning the years between eleven and nineteen. The individual forms a unique identity and pulls away from the family unit. Some people don't reach maturity until their early to late twenties while others never progress from adolescence to maturity at any age. The same dictionary defines puberty as "the stage of adolescence in which an individual becomes physiologically capable of reproduction." It is the first stage of adolescence and includes physical and hormonal changes and the formation of a sexual identity. As these changes are internal, they are unobservable by others.

## Characteristics of puberty

During this time of enormous change, boys and girls grow rapidly and are oftentimes confused by these changes which can cause wide mood swings. At times they may act like the children they used to be while at other times they show flashes of the adolescent which they are becoming. They begin to show an interest in that which is happening to their bodies, such as boys becoming concerned with their height while girls begin noticing the need for a brazier. They may develop problems with their complexion, seem to be continually hungry, sleep more and may have difficulty rising in the morning. As they move through this stage of development, adolescents begin to question their place in the world and may rebel against parents, teachers and other authority figures. They may also experiment with alcohol and drugs, discover the opposite sex and become sexually active.

## Onset of puberty

The biological changes experienced during puberty are dramatic, happening at different times for boys and girls and have unique consequences for each gender. During these years both boys and girls experience a growth spurt and develop primary and secondary sexual characteristics. Children this age experience increased sexual feelings and their bodies become fertile. For boys, puberty enhances their physical abilities, thus increasing their potential for success athletically, which leads to a higher social standing in school. Girls tend to mature, on average, about eighteen months earlier than boys. Their body fat increases, which changes their shape from a childlike androgynous profile to the curvaceous female form. Since some girls this age are yet mentally and emotionally unchanged, such as still playing with dolls, those who mature early may have a difficult time accepting these noticeable changes, which can lead to a negative self-image and self-esteem problems later in adolescence.

## Pubescent timeline for boys

As both primary and secondary physical changes occur gradually over a period of time, it can be difficult to determine precisely when they begin. Therefore the following timeline is approximate as age will vary:.
- Puberty begins between nine-and-a-half to fourteen (9.5 to 14) years of age.
- The first noticeable change is an enlargement of the testicles, and approximately a year after this the penis becomes larger.
- Pubic hair appears at about age thirteen-and-a-half (13.5).
- Nocturnal emissions ("wet dreams") begin at about fourteen (14) years of age.
- At about fifteen (15), hair starts to grow on the face and under the arms as the voice begins to change. Acne may develop as well.

## Characteristics of pubescent boys

Adolescent boys during puberty gain weight and are seemingly always hungry, unable to satisfy their appetites. In early adolescence boys are clumsy, boisterous and aggressive, while practicing poor hygiene. In middle adolescence, boys may become fascinated with and practice masturbation regularly and have frequent nocturnal emissions. Some even experiment with same-sex encounters, a behavior happening often enough to be considered normal by many. Adults should answer questions and concerns about sexuality directly and shouldn't be judgmental during discussions about sensitive subjects. The boys may become secretive and refuse to talk to family members and spend a lot of time in their bedroom. As they move into the middle and later teen years, they feel invulnerable and often engage in risky activities.

## Pubescent timeline for girls

Primary and secondary physical changes occur in girls earlier than in boys of the same age. Every girl is different and will experience the changes in her own way and at her own time. The following timeline is approximate and the actual age will vary with the individual girl:
- Puberty begins between eight and fourteen years of age (8 to 14).
- The first noticeable change is the development of breasts, and pubic hair begins growing shortly thereafter.
- The menstrual cycle begins between the ages of ten to sixteen-and-a-half (10 to 16.5).
- Underarm hair begins to grow at about twelve (12) years of age.

## Characteristics of pubescent girls

Young adolescent girls talk a great deal but don't really communicate with parents or peers. They are vague, can be mean and vindictive and giggle often. They enjoy playacting and firmly believe in romantic love. They frequently develop crushes on older men. As girls begin menstruating and develop breasts, a waist and hips, they become very conscious of their bodies: how it looks, what it can do and how it affects the opposite sex. Adolescent girls often have strained relationships with their mothers but still watch and learn from them as well as other adult females. Girls form strong bonds with friends and cliques are formed that can cause tense relations between the "in" crowd and the "out" crowd. Girls are usually interested in making and maintaining friendships with other girls and developing relationships with the opposite sex. In the past several years, there has been a shift to and focus on college and career choices.

## Adolescent development

Throughout adolescence, young people are dealing with a wide range of complex issues—most of which they feel but are unable to describe and do not understand. These changes are physical, hormonal, sexual, emotional and social. They are developing a unique identity separate from their parents and forming relationships with peers and adults outside of the family. Adolescents are searching for emotional support from friends before they have the maturity to determine the effect and appropriateness of these influences. They may also start behaving recklessly, oftentimes not thinking about or having any fear of the possible consequences of their actions. Their bodies are changing rapidly. This is the time when young people become aware of and begin to explore their sexuality. They begin to form intimate relationships with the opposite sex as well as strong ties to members of their own gender.

## Adolescent sexuality

Both male and female adolescents' acceptance of and adjustment to their emerging sexuality depends on several factors. The first is the adolescent's overall self-esteem, coping skills and willingness to recognize the need for help and to ask for it. The second is how much and what kind of support he or she receives from family, friends and other significant people with whom he or she interacts. The amount and quality of knowledge the adolescent has before the changes begin and as the maturation process proceeds will also determine how well the changes are understood and how easy they are accepted. Parents and teachers should be non-judgmental and provide positive support. They should also make sure these adolescents receive accurate information in a timely manner on topics of health arising due to sexuality and sexual activity.

## Pulling away from parents

Even though adolescents distance themselves from their parents, they instinctively know they still need and will seek out relationships with other adults. They want to talk to and benefit from the wisdom and experience of their elders. Programs away from school and family, such as church youth groups, scouting, social clubs, and volunteer activities provide fertile fields for young people to find caring, competent, and safe adults to confide in, share with, and learn from. Most of the time the reason adolescents turn to peers for guidance is that they don't have or are not allowed to develop relationships with adults outside of the family unit. When adolescents are encouraged to participate in family decisions and are provided with opportunities to develop relationships with adults outside the family, these young people are more self-reliant, have better self-esteem and positive relationships with teachers, perform on a higher level in school, and exhibit advanced moral reasoning skills.

## Adolescent cognitive changes

The cognitive changes that occur in early adolescence affect the way young people understand themselves and how they relate to their parents and their peers. They are able to think in the abstract, consider hypothetical situations, and recognize multiple aspects of a problem. Their information processing becomes more sophisticated and they are increasingly capable of dissecting complicated issues. As they become aware of their own strengths and weaknesses, they begin applying their hard-learned knowledge and experience to new situations in unfamiliar circumstances. As they pull away from their parents, a task that is not always easy for either side, adolescents begin to develop a sense of independence and a feeling of competence. As they form friendships with people of their own age, they found these friendships on the perception of personality compatibility. In other words, for the most part, adolescents seek out people who look, think, and act the same as they do.

## Early adolescence

Early adolescence lasts from approximately eleven to fourteen years of age. These are years of great change in multiple areas, including the biological, educational and psychological. Puberty begins and the changes are dramatic physically and hormonally. Cognitive growth causes a striking shift in thinking and problem-solving abilities. Profound changes in their relationship with parents include seeking advice from adults outside the family and developing strong ties to friends their own age. These all have a great deal of influence on the adolescent's psychological evolution. Most children pass through these years with minimal stress, yet some have a difficult time navigating these changes which can have a profound effect on the rest of their lives. A loving and supportive environment which recognizes and nurtures rather than ignores or criticizes will ease these years for parents, teachers and adolescents.

## Middle adolescence

The years between fourteen and sixteen are considered middle adolescence, yet these age parameters can and do vary with the individual. This is often a time of experimentation and risk-taking. Both boys and girls think that they are omnipotent and invulnerable. They want to spend less time with the family and more time with friends. These young people do not understand the concept of cause and effect and that all actions have consequences. This attitude can lead to drinking, drugs, smoking, and sexual encounters; behaviors which, if uncontrolled and misused, can have serious repercussions for the rest of their lives. Middle adolescents are seeking independence; they want to be their own person. This search, coupled with risky behavior, can and usually causes conflicts with parents. These conflicts are a normal part of the maturation process and must be confronted and resolved so that the youth can move into the next stage of adolescence.

## Peer pressure

While conforming to peer pressure is extremely important and very effective during adolescence, good teens being corrupted by bad influences is a simplistic answer to a complex issue. There are a myriad of reasons, and a multitude of thought processes used by an adolescent, to make the choices he or she does. According to psychologist Jacquelynne S. Eccles, experts believe that "poor parenting usually leads children to get in with a 'bad' peer group, rather than the peer group pulling a 'good' child into difficulties." Friends influence clothing, music and movie choices, and leisure activities pursued; they reinforce inherent strengths and weaknesses. Research indicates most young people agree with and accept their parents' position on and follow their example in vital areas like morality, educational goals, politics, and religion.

## Communication barriers

Privacy, trust, and respect are huge issues with adolescents, and when one couples those real psychological needs with a fragile sense of self and adds a general distrust of most adults and authority figures, communication becomes tricky at best and contentious at worst. Adolescents have a great fear of revealing their vulnerabilities. If they share their thoughts, feelings, and activities, these potential peeks behind the armor of self-protection opens them up to possible humiliation and ridicule. If they tell parents or other adults what they are doing, questions are asked and truthful answers are expected. Since adolescents worry about disapproval and want to avoid punishment, it is easier and safer to just not talk at all. Parents, teachers, and other authority figures that interact with adolescents need to show a willingness to listen and create an open atmosphere of honesty and fairness if they expect to be able to communicate effectively with teenagers.

## Cultural differences

The adolescent's cultural identity can play a major role in the development of a healthy self-esteem. As he becomes aware of his ethnicity, the values, traditions, and practices of his cultural group can shape the adolescent's view of society and his place in it. This can be a challenge in America because some minority groups carry negative stereotypes. This bias can potentially cause problems for the youth should he be a member of a certain cultural group. Since it is impossible to escape one's ethnic identity, he may decide that as he is expected to behave in a certain way, he might just as well act accordingly. On the positive side, he may use the negative expectations as an incentive to improve his position in society and help change the negative stereotypes. An involved, compassionate, and caring teacher can have an enormous influence on the choice he makes and the path he follows.

## Adolescent social development

Both family and friends impact adolescent social development. Just because peers seem to have more influence than the family does not mean that the youth is immune to family mores, traditions, and expectations. Even though he appears to be ignoring his parents, this does not mean that the adolescent is not hearing and absorbing what is being said and paying attention to parental behavior. In many situations, actions do speak louder than words. Scientific studies and anecdotal evidence show that family involvement is extremely influential on a teen's behavior and has a great deal of impact, especially when he is away from home and making on-the-spot choices. In early and middle adolescence, about eleven to sixteen, despite the increase in conflicts a youth might have with his parents, family closeness is a critical factor in preventing high-risk behavior. Around age seventeen, the influence of family and peers evens out and is given about equal weight.

## Stages of social development

According to the American Psychological Association, adolescent social development follows a discernable pattern. The ages given are approximate. Each youth will progress at his or her own pace and in his or her own way and timeframe.
- Early Adolescence: eleven to thirteen (11 to 13)
  - One's social world shifts from family to friends.
  - One tends to be involved with a same-sex peer group.
  - One has a strong desire to conform and be accepted by chosen peer group.
- Middle Adolescence: fourteen to sixteen (14 to 16)
  - Peer group acceptance fades in importance.
  - One's peer groups include both boys and girls.

- o One is more tolerant of individual differences.
- o One-on-one friendships develop.
- o Romance becomes important and dating begins.
- Late Adolescence: seventeen to nineteen (17 to 19)
  - o Intimate one-on-one relationships form.
  - o Peer groups begin to lose their importance.

## Gender differences

Each adolescent develops emotionally in his or her own way, in his or her own time. Even though the genders face different challenges and have different needs during this time, the exploration will be unique for every youth. Studies show that certain tendencies are common in all boys and all girls. Boys may need to learn cooperation. They also need to understand that anger is not the only emotion and that it is perfectly acceptable to express other feelings. At this age, girls tend to have low self-esteem. Some may need to learn how to be more assertive in their relationships and that it is acceptable to express their anger. If either gender gets stuck at this stage of development, it can have serious, long-term personal and professional consequences in later life.

## Etiologies of severe and profound intellectual disabilities

In addition to anoxia or hypoxia (lack of oxygen or insufficient oxygen to the brain) and genetic syndromes, other sources of neurological damage may also cause severe and profound intellectual disability. For example, "shaken baby syndrome" is the result of shaking a baby violently or too hard. This can cause rebound injury when the brain is bounced against the inside of the skull. Such damage may be extreme, even resulting in death. Infants who survive may suffer from enough brain damage to cause severe or profound intellectual disabilities and/or cerebral palsy. Another source of neurological damage is the maternal ingestion of or exposure to toxins during pregnancy. Many substances affect the development of an embryo or fetus, including prescription medications, street drugs, alcohol, tobacco, and caffeine; metals like lead and mercury; radiation; airborne pollutants; and others. There have also been cases of unsuccessful abortion attempts, including multiple attempts, wherein the unborn child survives but suffers severe to profound neurological damage from the procedure(s).

Severe and profound intellectual disabilities can be caused by damage to the brain during intrauterine development or during childbirth. One common cause of such damage is anoxia (no oxygen to the brain) or hypoxia (insufficient oxygen to the brain). This can happen from many sources, such as maternal distress, medication, and umbilical cord obstruction. Some babies have brain damage in areas that cause multiple disabilities, such as cerebral palsy plus intellectual disability. Another source of neurological deficits are various genetic syndromes. Down syndrome, caused by having a third, extra copy of chromosome 21 (hence the descriptor trisomy 21) is one example. This genetic abnormality produces a variety of symptoms, including short physical stature, facial stigmata, congenital heart defects, and intellectual disabilities. Down syndrome individuals can range from normal IQ scores to profound intellectual disability and anything in between. Other genetic syndromes, such as Marfan syndrome, Turner syndrome, Rhett syndrome, and many others, may also cause intellectual disabilities.

## Cerebral palsy

Cerebral palsy is a developmental disability resulting from neurological damage or defects. These most often occur in utero or during birth. One common reason that parts of the brain are damaged or do not develop normally is insufficient or absent oxygen (hypoxia or anoxia) to the brain, which can have various causes. In cerebral palsy, the parts of the cerebral cortex responsible for controlling motor functions are affected. This causes weakness and lack of coordination of muscular movements. While an individual with mild CP may only have a slight limp, persons with severe and profound CP are frequently paralyzed, unable to walk or even sit up without support. Many severe and profound CP patients also cannot speak. Some cases of CP are primarily spastic, that is, the individual's body parts are rigid and difficult to move; primarily athetoid, meaning the individual has excessive, uncontrolled body movements; or have combined spasticity and athetosis.

## Spina bifida

Spina bifida is a developmental disability occurring during fetal development in utero wherein the spinal column's neural tube does not completely fuse shut at the midline, leaving some of the spinal cord exposed. The most common type is myelomeningocele, wherein incomplete bone formation leaves the spinal cord and meninges (tissues covering it) protruding out the back. Surgery can correct this, but not the associated neurological damage. In the meningoceles type, the spinal cord stays in place, but the meninges protrude through the spinal defect's opening. In spina bifida occulta, spinal bones do not close, but the spinal cord and meninges remain in place and are usually covered by skin. Most spina bifida patients use wheelchairs or crutches, as paralysis below the waist is common. Up to 90% of children with myelomeningocele have associated hydrocephalus (fluid buildup in the brain). Even managed with shunt implantation, this can cause severe or profound intellectual deficits.

## Diabetes mellitus

Diabetic students, especially those with Type I diabetes, must monitor their blood glucose (sugar) levels regularly, in some cases many times during a typical school day. Such students usually (or should) have been provided with a portable glucose meter for school. However, students with severe or profound intellectual disabilities can often require assistance from school personnel to remind them, to help with the actual procedure, and to record each reading. Students with severe and profound disabilities will also need reminders and monitoring relative to exercising, choosing appropriate foods, eating appropriate amounts, and eating frequently enough throughout the school day to keep their blood sugar more stable. Snacks during class times may be necessary. Teachers and other school staff should also be trained in emergency recognition and response if a student goes into diabetic shock, experiences hypoglycemia or hyperglycemia, and other dangers of this disease.

## Profound autism spectrum disorders

Students with severe and profound autism spectrum disorders typically have very observable differences in their communicative skills and behaviors. Of all autistic individuals, roughly half are verbal and half are not. Those with higher-functioning profiles (as with those with Asperger's syndrome or higher IQs) are more likely to be verbal. Those with severe and profound autism are typically lower-functioning in general. Some of those diagnosed with autism are dually diagnosed with coexisting intellectual disability and some are not. Students with severe or profound autism who are verbal and have higher IQs tend to deliver monologues full of technical information or great detail, but find the give-and-take of normal conversations difficult or impossible to master. These same deficits interfere with social skills development. Those with lower intellectual levels who are verbal may display echolalia (repeating what others say), frequently repeat the same few phrases, or speak in odd, sing-song tones or rhythms.

## Disabilities pertaining tocognitive development

Young children with severe or profound intellectual disabilities are likely to be delayed in their cognitive development. They are likely to begin talking and walking at later ages than other children, and their gross and fine motor skills tend to develop later. The discrepancy between normal/average developmental milestones also becomes larger and more evident with increasing age. Individuals who score around 20 to 34 on most standardized IQ test measurements are classified as having severe intellectual disability. Their levels of cognitive development are similar to those of a normally developing younger child. Individuals who score below 20 on IQ measures are classified with profound intellectual disability. Scoring below 20 is synonymous with being unable to obtain an exact IQ score as existing tests cannot measure it. Individuals in this category are considered to be at a level of cognitive development similar to that of a normally developing infant.

## Psychological needs

It is not unusual for students with severe and profound intellectual disabilities also to exhibit behavioral problems. There are various reasons for these. Some students have neurological conditions that interfere with normal social inhibitions, for example, and they exhibit socially inappropriate behaviors, such as sharing overly personal information, asking embarrassing questions, or engaging in private behavior publicly (belching, passing gas, undressing, eliminating, masturbating, sexual advances, and similar behaviors). Neurological conditions causing intellectual disability may also cause extreme emotional behaviors. For example, tuberous sclerosis has led to rage disorders, as well as ID in some individuals. Nonorganic causes of behavior problems include frustration over skill limitations, slow learning, and/or task difficulty; resentment of faster-progressing peers; reactions against teacher demands; and difficulty making transitions. Problem behaviors with nonorganic causes are strongly related to inadequate skills for expressing feelings and meeting one's needs in more acceptable ways.

## Motor development and functioning

Children with severe or profound intellectual disability are slower to develop and to learn overall, including development of motor skills. Regarding gross motor skills, these children are likely to be unable to perform activities such as walking, jumping, hopping, going up and down stairs, throwing and catching objects, sweeping, vacuuming, and coordinated arm and leg movements at the same ages as their normally developing peers. In special education classes, they should be taught appropriately to their developmental level. When mainstreamed in regular classes, their developmental level must also be considered; they should not be expected to have gross motor development equal to that of age peers. Generally, students with severe or profound ID are likely to have less developed fine motor skills, such that they cannot do very small, fine, or delicate tasks—for example, painting figurines, chess pieces, or action figures, or hand-sewing, and may need help with buttons and zippers on clothing.

## Social development and functioning

Students with severe and profound intellectual disabilities may not learn as their normally developing peers do how to start a conversation and to maintain it. If they have not learned this skill, they will have more difficulty making and keeping friends. This may result in loneliness, lack of good peer models, and lack of social interaction, both with children having similar disabilities and with normally developing age peers. Many students with these disability levels can be taught the basic social skills to initiate conversations and continue them through give-and-take. These students may also not have learned the social skills for interacting appropriately in social situations, including classrooms; school activities outside of classrooms; and home and community activities, such as parties, play dates, and so forth. For instance, they may interrupt others; not respond when spoken to; grab toys from other children; or poke, shove, or slap others. Allowing enough time, patience, repetition, and reinforcement, educators can teach more appropriate social skills to these students.

## Important terms

*Dyslexia*—a chronic neurological disorder in which a person has trouble learning to read and spell. He sees letters and words in reverse order (backwards); his handwriting is frequently illegible.

*Dyscalculia*—a brain disorder that causes impairment in the ability to solve arithmetic problems and difficulty understanding mathematical concepts.

*Dysgraphia*—a disorder that makes it difficult to form letters and numbers. A person suffering from this problem finds it almost impossible to write within a defined space.

*Auditory and Visual Processing Disorders*—cover a range of sensory problems in which a person, even though his hearing and vision is are normal, has difficulty understanding language.

*Nonverbal Learning Disabilities*—neurological disorders in the right side of the brain that cause problems with processing spatial, intuitive, organizational, evaluational and holistic functions.

# Assessing Students and Developing Individualized Programs

## IEP

The Individualized Educational Program, or IEP, is a comprehensive written document required by the Individuals with Disabilities Education Act (IDEA). Schools are required to conduct an evaluation of all students diagnosed with a learning disability. The IEP includes various assessment tests to determine the child's strengths and weaknesses. It includes the results of interviews with the child, his parents, teachers, and other significant adults and also contains notes from conferences with professionals familiar with the child. The document provides a review of the child's medical history and current educational performance as well as comments from direct observation of him in various settings. The plan describes annual goals and sets short-term objectives. The IEP spells out the type and length of special services required and establishes methods for evaluating progress. If the student is sixteen or older, the IEP must also include a plan to move him out of school and into the real world.

## Potential attendees at a student's IEP team meeting

Who attends the IEP meeting will vary depending on the reason for the meeting. Attendees may include the principal or other school administrator to manage the meeting and assure that the IDEA's requirements are satisfied; a special education teacher to give information on instruction suitable for the student's disability; a regular education teacher to give information on general education requirements and how the school will meet the disabled student's needs; a school psychologist or another evaluation professional to address suitable evaluations for the student, explain evaluation results, and give information on the student's various abilities; related service providers if the student needs their services to benefit from the special education program, such as a speech-language pathologist, physical therapist, occupational therapist, and/or mental health professional; a guidance counselor to help with counseling and curriculum matters; and an advocate or support person. Doctors or others who cannot attend may submit important information in writing or by telephone or video conference.

## Arriving prepared at an IEP meeting

A student's Individual Education Plan (IEP) is a central part of his or her special education program. IEP team meetings are held to discuss initial referrals for evaluation, to discuss evaluation results, to plan and produce the student's IEP, for annual IEP reviews, for transitions between programs or schools, and to address other issues as needed. Parents should review their child's report cards, test and assignment grades, progress reports, and any assessment results to focus on strengths and needs to be addressed in the IEP. They should consider what issues are important to them to discuss at the meeting. It is often helpful for parents to make notes in advance to bring to the meeting in order to be sure all their concerns are addressed. They may also want to find out in advance who will attend the meeting and what their roles are. Additionally, it is good for parents to have a copy of their rights, guaranteed under the IDEA law and familiarize themselves with those rights. Parents with questions about their legal rights can ask the IEP team's chairperson or the school district's special education coordinator.

## Typical elements of an IEP team meeting

Typically, IEP team meetings start with participant introductions and short explanations of their involvement with the student and school roles. Parents are given a copy of the IDEA Procedural Safeguards, sometimes called "parents' rights." They may ask the team chairperson for explanations as needed or waive discussion if they understand or are already familiar with this material. The team may discuss need for referral; discuss evaluation results already obtained; determine eligibility for special education services and/or general education accommodations; review IEP progress annually, adjusting goals and objectives as indicated; plan for transitions; and/or address concerns at any time. The team establishes the student's present level of performance through assessment results and writes student goals and objectives for improvement. A designated team member records a meeting summary; parents should receive a copy of this summary. They may voice any disagreements with team decisions, which should be consensual, and record their objections in the written summary.

## Evaluating intellectual abilities

Today, both intellectual ability and adaptive behavior are measured to assess intellectual disabilities. For assessing intelligence, a number of valid, reliable IQ tests exist. David Wechsler's series includes the Wechsler Preschool and Primary Scales of Intelligence (WPPSI) for ages 2 years 6 months to 7 years 3 months; Wechsler Intelligence Scales for Children (WISC) for ages 6 to 16 years 11 months; and Wechsler Adult Intelligence Scales (WAIS) for ages 16 to 90 years. The Stanford-Binet Intelligence Scales constitute another standardized IQ test for individuals aged 2 to 23 years. The Woodcock-Johnson (WJ) Tests of Cognitive Abilities for ages 2 to 90+ years, the Differential Ability Scales (DAS) for ages 2 years 6 months to 17 years 11 months, and the Kauffman Assessment Battery for Children (KABC) for ages 3 to 18 years are additional good formal, standardized intelligence measures. All these tests measure specific cognitive abilities in addition to general intelligence.

## Adaptive behavior assessment

To make an informal assessment of adaptive behavior, that is, how functional the student's behaviors are, the assessor should interview the student, and also separately interview a reliable adult third party who knows the student very well. This may be a parent, teacher, therapist, babysitter, neighbor, family friend, or other individual who is very familiar with the student. This adult should know about things like self-care routines the child can perform independently, amounts and types of assistance are needed with various activities, how the student communicates and interacts with others socially, degrees and types of motor control the child does or does not display, whether the student displays maladaptive behaviors, and if so, what types. Most formal standardized adaptive behavior scales depend strongly on how well the third party knows the student and the third party's response style. Therefore, multiple information sources, including both formal and informal assessments and more than one third-party respondent, are advised.

## Modifying assessments to accommodate students

Teachers and other test administrators should try to find quiet places for mildly or moderately disabled students to take tests. For students with difficulty writing, they should allow oral responses or provide scribes to write down students' responses. If possible, students with mild or moderate intellectual disabilities should be exempted from district-wide standardized tests, which are normed using students without intellectual disabilities. For students who can or must take a test, the teacher or other administrator should divide it into smaller, more manageable parts. Teachers should grade disabled students' response content separately from their spelling for fairness. Students with intellectual disabilities should be given as much time as they need to complete tests. In fact, administrators should avoid giving this population timed tests at all. Another modification is to adjust the percentage of correct responses required for a passing score. Disabled students should be allowed to retake tests if needed. Administrators should also enable monitored breaks during testing for these students.

## Historical and current methods of assessing intellectual disabilities

Historically, only intelligence measures were used to assess intellectual disabilities. However, educators eventually realized that an individual's success in school and life depends not only on cognitive ability, but also equally on adaptive behavior; so now both types of measures are used. IQ tests are used to determine an individual's cognitive developmental level, while adaptive behavior scales are used to test how well the individual's behaviors adapt to his or her environment—that is, how functional or effective those behaviors are. The Vineland Adaptive Behavior Scales (VABS) is a time-honored, popular standardized test for assessing adaptive functioning. It covers the domains of communication, daily living skills, socialization, and motor skills, and includes an optional Maladaptive Behavior Index. Another useful instrument is the Adaptive Behaviors Assessment system, published by Pearson Education. The American Association for Intellectual and Developmental Disabilities (AAIDD, formerly AAMR) has also recently developed its own Diagnostic Adaptive Behavior Scale (DABS).

## Complete educational assessment

For a complete educational assessment, the assessor should collaborate with the student's teachers to compile background information on the student's academic history. The assessor will create and maintain records of relevant student information. The assessor must also establish and maintain rapport with the assessed student and administer formal test instruments to him or her, then score and interpret those results. To accommodate the student's individual needs, the assessor must be able to modify any existing tests or tools as needed. The assessor will have to determine the student's current level of functioning through interpretations of formal and informal assessment measures. The assessor will discuss the evaluation results with the student's teachers. The assessor will then suggest plans for instruction and/or modifications to the student's existing instructional plan. All assessors must take ethical procedures for confidentiality of communication into consideration when sharing student information. Finally, the assessor will complete a written report of the assessment results.

## Selecting formal tests for assessment

Educators should consider where to obtain a published test, its price, and any purchasing restrictions. They should determine whether the test is available in other languages and identify the population used for the test's norm group, including their ages and ethnicities, and whether students with disabilities are represented. It is also important to examine test content for signs of cultural bias. Furthermore, they must consider what accommodations of a test are possible in order to enable students with disabilities to take it. They should review the test's materials, administration and scoring procedures, and what types of scores it yields. They should examine the test's validity, reliability, applications, and limits. Additionally, they should take all this information into account to arrive at their own judgment of a test's value as a psychoeducational assessment instrument for students with mild to moderate disabilities.

## Minimum competencies for those administering standardized tests

Those giving students tests should establish a rapport with them in order to ensure accurate scores. They should scrupulously guard against scoring and recording errors. They should not make their own scoring sheets that do not match the test's official scoring sheets, and they must protect test materials' and scoring keys' security. They should provide settings (as possible) to assure students' best test performance, like sufficient space and lowest noise levels. As far as possible, they must assure every student understands and follows all test instructions for accurate scores. However, they must not coach or train students, individually or in groups, on test items, which would misrepresent students' abilities. They should be willing, though, to provide guidance and interpretation in counseling situations to test-takers. Test administrators should not answer test-takers' questions in more detail than allowed by test manuals. They also should not assume a norm for one student group or subtest applies to a norm for another group or subtest.

## Woodcock-Johnson (WJ) Tests of Cognitive Abilities

### Short-term and long-term memory abilities

Short-term memory (immediate, temporary memory) is tested by the Woodcock-Johnson (WJ) subtests of Numbers Reversed and Auditory Working Memory, measuring working memory and memory span; and Memory for Words, also measuring memory span. Working memory is the ability to retain current information temporarily well enough to manipulate it, such as combining additional parts to form a coherent whole, as in understanding words in a sentence or sentences in a paragraph. Memory span measures the ability to recall information presented once, immediately and in correct sequence. Long-term memory storage and retrieval are tested by the WJ subtests of Visual-Auditory Learning and Visual-Auditory Learning - Delayed, which measure associative memory, or the ability to recall one item from a previously learned (unrelated) pair when presented with the other item; and Retrieval Fluency, which measures ideational fluency, or the ability to generate many varied responses to one stimulus.

### Processing speed and quantitative knowledge

Processing speed refers to the ability to perform easy or familiar cognitive operations quickly and automatically, especially when they require focused attention and concentration, that is, high mental efficiency. The WJ tests this ability through four subtests: Visual Matching measures perceptual speed that is, finding, identifying, comparing, and contrasting visual elements. This includes pattern recognition, scanning, perceptual memory, and complex processing abilities. The Decision Speed subtest measures semantic processing, meaning reaction time to a stimulus requiring some encoding and mental manipulation. The Rapid Picture Naming subtests measures naming facility ("rapid automatic naming" in reading research), meaning the ability of rapidly naming familiar presented things (objects, concepts, their images, or descriptions) with names retrieved from long-term memory. The Pair Cancellation subtest measures the student's ability to attend to and concentrate on presented stimuli. Quantitative k knowledge is acquired numerical or mathematical information. The WJ does not have any subtests for measuring quantitative knowledge.

### Crystallized and fluid intelligence

Crystallized intelligence, or the solidified knowledge that an individual has acquired from his or her culture through life experiences and formal and informal education, is measured on the WJ by its subtests of General Information and Verbal Comprehension. The latter subtest measures language development and lexical knowledge (vocabulary). Fluid intelligence or reasoning stands in contrast to crystallized intelligence or knowledge. This is the ability to solve novel problems by performing mental operations. Fluid reasoning is measured on the WJ by its Concept Formation subtest, which tests inductive reasoning—the ability to relate a specific problem to a generalized, underlying rule, concept, or principle—and Analysis-Synthesis, which tests deductive or general sequential reasoning—the ability to apply a general rule, concept, or principle to a specific problem. Thus inductive (specific to general) and deductive (general to specific) reasoning, which are opposite processes, are both part of the cognitive ability of fluid intelligence.

## Visual and auditory processing

The WJ tests visual processing through subtests of Spatial Relations, which includes visualization; Picture Recognition, measuring visual memory; and Planning, which includes spatial scanning. The term "spatial relations" means the ability to perceive objects in space, their orientation, and visual patterns, and to maintain and manipulate these rapidly. Visualization is the ability to match objects in space, including mentally manipulating them three-dimensionally more than once, regardless of response speed. Spatial scanning involves quickly and accurately identifying paths through complex, large, visual, or spatial fields. Auditory processing, the ability to interpret sound signals from one's sense of hearing, is tested by the WJ subtests of Sound Blending, measuring phonetic coding for synthesis; Incomplete Words, measuring phonetic coding for analysis; and Auditory Attention, measuring ideational fluency. Phonetic coding for synthesis involves putting sounds together meaningfully as in words. Phonetic coding for analysis involves breaking words down to their component sounds. Ideational fluency is the ability of rapidly generating many diverse responses or ideas to one stimulus.

## Wechsler intelligence scales (WPPSI, WISC, WAIS)

### Crystallized intelligence

Crystallized intelligence is the knowledge that students have amassed from their culture through their life and formal and informal educational experiences, including the ability to retrieve this information from memory. David Wechsler's intelligence scales measure this capacity through four subscales: Information, which measures the student's store of general information; Vocabulary, which measures language development and lexical knowledge; Similarities, which also measures language development and lexical knowledge, in the context of the ability to make comparisons; and Comprehension, which measures language development and general information. Fluid intelligence or reasoning is the ability to perform mental operations that manipulate information to solve new problems, requiring cognitive flexibility, as well as existing knowledge. The Wechsler tests measure this capacity through the Matrix Reasoning subscale, which tests inductive reasoning. Inductive reasoning is the ability to generalize from a specific task, problem, or set of observations to a broader underlying principle, concept, or rule.

### Short-term memory and long-term memory

Short-term memory is the ability to maintain immediate awareness of information received in the last few minutes. Three Wechsler subscales address this: the Digit Span subscale measures memory span, or the ability of sequentially accurate, immediate recall of a series of numbers presented only once. The Letter-Number Sequencing subscale measures both memory span and working memory, or the ability to temporarily store information and perform mental operations on it, requiring divided attention. The Sentences subscale measures both memory span and the level of the student's language development. Information used in working memory and memory span, that is, in short-term memory, is not retained beyond the few minutes when it is needed, unless it is also stored in long-term memory. Long-term storage and retrieval can be reproductive, meaning recalling facts from memory; and/or reconstructive, that is, generating new material based on rules, principles, or concepts stored in memory. The Wechsler intelligence scales do not contain any subscales to measure long-term memory storage and retrieval.

### Auditory processing, processing speed, and quantitative knowledge

Auditory processing is the ability to interpret information received through the sense of hearing. The Wechsler intelligence scales do not contain any subscales specifically measuring auditory processing. Processing speed is the ability to perform easy or familiar cognitive operations quickly and automatically, especially when they require focused attention and concentration, that is, high mental efficiency. Three Wechsler subscales measure this: the Coding-Digit Symbol and Animal Pegs subscales measure rate-of-test-taking. This does not reflect test content, but is rather a general measure of rapidity in taking easy or over-learned tests requiring very simple decisions. The Symbol Search subscale also measures this, plus

- 23 -

perceptual speed, or finding, identifying, comparing, and contrasting visual elements. Perceptual speed includes pattern recognition, scanning, perceptual memory, and complex processing abilities. Quantitative knowledge is numerical or mathematical knowledge. Wechsler's Arithmetic subscale measures math achievement, which relies on quantitative knowledge, as well as quantitative reasoning (inductive and deductive reasoning about mathematical properties and relations).

Visual processing
Visual processing is the brain's ability to interpret signals received through the sense of vision (eyesight). Six Wechsler subscales measure this area: the Block Design tests visualization, or the ability to match objects in space, including mentally manipulating them three-dimensionally more than once, regardless of response speed; and spatial relations, or the ability to perceive objects in space, their orientation, and visual patterns; and to maintain and manipulate these rapidly. The Object Assembly subscale also measures spatial relations, plus closure speed, the ability to quickly identify meaningful familiar visual objects from incomplete (partial, unconnected, or vague) stimuli by filling in missing parts. The Mazes subscale measures spatial scanning, that is, the ability to quickly and accurately identify paths through complex or large visual/spatial fields. The Picture Completion and Picture Arrangement subscales measure general information. Picture Completion also measures flexibility of closure—recognizing a figure or pattern within a complex or distracting background. Picture Arrangement also measures visualization, as does the Geometric Designs subscale.

## Woodcock-Johnson Tests of Cognitive Abilities (WJ) vs. Wechsler intelligence scales (WPPSI, WISC, and WAIS)

Controlled learning, timed testing, preschooler-targeted subtests, and long-term follow-up capacity
The WJ cognitive tests include three controlled-learning tests, meaning tests measuring learning with corrective feedback provided throughout their administration: the Visual-Auditory Learning, Concept Formation, and Analysis-Synthesis subtests. These are useful, as many students with mild to moderate deficits do not have the same automaticity in these cognitive abilities as others, yet are able to learn them with instruction. The Wechsler scales do not include controlled-learning tests. The Wechsler subscales are generally timed. The WJ tests are not timed except for those specifically measuring speed. The WPPSI, whose age range includes preschoolers, includes subtests specifically designed for preschoolers using diverse printed and manipulative test materials. The WJ tests do not include subscales specifically targeting this age group. Both the WJ and Wechsler cognitive tests have the capacity for longitudinal follow-up testing using the same measures across the age ranges specified for each test.

Nonverbal measures, subtest norms, and aptitude measures
The WJ cognitive tests are administered in pantomime and require no verbal responses, so they are suitable for students with deficits in both receptive and expressive language. The Wechsler tests have a composite needing no expressive verbal responses, but demanding receptive language comprehension. All 20 WJ cognitive subtests are normed for ages 4 to 90+; seven of these are normed for ages 2 to 90+. The WPPSI has 12 subscales normed across its age range of 2 years 11 months to 7 years 3 months. The WISC has 13 subscales normed across its age range of 6 to 16 years 11 months. The WAIS has 14 subscales normed across its age range of 16 to 89 years. The WJ tests include differentiated measures of aptitude to help predict potential future achievement according to specified criteria. These measures include Oral Language Aptitude, Reading Aptitude, Mathematics Aptitude, Written Language Aptitude, and Knowledge Aptitude. The Wechsler scales do not use aptitude measures to predict achievement.

Recorded tests, selective testing, examiner training, and Spanish versions
The Woodcock-Johnson cognitive tests include recording of subtests for memory and auditory processing to standardize their administration; the Wechsler intelligence scales do not. The Woodcock-Johnson test

manual emphasizes the principle of selective testing in that its authors recommend customizing the battery's subtests for specific referral matters. Wechsler does not emphasize selective use of his subscales for referral purposes. The Woodcock-Johnson manual includes examiner training activities such as examiner training checklists, observation checklists, and so forth, while the Wechsler test manuals do not. There is not presently a Spanish language version of the Woodcock-Johnson cognitive tests. However, Wechsler has produced a revised version of the WISC (Wechsler Intelligence Scales for Children) using Mexican Spanish (WISC-RM), and another version normed on Puerto Rican Spanish students (EIWN-R-PR, or Escala de Inteligencia Wechsler para Ninos - Revised – Puerto Rico).

Administration time
Overall, the Woodcock-Johnson standard battery of tests take less time to administer than Wechsler's standard battery for children and younger teens (WPPSI and WISC). The Woodcock-Johnson extended battery can take as long as Wechsler's standard battery for older teens and adults (WAIS), but if optional subtests in the WAIS are also administered, it can take longer than even the extended battery of the Woodcock-Johnson tests. The Woodcock-Johnson's standard battery of tests normally takes about 35 to 45 minutes to administer. The Woodcock-Johnson extended battery normally takes about 90 minutes total. Most of these subtests are not timed, while the Wechsler subtests are. The WPPSI and WISC for preschoolers and primary students respectively, and for children, each take about 50 to 70 minutes to administer; including optional subtests adds approximately 10 to 15 minutes more. The WAIS, for ages 16 to 89, takes approximately 60 to 90 minutes to administer, with optional subtests adding about 10 to 15 minutes more to the total time.

Developmental and proficiency levels, peer comparisons, and co-norming with related achievement tests
To determine developmental levels, the Wechsler scales give a Composite Test Age, while the WJ tests give an Age Equivalent and a Grade Equivalent. Wechsler does not score proficiency levels in his tests. The WJ tests give Instructional Ranges, Developmental Level Bands, and a Relative Mastery Index to assess proficiency levels. The Wechsler intelligence scales give Percentile Rank and IQ/Index for peer comparisons. The WJ cognitive tests give Percentile Rank, Standard Score, T-Score, Normal Curve Equivalent, Stanine, and CALP for peer comparisons. In addition to providing age norms, which include students in the same age range whether they are enrolled in colleges and universities or not, the WJ tests give separate grade norms for post-secondary students, while the WAIS does not. The WJ cognitive tests are co-normed with the Woodcock-Johnson Tests of Achievement (WJ ACH), and the WAIS is co-normed with the Wechsler Memory Scale (WMS).

**Links to certain achievement tests and/or special-purpose test batteries; Contrast how WJ and Wechsler tests analyze ability and achievement relative to discrepancy norms**

The Woodcock-Johnson Tests of Cognitive Abilities (WJ) are not linked to any specific tests of achievement or special-purpose test batteries.

The Wechsler Preschool and Primary Scales of Intelligence (WPPSI) and Wechsler Intelligence Scales for Children (WISC) are linked to the Wechsler Individual Achievement Test (WIAT). The WISC is additionally linked with the Children's Memory Scale (Cohen). The WISC and the
Wechsler Adult Intelligence Scales (WAIS) are both linked to the Wechsler Abbreviated Intelligence Scale (WASI).

The WJ cognitive tests basetheir aptitude/achievement analyses on actual discrepancy norms, that is, without correction for statistical regression procedures. This permits student discrepancies between ability and performance to be compared with national distribution norms for discrepancy scores. The

WPPSI andWISC, with the WIAT, base their aptitude/achievement analyses on estimated discrepancy norms, using correction for regression procedures.

The WAIS gives analyses of discrepancies between ability and memory with the Wechsler Memory Scale (WMS) based on actual discrepancy norms.

**Sample sizes of student scores used for establishing norms for the general measure of intelligence**

The Woodcock-Johnson Tests of Cognitive Abilities (WJ) instrument has a total sample size of 6,085 students for establishing its norm for the general intelligence measure.

The WPPSI for preschool and early primary school-age children (ages 2 years 11 months to 7 years 3 months) has a sample size of 1,700, with an average per year of age of 283.

The WISC, for older primary and early secondary school-age children (ages 6 years to 16 years 11 months), has a sample size of 2,200, with an average of 200 per year of age.

The WAIS, for older adolescents and adults (ages 16 to 89 years), has a sample size of 2,450, with an average of 200 per age group.

The WJ covers ages 2 to 90+ years while the Wechsler tests are divided by age range so the latter can be added together: 1,700 + 2,200 + 2,450 = 6,350. Thus, the WJ's total sample size of 6,085 and the Wechsler tests' total samples for all age ranges of 6,350 are comparable with the Wechsler tests' total having 265 more students than the WJ's total sample.

**Person and community variables used respectively in establishing norms**

For its norms—normally distributed test scores of a sample of students representative of the general population—the WJ cognitive tests use the person variables of sex, race, Hispanic origin, parent education, school type (public, private, home), occupations of adults, occupational status, and education of adults. The Wechsler intelligence scales use the person variables of gender, race/ethnicity (no separate category for Hispanic origin), and family socioeconomic status, including occupation and education. The Wechsler tests use community location and size as community variables for establishing norms. The WJ cognitive tests use location, size, and 13 additional socioeconomic community variables, distributed as these controlled values: three adult educational levels; three levels of occupational status; three classes of occupations; and among colleges and universities, two types of institutions and two types of funding.

**Prereferral screening**

When adults suspect deficits in a child's ability to learn, speech-language development, or school achievement, qualified educators can give the child brief screening tests. Screenings are made prior to making referrals for formal evaluation to determine if there is a need for special education services. Screenings may determine whether a student has academic weaknesses that would affect formal response to intervention in regular education programs. They can determine whether or not the student has any learning disability in addition to or instead of mild to moderate intellectual disability. They can determine whether the student has a visual and/or hearing disability instead of, or in addition to, intellectual disability. Emotional and/or behavioral disability can also be ruled in or out as compounding, creating, or mimicking intellectual disability. The IDEA (Individuals with Disabilities Education Act) requires schools to rule out instruction or other variables addressable in regular education as causes for learning problems before conducting full assessments.

## Referring a child for assessment of disabilities

When an adult observes and has concerns about a child's cognitive development, or about the child's level of functioning or school progress, the adult can refer the child for testing. However, one prerequisite to a complete evaluation is a prereferral screening, involving brief tests to determine if full assessment is indicated. Any involved adult can refer a child, though it is most commonly a teacher or parent. The Individuals with Disabilities Education Act (IDEA) law mandates referral to ascertain eligibility for special education services, and Section 504 of the Americans with Disabilities Act (ADA) mandates eligibility for accommodations to be made within the regular education classroom. Following referral, the assessment can determine whether the child's intellectual ability is considered normal for his or her age/grade level or not; whether the child has any specific learning disabilities; whether there are physical, emotional, and/or behavioral disabilities; and whether the child's performance is consistent with intellectual ability.

When a parent, teacher, counselor, other school staff member, or other familiar concerned adult believes a child should be referred for assessment, he or she should write a referral letter to the school's principal or other designated administrator. Educators estimate it should take roughly 30 minutes for most adults to write a referral letter. Letters should be typed or neatly handwritten, using business letter style or a district form if the school district uses forms. Letters should include the child's name, birth date, school name, and grade, plus the sender's mailing address, phone numbers, e-mail address, and any additional relevant information, including relationship to the child. In addition to contact information, the writer should describe as specifically as possible what kinds of learning or functioning problems s/he has observed in the child. The letter should state that the writer is referring the child for evaluation and requesting an Individual Education Plan (IEP) meeting to discuss this referral, providing several dates and times s/he is available to meet with school personnel.

## Technical quality of assessments

One issue that must be considered when developing academic assessments is the technical quality of the examination.

The National Center for Research on Evaluation, Standards and Student Testing (CRESST) developed the following criteria to evaluate technical quality:
- Cognitive Complexity: requires problem-solving, critical thinking and reasoning ability.
- Content Quality: correct responses demonstrate knowledge of critical subject matter.
- Meaningfulness: students understand the value of the assessment and the tasks involved.
- Language Appropriateness: clear to the students and appropriate to the requested task.
- Transfer and Generalization: indicates ability to complete similar tasks and the results permit valid generalization about learning capabilities.
- Fairness: performance measurements and scoring avoid factors irrelevant to school learning.
- Reliability: consistently represents data added to students' background knowledge.
- Consequences: it results in the desired effect on students, instructors and the educational system.

## Content standards

Content standards define the specific areas of knowledge every student needs to learn. These areas are usually the traditional subjects of English (or language arts), mathematics, science, social studies,music,art, and drama; some also include general concepts and interdisciplinary studies. Some reflect one grade level and specific academic content, while others combine grade levels and integrate the content across academic disciplines. Standards should not be so broad they cannot be used as instructional guidelines or to evaluate students effectively.

Specific standards are created by individual states and various national educational organizations; ideally, the groups work in tandem. The content standards should be a result of community meetings that include academic and business representatives so that the requirements of both are recognized and met. These meetings should be moderated by state leaders and open to the public so that everyone helps define what needs to be taught and the methods used to teach it.

## Performance standards

Evaluating students' progress using performance standards is tricky because there is no clear definition of the term. Are the standards based upon test performance? If so, do they take into account test grading practices? Do they mean the method of reporting test scores, e.g., basic equates to unacceptable, proficient to adequate, and advanced to excellent? How good is good enough? The Goals 2000: Educate America Act says "performance standards means concrete examples and explicit definitions of what students have to know and be able to do to demonstrate that such students are proficient in the skills and knowledge framed by content standards." Performance standards must also be appropriate for the age, feasible to administer, and useful for evaluating progress. According to this definition, content and performance should be evaluated together in order to obtain a clear picture of the student's progress or lack thereof.

## Articulation matrix and Bloom's taxonomy

An articulation matrix is the relationship between activities and outcomes. It is a defined set of goals and the methods used to reach them. For example in a graduation matrix, completing the required courses is the outcome, and the lectures, homework assignments, projects, papers, tests, and evaluations are the activities.

Bloom's Taxonomy, which is a hierarchical classification system, is an articulation matrix that outlines six levels of cognitive learning. At each step, students reach a predictable level of mastery:
- Knowledge Level: ability to define terms.
- Comprehension Level: finish problems and explain answers.
- Application Level: recognizes problems and uses methods to solve them.
- Analysis Level: ability to explain why the process works.
- Synthesis Level: can use the process or part of it in new ways.
- Evaluation Level: can create different ways to solve problems and use designated criteria and can select the best method to obtain the correct solution.

## Credibility and feasibility

For any assessment method to be successful, it must be introduced to the community in a way that builds support rather than causing confusion, resentment, and skepticism. Parents, teachers, students, and the public need to understand the purpose of the assessment, what it is intended to accomplish, why it is necessary and how it will logically integrate with methods already in place. Allowing the community to review the test and try to answer some of the questions will usually help generate acceptance of the new tool.

Development, scoring and reporting costs, and teacher expectations should be considered before a new assessment is introduced and implemented. Sometimes the cost is prohibitive. Teachers may not be qualified to prepare students or to administer the test and training may not be available or affordable. These potential stumbling blocks need to be addressed before a new assessment is added to the existing requirements.

## Assessment station

An assessment station is a designated area, inside or outside of the classroom, used for the specific purpose of evaluating students' progress performing a task. Individuals or groups can be assigned to complete a task, use a piece of lab equipment or work with some technological device. The purpose is to assess the knowledge acquired, processes used, skills displayed, and general attitude about the task, and if working in a group, how each student interacts with the other members of the team.

The assessment station should function the same way every time it is used. This builds consistency and reduces the time needed for explanations and demonstrations before and during future assessments. Instructions should be clear, concise and specific and explain exactly how the area should be left for the next student. Activities performed in the assessment station should be simple, straightforward and relate to the material being studied.

## Using an assessment station

Because the assessment station is an interactive tool, the area needs to be equipped with the appropriate equipment necessary to complete the task. If the activity is an experiment, the area needs to be ventilated and appropriate safety precautions taken, e.g., having water available and a fire extinguisher at hand. The students need to understand how to operate the instruments in a safe manner and therefore instructions should be provided both in writing and verbally. Questions should be asked and answered before any activity is started. If it is a group activity, each student needs to contribute to the assigned task.
The work submitted by each student is evaluated using a rating/grading scale or a checklist. For example if the task required the use of a microscope, the checklist should have points related to its use. If it was a group project, cooperation, helpfulness and leadership skills should be noted.

## Individual assessments

Individual assessments focus on the progress each student made during a defined period of time (e.g., every six weeks, at the end of the semester) rather than in a team collaboration. A variety of activities such as written assignments, oral presentations, and class participation should be incorporated into the assessment in order to obtain a broader, more realistic view of the student's understanding of the material. The assessment process should be fully explained so that the student knows what is expected. He is evaluated using one or all of the following standards:
- self-referenced —based on his previous level of progress
- criterion-referenced — a defined, school or district-wide standard
- norm-referenced — based on the progress of groups of students the same age or grade level

Using a combination of standards instead of relying on one method presents a clearer, more accurate picture of the student's growth.

## Group assessments

Group assessments focus on how students cooperate and collaborate in completing a project assigned to the group rather than to a single student. The same activities used in individual assessments are used, such as written assignments, oral presentations, and group participation, but they are used to evaluate social and interactive skills as well as the work produced. The students' willingness to accept being evaluated for a group project is based on if and how long they have been exposed to this type of cooperative collaboration and if they feel the grading system is applied fairly. If this project is the first time students in a competitive environment are expected to work together, there may be some misunderstandings and objections about what is expected, how it works, and how each student will be evaluated. It is critical the teacher explains the evaluation process clearly, answers questions, addresses reservations, and closely monitors individual contributions as well as the progress of the project.

## Advantages and disadvantages of assessments

Individual assessments are easily understood by students and parents and mesh with most school districts' systems. Because each student is evaluated based on criteria established by state performance and/or content standards, it is easy to measure the success of department curricula. Self-referenced standards provide feedback about the student's strengths and weaknesses. They can help motivate the student to work harder and take more responsibility for his learning. Students sometimes set personal goals and expectations. Individual assessments help them measure their success. These evaluations provide the teacher insight into any special help the student might need. Individual assessment can create and encourage a very competitive environment in which some students are unable to compete effectively. It makes it difficult to evaluate students' ability to work with a team and judge their interaction with others both of which are important to the educational experience. They can also be also very time consuming for the teacher to complete fairly and accurately.

There are three ways to evaluate a group project: group grade only, individual grade only, or a combination of both. The reason for group projects is to teach cooperation in a team environment. Giving everyone the same grade can foster some degree of esprit de corps. It also frees the teacher from having to decide who was responsible for what part of the project. A group grade, however, can cause resentment, especially if students are not used to working in a group and are used to earning grades based on a competitive scale. Students understand individual grades, but in a group project environment the competitive scale diminishes the spirit of cooperation because everyone is working for himself rather than for the good of the team. Giving a group grade and an individual grade addresses both issues. Basing eighty percent of the grade on cooperation and collaboration and twenty percent on individual production recognizes the importance of working for the group and the necessity of individual contributions.

## Performance contracts

A performance contract is a written agreement between an individual student or a group of students and a teacher about a specific activity. The assignment can be a research paper, an oral presentation with props, or some other project. The contract clearly states the goal, explains the activity, establishes a timeline, and describes who will do what and how it will be done. Sometimes the agreement also details the criteria to be used to evaluate the finished product. This tool helps students learn to plan a project by breaking it into manageable parts and shows them how to utilize their time more efficiently. Not only can the completed project be graded, but the performance contract itself can be evaluated. The teacher should assess the student's participation in setting up the contract, his willingness to compromise when necessary and his general attitude about the concept and the process.

Performance contracts can be a great learning experience for students by teaching them how to plan and prioritize and encouraging them to avoid procrastination. However, some students may have trouble understanding the concept, so it may be necessary to review the planning, organizing, and writing steps several times before they are able to grasp the idea. Using contracts can also help a struggling student in other areas of his life. These agreements can be developed to address attendance requirements and expected behavior standards or to plan weekly or monthly homework schedules.

If a teacher has never used performance contracts, he needs to understand that setting up the system and helping the students write their agreements is very time consuming, especially in the beginning. It can help, as a class project, to create a performance contract based on a completed project. This strategy sometimes reduces the learning curve for all the students.

In order for a performance contract to be a learning experience, the guidelines for writing one should be very general. The teacher can either give the student a written list of suggestions or, preferably, discuss them one-on-one. Some questions that might be used:
- What work items are you planning to include?
- Where you will find the necessary data: Personal reference books, the internet, the library? Do you have additional sources?
- How long will it take to outline a plan, research the topic, and finish the project?
- What criteria should be used to evaluate the finished product?

Questions that might be used to evaluate the completed contract:
- Is the contract realistic relative to required completion date?
- Are the contract questions appropriate to the project objectives?
- Were reliable and appropriate sources chosen?
- How comprehensive is the plan?
- Does the student understand his capabilities and recognize his limitations?

## Example of a performance contract

Student's Name: _____

Teacher's Name: _____

Contract Dates: _____

Purpose of Contract: _____

I am planning a study of: _____

Reason for choosing this topic: _____

Main focus of the study: _____

Questions I want to answer (add as many lines as needed):

_____

Sources I plan to use (check at least 5):
*Books ___; Interviews ___; Experiments ___; Magazines___; Encyclopedia___; Newspapers___; Museums___; Pictures, Films, Videos___; Other Sources/ My Research___*

Explain: _____

The finished product will be in the form of: _____

The learning skills I will use: _____

The study will be completed by (different dates may be given for various segments):

_____

The study will be reviewed by: _____

Evaluated by: _____

The evaluator will be looking for: _____

Student's Signature _____

Teacher's Signature _____

## Portfolio

Once decisions have been made about what will be included, it is important to begin with baseline data for comparison as the portfolio grows. Selected material can be placed in a folder or large envelope with the student's name on the front. Each addition needs to be dated with an explanation attached stating why the item was included and what features should be noted. Teachers who use portfolios will often create assignments with the intention of including it in the package. As the contents grow, it may become necessary due to space limitations to review the items and remove some daily work, quizzes, or tests. Once the portfolio is complete, the teacher needs to have a method to evaluate the contents and review the student's progress in areas such as creativity, critical thinking, originality, research skills, perseverance, responsibility, and communication effectiveness. A checklist can be useful (see card 192).

## Portfolios and student assessment

A portfolio is a collection of the student's work assembled over a period of time (e.g., six week grading period, one semester, the entire year). Various items can be included: contracts, copies of completed activities such as papers; presentations and pictures of props; performance assessments made by the student, his peers, and the teacher; copies of class work and homework; classroom tests; and state-mandated exams. A portfolio is a powerful aide in assessing the student's progress and an excellent format to present to parents so they can review their child's progress. The decision on what to include should be a collaboration between the student and the teacher. What will be included: examples of best work, worst work, typical work, or perhaps some of each?  Will the student keep a copy as a reference point? Decisions need to be made and rules established as early as possible in the process so that progress is accurately and fairly recorded.

## Student feedback form

---

### Rating For Group Project

Student Name: _____

Date of Project _____ to _____

*Circle the phrase that describes how you feel.*
Choosing the members of your group:

**I really like it.**          **It's okay.**                    **I don't like it.**

Having the teacher choose group members:

**I really like it.**          **It's okay.**                    **I don't like it.**

The group deciding how you are going to complete the project?

**I really like it.**          **It's okay.**                    **I don't like it.**

Comments:

_____
_____
_____

---

## Work products, response groups

Work Products are completed assignments that are evaluated on the basis of the topic chosen as well as creativity, originality, organization, understanding of the subject matter, social and academic progress, and success in meeting and/or exceeding predetermined criteria along with any other items deemed important by the individual teacher. Work products can take many different forms, including but not limited to research papers, poems, fiction and non-fiction stories, bulletin boards, video and audio tapes, computer and laboratory demonstrations, dramatic performances, debates and oral presentations, paintings, drawings and sculptures, and musical compositions and performances.

Response Groups are discussions about a particular subject. Frequently, the students themselves start them spontaneously in response to a shared experience. They want to talk about the event because it affected all of them in some way. Teachers can gain insight into the students' critical thinking skills, information and observations shared, willingness to participate in the discussion and behavior within the group.

## Self and peer-assessment

Self-assessment allows the student to become involved in the evaluation process. He takes more responsibility for the learning process because he is expected to reflect upon his attitude about and attention to assigned activities and the product produced. To be truly effective, the student should be involved in developing the evaluation criteria. It gives him more control. Instead of the teacher having all of the power and being perceived as such, some power shifts to the student in allowing him to help determine the rating scale used, to participate in evaluating the finished product, and to provide direct input into the grade which he receives.

During peer-assessments, students learn by listening to other students critique their work and make suggestions on ways to improve it. The student doing the evaluation must think analytically about their peer's work product; in doing so, it should help him become more critical about his own work. Teachers need to moderate these discussions and stress consistency, being descriptive and not judgmental, realistic, positive, and reflective.

**Book response journal, comparison chart, conferences**

The Book Response Journal is a place for students to express their feelings about concepts and ideas discovered in the literature they read whether in a book, magazine, on the internet, or some other source of information. Students are encouraged to use these journals to comment on everything which they read. Teachers can use the journals as a way to ask questions, comment on the student's observations, and suggest additional reading material. Book response journals can and probably should be reviewed in student-teacher conferences.

Comparison Charts are a graphic way to organize ideas, events, characters, plot lines, and the like so that they can be compared and contrasted. They can be used by individual students and are a very effective tool for small groups to use in order to generate lively discussions.

The main purpose of a Conference is to collaborate, assess, and guide. They can be used for setting goals, coaching and mentoring, and evaluating the student's progress.

**Graffiti wall, interview, KWL technique**

A graffiti wall is a designated area to brainstorm ideas, concepts, observations, questions, and conclusions about a topic. It can be used as an evolving record of the progress made by the group as they begin to understand the subject being researched and discussed. It can develop into a class dictionary and thesaurus used to enrich the students' vocabulary.

An interview is a dialogue between the student and the teacher. Typically one or more questions are asked or problems posed in such a way as to determine the depth of understanding rather than to elicit specific answers.

A KWL is an effective way to assess how well the student grasped the concepts and can be used to judge the effectiveness of the teacher's lesson plan. The acronym stands for "Know," "Want," "Learned," and refers to what student knows and wants to know at the beginning of the lesson and what he has learned at the end of the lesson.

**Demonstration, discussion, goal setting, I learned statement**

A demonstration turns a concept into a concrete, observable experience using one or more of the five senses. It can be an audio-visual presentation, a piece of art or music, or a personal interpretation using drama or dance. It can be an experiment or an explanation of how something works.

A discussion should be a safe forum for students to explore and explain ideas and concepts. They should be encouraged to speak, listen, and comment on and respond to their own and others' opinions, feelings, and reactions to a specific topic.

Goal Setting is an excellent way to help students learn to plan a project and experience success. It should be a collaborative effort with the teacher and encourage the student to reflect on his performance or lack thereof.

The purpose of an I Learned Statement is to encourage the student to express what he learned from a lecture, class discussion, homework assignment, or some other activity.

---

**Rating Scale**

Student Being Rated: _____

Activity: _____

Student Doing the Rating: _____

Date: _____

| Presents Argument Clearly | | Demonstrates Background Knowledge | |
|---|---|---|---|
| ☐ | 5. Very Logical | ☐ | 5. Very Knowledgeable |
| ☐ | 4. Logical | ☐ | 4. Knowledgeable |
| ☐ | 3. Average | ☐ | 3. Average |
| ☐ | 2. Not Very Logical | ☐ | 2. Not All That Knowledgeable |
| ☐ | 1. Totally Illogical | ☐ | 1. Not Knowledgeable At All |
| Answers Relevant Questions | | Organization | |
| ☐ | 5. Very Relevant | ☐ | 5. Very Organized |
| ☐ | 4. Relevant | ☐ | 4. Organized |
| ☐ | 3. Average | ☐ | 3. Average |
| ☐ | 2. Some Relevance | ☐ | 2. Not Always Organized |
| ☐ | 1. No Relevance | ☐ | 1. Not Organized At All |

NOTE: can be modified to address different topics.

---

**Learning logs, oral attitude survey, oral presentation, problem-solving activity**

A learning log is similar to a book response journal except that the student records his feelings about and responses to concepts and ideas covered in all of his classes. Keeping a log is a way to encourage critical thinking and improve writing skills.

Oral attitude surveys is a method to encourage students to share their own ideas, learn about the ideas of fellow students and think about topics from different perspectives. They can also evaluate their performance and rate the effectiveness of the discussion.

An oral presentation can be a speech, a dramatic recitation of a story or a poem, a video, or a debate that is evaluated using particular criteria.

A problem-solving activity presents a question to the class. The group is expected to develop a method to find the answer and then solve the problem. Both the method and the solution are evaluated.

## Anecdotal record

An anecdotal record is a written description of observed behavior. They are usually kept in an alphabetized book, binder, or folder and should be organized so it is easy to find notes concerning a particular student. There are computer programs available that make retrieving the data simple.

To be effective, observations need to be made frequently and incidents need to be described completely and objectively; the teacher's analysis should be used as a guide for appropriate responses. Both successful situations and unsuccessful attempts need to be recorded in order to present an accurate picture of the student's progress.

The evaluation context is:
- Formative: recalling the incident may raise an alert that something that needs to be addressed.
- Summative: since observations are made over a period of time, they are an effective way to track student attitude, behavior, knowledge acquired, cognitive skills learned, etc.
- Diagnostic: consistent attention to performance may spotlight areas that need special attention.

## Sample form for an anecdotal record

---

### Anecdotal record for a group discussion
Subject Under Discussion: _____

Students' Names:

Date and Time Period of Observations:

***Characteristics to be evaluated:***

Balance between talking and listening: _____

Respect for others: _____

Actively participating in discussion: _____

Stating own opinion: _____

Acted as scribe: _____

*Effectiveness:* _____

Acted as reporter: _____

*Effectiveness:* _____

Acted as participant: _____

*Effectiveness:* _____

Acted as time-keeper: _____

*Effectiveness:* _____

---

## Observation checklist

An observation checklist is a list of specific skills, behaviors, attitudes, and processes that are relevant to a student's development and contribute to his ability to successfully complete learning activities. To be effective, these checklists need to be used frequently and be collected over a period of time. One or two observations can be misleading and will not provide an accurate measurement to reach a fair evaluation. Before a using a checklist, a teacher must decide upon its purpose, how and when it will be used, and what the criteria will be. During the observation period, all occurrences of each item shown on the list need to be recorded. It is helpful for later evaluation if the teacher has a quick reference shorthand system to describe each appearance, e.g., ! equals excellent, @ equals adequate, ? equals iffy, X equals inappropriate. After the session, notes should be added to clarify or elaborate the shorthand ratings.

## Developing an observation checklist

Developing an observation checklist takes time. It can be helpful to write down all the skills, behaviors, attitudes, and processes required to acquire mastery of the subject and that are appropriate for the particular age group. The language should be simple and easy to understand, so that the checklists can be used during student and parent conferences. Items needed for the specific task or activity to be evaluated can be chosen from the master list. There should be no more than twelve items on a checklist: any more than that becomes difficult to track, especially when observing several students at the same time. Individual checklists can be developed for specific functions, e.g., participation in a class discussion, proficiency at using a microscope, the mechanics of preparing a term paper. Whatever the rating scale, it must be used consistently, applied fairly, and easy to use during the observation period.

### Observation Checklist

Subject Being Discussed: _____

Date: _____  Class: _____

Time Elapsed: _____

| | Student Names | | |
|---|---|---|---|
| | | | |
| Spoke Clearly | | | |
| Listened to Other Opinions | | | |
| Waited for turn | | | |
| Comment was Relevant | | | |
| Challenged a Comment | | | |
| Stated Reasons for Challenge | | | |
| Noticed a Discrepancy | | | |
| Stated a Relationship Between Ideas | | | |
| Offered a Conclusion | | | |
| Inclusive Behavior Shown | | | |

## Methods of data recording

There are three ways to record data about individual student performance. Each provides important information and lends itself to evaluating different aspects of student growth.

Anecdotal Records are observations of day-to-day activities, e.g., how the student interacts in a group, his ability to complete a hands-on assignment, his demeanor while taking tests, and his development of particular cognitive skills. All these offer opportunities for teacher comments.

The criteria on Observation Checklists vary depending on what the teacher wants to evaluate. They can be used to measure the growth of knowledge, a change in attitude, or the understanding of new skills. Checklists can also be used to evaluate written assignments, oral presentations, class participation, completion of individual and/or group work, or any activity that requires assessment.

Rating Scales are similar to observation checklists. The difference between the two is that checklists are used to determine the presence or absence of a skill, while rating scales measure the quality of the performance.

## Oral presentations

Oral presentations offer a wealth of possibilities to evaluate student growth and development in several areas, including:
- Understanding of the subject,
- Planning and organizing abilities, and
- Communication skills.

This flexible assessment tool can be assigned to an individual student or as a group project. If given to a group, additional skills can be evaluated including response to other opinions, listening behaviors, active participation in discussions, and contributions to the work product. Teachers need to recognize that some students may have difficulty with or little or no experience conceptualizing, organizing, and delivering a presentation. To address these issues as well as any performance anxieties, it is necessary to establish a classroom atmosphere of acceptance so that students feel confident when giving a presentation. Allowing students some control over the choice of topic also helps alleviate some of the stress involved in standing up in front of the group.

## Rating scale

A rating scale is used to evaluate a student against a predetermined continuum. It is particularly useful for rating an oral presentation such as a speech, debate or stage performance, and for students to use as a self-assessment tool. To increase the scale's reliability, when developing the criteria to be evaluated, the activity needs to be broken into specific, manageable parts. Each criterion may need its own rating system. Scale points need to be created.
- Will the evaluation be based upon the one to five number scale with five being the highest, or
- Will the Very Good/Good/Average/Poor/Very Poor standard be used?
- Will another system be developed?

It is helpful for the teacher to decide at the beginning of the semester which units of study will be evaluated using this method and to develop the criteria and rating system ahead of time.

## Written assignments

Written assignments can take many forms, including essays, reports, term papers, short answers questions, journal and log entries, letters, articles, poetry, solutions to math puzzles, and research, to name a few. It is important that the teacher's expectations and the rating scale are explained with as much detail as possible, especially if students are unfamiliar with the process or are afraid of writing in general. The entire process should be reviewed: choosing a topic, planning, organizing, researching, outlining, writing a first draft, reviewing content, editing, writing a second draft, proofreading, asking someone to read the final draft, and meeting the deadline. Criteria need to be developed for each segment so that when the student and teacher meet for regular consultations during the process, there is a framework for discussion. If it is a group project, it is critical for the teacher to monitor the progress and make sure that every student is contributing to each phase of the process.

## Written assignments, presentations, performance assessments, homework

Students are expected to engage in and complete various activities as a normal part of daily classroom participation. Teachers not only rate work products but they can and should use these activities to gauge progress in other goals such as social development, communication skills, and cognitive growth.

- Written Assignments: The ability to plan, organize, and produce a coherent, well-written essay, report, or term paper is just as important as the content of the finished product.
- Presentations: Whether planned or spontaneous, oral presentations need to be organized, logical, and engage the attention of the audience.
- Performance Assessment: Evaluating a student's participation and performance is important for helping him develop social and communicational skills.
- Homework: Homework requires independent study, planning skills, and the ability to prioritize. The student is expected to remember to do the work and turn it in by the required deadline.

## Rating scale for oral presentation

### Rating Scale For An Oral Presentation

Student's Name: _____

Date & Class Period:

| | 5 | 4 | 3 | 2 | 1 |
|---|---|---|---|---|---|
| Voice is well modulated. | | | | | |
| Presentation is well paced. | | | | | |
| Pauses and emphases are appropriate. | | | | | |
| Can be heard easily by everyone. | | | | | |
| Material is: Organized | | | | | |
| Logical | | | | | |
| Interesting | | | | | |
| Good preparation is evident. | | | | | |
| Information used is on topic. | | | | | |
| Language is appropriate. | | | | | |
| Creativity in preparation and presentation. | | | | | |
| Audience is involved. | | | | | |

## Oral assessments

Oral assessments are used for two reasons: when written assessments are not feasible, and to evaluate a student's mastery of such topics as verbal language proficiency, debating skills, and the ability to think and respond quickly. These types of assessments can be stressful and some students may have trouble responding and become tongue-tied; and therefore it is important to conduct the session in private or in an atmosphere of acceptance. As an interactive form of communication, the teacher needs to avoid filling in the blanks and providing body language clues that might influence the student's response. It is also important to avoid accentuating gender, race, or cultural differences in the content or delivery of the questions and/or tasks. The examination period should be long enough and the tasks required general enough in order to ensure that the student's knowledge and proficiency can be adequately presented and evaluated.

## Performance assessments

- Performance assessments are used to evaluate students' progress in specific tasks like demonstrating a skill, solving a complex problem with multiple parts, or participating in a general classroom discussion. The teacher is looking for what the student has learned and retained through what he does and not merely what he says. Information gathered through performance assessments is easy to communicate to students and parents because it describes observable, verifiable actions and offers concrete discussion points to use during conferences. There are four steps to successfully integrate performance assessments into a balanced, comprehensive view of student progress:What is to be observed and assessed.
- Develop the criteria to be used.
- Decide which recording method to use between anecdotal records, an observation checklist, or a rating scale.
- Inform the students that they are being evaluated, on what they are being evaluated, and the criteria being used.

## Performance test

A performance test is used to evaluate a particular skill that is one of the primary objectives of the class. Playing a musical instrument, using the backhand stroke in tennis, making a dress, doing a tune-up on a motor vehicle, and conducting a lab experiment are all skills that can be tested using this method. The teacher must ensure that the same criteria are used to evaluate each student and that every student has the same amount of time to demonstrate the skill. If it is an outdoor activity, climate conditions should be considered. Students need to be informed ahead of time on what they will be evaluated and when it will take place. In designing a performance task, teachers should be as specific as possible and consider the objective carefully. Students should be evaluated on both the process and the results. An observation checklist or rating scale is helpful in evaluating a performance test.

## Quality tests and quizzes

Tests need to ask the right questions to accurately measure students' knowledge. There are several things to consider:
- Does each item represent an important idea or concept? If students understand the main objectives, their knowledge should be evident in their responses.
- Is each item an appropriate measure of the desired objective? Consider information presented and teaching strategies used.
- Are items presented in easily comprehensible language with clearly defined tasks? Students should not have to decode words or wonder what the item is asking them to do.
- Is the difficulty of the item appropriate? It should not be too difficult or too easy to complete.
- Is each item independent and free from overlap? Completing one item should not lead to completing additional items.
- Is the subject matter covered adequately?
- Is the test free of gender, class, and racial bias? Choose examples that are either familiar or unfamiliar to everyone.

## Checklist for written assignment

### Checklist for written assignment

Student Name: _____

Class: _____

Title of Paper: _____

| | Yes | No | Comments |
|---|---|---|---|
| Understood objectives & requirements | | | |
| Met the timeline due dates | | | |
| Understood criteria for evaluation | | | |
| Actively participated in consultations | | | |
| Responded appropriately to suggestions | | | |
| Used reliable research sources | | | |
| Developed & followed a workable outline | | | |
| Used examples of prior knowledge | | | |
| Used good analytical & reasoning skills | | | |
| Developed good questions & answered them | | | |
| Worked in a methodical manner | | | |
| Used good grammar, sentence structure, spelling | | | |

## Homework

Homework should never be assigned as punishment or due to the teacher falling behind as a result of a poorly executed lesson plan or due to outside circumstances. It should be used if students are unable to complete a project during class, to gather information, to practice new skills, or to devise a solution to a complex problem based on a real life situation. Assigned tasks should be interesting and relevant to the students' daily experiences.

Guidelines for assigning homework:
- Provide clear, unambiguous, written instructions. What is expected and how the results will be evaluated.
- Answer questions and address concerns.
- Make sure the due date is reasonable.
- Consider other academic requirements students may have.
- Be sure resource material is adequate and readily available.
- Collect the assignment on the date specified, grade it, and return it promptly.
- Be consistent with assessment protocol and provide thoughtful, helpful comments.

## Test effectiveness

Teachers should have confidence that a test accurately measures students' knowledge: therefore it is important to monitor its effectiveness each time it is used. Before the test is given, all items should be reviewed to ensure that they still meet the criteria established for understanding the material and if one item does not meet the criteria, either rework it or remove it. If most students, including the better ones, miss the same question, perhaps it is too difficult or is not worded properly. If the item is salvageable, rework it, and if not, delete it. Asking for student feedback on one or two items is an effective way to determine if they are still appropriate or if they should be reworked or removed. Veteran teachers usually develop a "feel" for whether a test is an accurate reflection of what students know. If individual items or entire tests are reused, it is imperative to keep them in a secure place to minimize the possibility of cheating.

---

**Assessment of Subject Understanding And Ability To Orally Present Concepts**

Student Name: _____

Class: _____

Brief Description of Topic:

| | |
|---|---|
| ☐ | Obviously read the material/watched the film/listened to the tape of background information. |
| ☐ | Able to identify main ideas and concepts. |
| ☐ | Information organized and presented logically. |
| ☐ | Showed evidence of prior knowledge and/or understanding of the topic. |
| ☐ | Creatively linked new data with prior knowledge. |
| ☐ | Defended position clearly and logically using good examples and solid reasoning. |
| ☐ | Accepted criticism from teacher and peers of reasoning used and position taken. |
| ☐ | Able to be heard by everyone. |
| ☐ | Spoke clearly with good cadence and used proper English. |
| ☐ | Keep audience interested and engaged. |

NOTE: may be modified to meet teacher requirements.

---

## Extended open-response items

Using an extended open-response item is a very effective method to determine how well students understand the subject matter. This type of item measures students' ability to evaluate and synthesize information and how effectively they communicate using the written word. Depending upon how the item is worded, it allows students to describe and explain, compare and contrast, and develop and summarize the ideas and concepts learned. Since one item might be easier to answer than another, it is better to give all the students the same information to consider so that the evaluation is based upon the same premise. It is important that students understand beforehand the criteria that will be used to assess the response. Accurate facts and figures; a clear, concise writing style; and persuasive arguments might be the focus of the evaluation or perhaps rather the focus is creative expression, personal opinions, and/or conclusions and critical thinking.

Extended open-response items can be evaluated using either holistic scoring or analytic scoring; there is not much difference in reliability and effectiveness between the two methods. Holistic scoring measures a list of specific elements, e.g., clarity of the objective, choice of ideas explored, persuasiveness of the arguments, effectiveness of vocabulary, sentence structure, and organization of the essay. Each item is recognized and noted and the final grade is based upon the response as a whole.

Analytic scoring can evaluate the same elements but the difference is that each one is given a rating and the final grade is a sum of those rating values. For example: clarity earns twenty of twenty-five, choice of ideas earns eighteen of twenty, persuasiveness earns twenty-five of twenty-five, vocabulary and sentence structure earns fifteen of fifteen, and organization earns twelve of fifteen for a final grade of ninety. Analytic scoring evaluates with a little more detail than holistic scoring.

## Short-answer items

Short-answer items require a specific answer to a specific question. They can be a one or two word response, a brief definition, or a short paragraph. They are helpful when a teacher wants to know how well students have learned individual facts, figures, dates, definitions, etc. When using a completion or fill in the blank item, the answer should be placed at the end of the statement. This gives the student the opportunity to read all available information before having to answer. For example: Bright, bold, beautiful is an example of _____. The response (alliteration) is a one-word answer. If the answer requires more information, the instructions need to clearly state how much data is required. For example, "Give three important reasons the United States became involved in World War II." Multiple choice and true/false questions can be turned into short answer questions by requiring a brief explanation justifying the choice.

## Multiple choice item lists

A multiple choice item has a direct question or a complete statement called the stem, which is followed by several possible answers of which usually only one is correct (multiple responses can be requested). These items are designed to test recall and recognition of facts as well as the ability to make associations. The stem needs to be stated in such as a way as to require a specific answer. The language needs to be simple, short, and concise but must include enough data and state the information clearly enough that there is no confusion. Avoid using clues that might indicate the correct answer and be wary of using "all of the above" and "none of the above" as possible responses. These too cause confusion. Ensure that the stem of one item does not include the answer to another. Asking for the correct or incorrect answer is common. Asking for the best answer requires using critical thinking skills.

## Matching item lists

Matching items are used to test recall of specific facts. This is a quick, effective method to determine how well students have integrated information and made associations. The first step is to group homogeneous facts together and then develop parallel lists of premises and responses. The information needs to be closely related; if it is not, common sense instead of knowledge of the subject will dictate the matches. List items randomly to avoid providing clues as to what premise matches which response, e.g., alphabetically by first word or by length of answer. Keep lists manageable as too many items can be confusing. The entire question needs to be on the same page; dividing it between two wastes time and changes the dynamics. Having the students group related facts and develop premises and responses as a class exercise is a good method to review the material. It also provides data to use on a future test.

## True/false item lists

Depending upon how they are worded, true/false items can be used to test content knowledge, recall of facts, ability to define and/or use an idea or concept, and to evaluate information. The most efficient way to develop true/false items is to review textbooks and other resource material and make a list of ideas, concepts, facts, and miscellaneous data. It is important to construct the statement using clear, concise language that is grammatically correct and unambiguous. In order to avoid confusion, use only one idea, concept, or fact in each question. Make the statement positive rather than negative. If using a negative statement, make sure its negativity is clear. The idea is to challenge, not confuse students. Use more false items than true ones because, statistically, guessers tend to check true more often than false. Try to include some plausible false answers but avoid trick questions.

## Preparing tests

It is a good idea to use several types of questions when preparing tests. This will prevent the students from getting bored, expose them to a variety of testing formats, and encourage them to recall and respond to information in different ways. Matching and true/false questions are an excellent way to quickly assess how well students remember specific facts, as well as their ability to memorize data. Multiple choice and short-answer questions require a little deeper knowledge of the subject and better reasoning and thinking skills. These four testing options are reasonably quick and easy to grade. Open-response questions can be used to evaluate in depth content knowledge, the use of critical thinking skills, and the ability to communicate thoughts and ideas through the written word. This option requires more time, effort, and concentration to evaluate fairly, and is a more effective tool in some situations and courses than it is in others.

## Time management ideas

Effective time management is crucial for every teacher. Accurate, fair assessment of students' academic and social progress is equally important. It is critical to develop ways to accomplish both efficiently. Organization is a key ingredient in the equation; time spent searching for things is time wasted. Collaborating with colleagues to develop assessment tools; sharing instructional methods, testing techniques, and formats that work; and establishing standards and priorities for evaluations take time in the beginning but ultimately save time. Teachers who expect perfection from themselves and/or their students are striving to reach an unrealistic goal. Using evaluation tools with appropriate frequency, assessing their value at regular intervals, constructing and saving good testing items, and using standard formats when possible are all ways to use time efficiently. Preparing lessons, organizing record keeping and evaluating the effectiveness of each on a regular basis will help develop a sensible, workable use of limited time resources.

## RTI approach

Many educators believe it is in the best interest of students with learning disabilities to remain, if possible, in a general education classroom rather than be placed in a special education setting. Proponents believe that as long as the necessary instructional tools are provided and progress is monitored, this scenario addresses the special needs of the students and helps them succeed without being placed in a special education environment. Using the response-to-intervention (RTI) approach, students receive the special education services that they need in a general classroom setting. Instructional tools are developed to address the student's particular issues and the effectiveness of the tools is monitored. If the student learns and shows progress, he stays in the general education classroom. If he does not thrive, however, and fails to achieve planned mandated milestones, a request for special education services is initiated. Both provide the appropriate environment for the student to succeed.

# Teaching and Modifying Instruction and Curricula

## Classroom management

Classroom management includes the procedures, strategies, and instructional techniques that affect student behavior and learning activities. When the classroom environment is calm, teachers can teach and the students can learn. With clearly defined rules and established routines, there is less need for disciplinary action and more time for teaching. According to teacher, lecturer, and author Harry K. Wong, "Student achievement at the end of the year is directly related to the degree to which the teacher establishes good control of classroom procedures in the very first week of the school year." In his book, The First Days of School: How to be an Effective Teacher, Wong says that in a well-managed classroom:

- Students are involved with the work.
- Assignments are posted and based on objectives students understand.
- Students know what is expected, are usually successful and encouragement is offered frequently.
- There is little wasted time, confusion, or disruption.
- The environment is work-oriented and relaxed.

## Behavior management

Behavior management is an essential key to creating a positive learning environment. If the students are misbehaving, they are not paying attention and they cannot learn. It is important to establish written expectations at the beginning of the year, review them with the students as needed and enforce them when necessary. When discipline is required, do it quietly and privately; never embarrass a student. Avoid talking the entire class period. Spend fifteen minutes lecturing and then give the students something to do and make sure everyone is actively involved. Break the time into predictable segments and move smoothly from one activity to the next. A wise teacher makes sure he and the parents are working as a team by communicating often, being specific and providing details. Teachers need to be consistent, patient with themselves and the students, keep situations in perspective, have a sense of humor and know when to ask for help.

## Classroom discipline and management

- Students respect a teacher who maintains control of the classroom, and students perform better in a quiet, orderly environment.
- Teachers should always have a disciplinary plan and they should follow it every day. Most students respect rules if they are clear and the consequences are understood and explained ahead of time, while being consistently and fairly enforced.
- Disruptions and interruptions need to be dealt with immediately to prevent an escalation of the situation.
  - However, teachers should never humiliate a student, use sarcasm, or yell: all semblance of control will be lost.
  - One effective way to avoid discipline problems is to have more material planned for class than can possibly be presented in the allotted time. Keeping students busy and engaged in the business of learning goes a long way toward preventing disciplinary problems.

## Behavior teachers should avoid

Teachers are human, and adolescents can be difficult at times. That combined with the fact that almost all students enjoy challenging a teacher can bear the potential for disaster. So it makes sense to avoid certain behaviors at all times before they can become catalysts for disaster.

- Teachers should not stop a lesson for minor infractions. It is much better to speak to the student afterwards than to create a potential no-win confrontation.
- A teacher should not create arbitrary rules that may be difficult to enforce.
- If a student should complain about another teacher, the listening teacher should remain noncommittal. If the issue is serious, it should be discussed with the teacher involved or brought to the attention of the administration.
- Teachers should never come to class without a lesson plan. Students will seize the opportunity to create chaos.

## Motivation

Motivation is considered the most important factor in education, but it is the most difficult to cultivate. Adolescents learn rap songs; memorize sports statistics; devour pop culture news; and acquire computer skills easily, quickly, and avidly, yet they have trouble remembering the previous day's homework assignments and fall asleep listening to a social studies lecture. Studies show that nearly everything a teacher does and says in the classroom has an influence on students, be it positive or negative, outwardly or inwardly. This includes what teachers say and don't say, and how they interact with the students, how material is presented, the activities used, and how much input the students have in the classroom. Research has concluded that the most effective way to motivate students is to satisfy their psychological need to feel in control, competent, and connected.

## Ideal learning environment

Middle and secondary students do their best in an environment that trusts and respects them as individuals; creates a caring, concerned climate; and provides a sense of community. Administrators can write policies and procedures and erect hall posters, but it is the teacher who is instrumental in fostering a positive learning environment. The adolescent is searching for adult mentors and role models, and therefore their relationships and interactions with teachers can and do determine how a student perceives learning as a whole and affect his performance in individual classes. While there are many ways to create a positive learning environment, here are a few to consider:

- Use active listening techniques.
- Provide detailed instructions.
- Clearly explain behavioral and academic expectations.
- Provide approval when earned and encouragement when needed.
- Recognize individual and group accomplishments.
- Discipline students privately, away from the rest of the class.

## Behavior modification

The American Heritage College Dictionary defines behavior as "the actions or reactions of persons or things in response to external or internal stimuli." Behavior modification is defined as "The use of basic learning techniques, such as conditioning, biofeedback, reinforcement or aversion therapy, to alter human behavior." When the goal is to alter inappropriate behavior, the conduct must be defined, observed and measured before techniques can be developed to change the undesirable activity. All behavior follows a particular, defined set of consistent rules; if the rules change, the conduct changes. All conduct is maintained, shaped and changed by the consequences of that conduct. All children and adolescents (with certain exceptions) function best when they know the rules and understand the consequences of those rules. Behavior can be changed by either reinforcement or punishment, and studies have shown that reinforcement strengthens behavior while punishment weakens it.

## Physical development and functioning

Some specific syndromes cause physical differences. For example, children with Down syndrome tend to have weak muscular tone; are generally smaller and shorter than others; and have short, stocky arms and legs. These symptoms may make physical activities more difficult for them in addition to developing more slowly. In regular education classrooms they will likely be unable to perform physical activities at the same level as age peers. In physical education classes, they can participate and should be encouraged to do their best and rewarded for their efforts, but they should not be expected to achieve the same levels of physical fitness, speed, strength, or coordination as age peers. While some students with profound intellectual disability, including those with Down syndrome, can demonstrate excellent physical coordination, this varies individually. Some students with severe or profound IDs appear physically normal, but educators should not expect them to have normal cognitive ability or performance. Others look younger, less mature, and/or smaller than normal, yet educators must take care not to treat them inappropriately as younger.

## Speech problems

Students with Down syndrome have genetically determined characteristics, including short, thick tongues, so they frequently "lisp" or distort /s/ and /z/ sounds. They also tend to have hypotonia, that is, weak muscle tone throughout the body. This can distort their articulation of speech sounds through weakness of the speech muscles. Beyond such specific syndromes, in general students with severe or profound intellectual disabilities have delayed development overall. Therefore, they will speak at later ages than other children. Also, their delayed speech development will reflect earlier developmental levels than their chronological ages. Since they are likely to distort more difficult speech sounds at older ages than others, a 10-year-old child with severe or profound ID might have the articulation of a normally developing 3- or 4-year-old, making the child's speech sound immature. Some children with these disabilities develop stuttering due to difficulty coordinating speech production with cognition, auditory feedback problems, anxiety, pressure, or other causes.

## Expressive language problems

Students with severe or profound intellectual disability are slower in their language development than normal, both receptively and expressively. They are most likely to have receptive language development that is superior to their expressive language development. This is also true of normally developing children. Infants cannot yet speak, but they are typically surrounded by others' speech and are always absorbing information and learning from their environments. Assuming no hearing or auditory processing deficits, learning to understand what one hears is easier than learning to formulate speech mentally and produce speech sounds physically. Severely ID children will speak later, speak fewer words, and use simpler words and concepts. They are also likely to speak in phrases, sentence fragments, and/or ungrammatical constructions, all reflecting levels of language development lower than their chronological ages. For the same reason, they may confuse concepts expressed by words, such as "hungry/thirsty," "walk/talk," and so on.

## Sensory abnormalities

Some students with severe or profound intellectual disabilities register sensory stimuli very differently from others. Some demonstrate such a high pain threshold that they do not feel injuries normally perceived as painful. For example, parents have reported their child cut her leg on a barbed-wire fence, did not realize or mention it, and showed no discomfort, yet the injury was sufficient to cause a scar that was still visible years later. These students need monitoring for injuries they may not notice and to prevent the behaviors causing them. Other students may be hypersensitive, feeling pain from physical stimuli that are not normally uncomfortable. Students with autism spectrum disorders, in addition to intellectual disabilities, are particularly likely to suffer hypersensitivity to tactile, visual, auditory, olfactory, and gustatory stimuli: when these are unpleasant to them, they are often experienced as painful. These students need modifications to their home and educational environments to lessen sensory distress and protection from public environments with overwhelming sensory input. At both extremes, these differences are attributable to differences in neurological structures and functions.

## Sensory development and functioning

Sensory development refers not only to the development of the senses of hearing, vision, touch, smell, and taste, but also to brain development of the ability to interpret signals received through these senses, integration of sensory information, and ability to respond appropriately to perceptions of sensations. Thus sensory development is related to all other aspects of development. Children with severe or profound intellectual disability develop more slowly than others, including with sensation and perception. Sensory processing is the ability not only to see, hear, touch, smell, and taste environmental stimuli, but also to pay attention to them and respond to them. Students with severe and profound intellectual disabilities may have difficulties in understanding the information they receive through their senses, even when their sensory mechanisms operate normally. For example, some might smell toast burning and not recognize it; some might recognize a food smell but not a burning smell, or vice versa; some might recognize the smell as toast burning, but not understand that this requires action.

## Emotional and psychological development

Individuals with intellectual disability have the same needs for love, affection, and positive relationships with others, regardless of their cognitive and adaptive functioning. However, because their cognitive development is at a level similar to that of a young child or infant, they are likely to have what Piaget termed an egocentric view of the world. In other words, they see everything as related to themselves and cannot view anything from another person's perspective. This means they will not understand that other people have feelings and thoughts different from their own. Moreover, they may have difficulty understanding even their own feelings. Some of these functions may be trained or taught to some degree, given sufficient time. Two other psychological factors to consider are that students with severe or profound disabilities are likely to experience frustration when they have difficulty performing tasks, and if they aware that they differ from other children, they may feel stigmatized as "slow" or "dumb." These students often benefit from developmental-age-appropriate counseling.

## Consequences and reinforcement

The American Heritage College Dictionary defines consequence as "something that logically follows from an action." Reinforcement is defined as "an event that increases the likelihood that a given response will reoccur in a similar situation." To effectively modify behavior, the consequences must be relevant and follow immediately after the action. Paying attention to unacceptable behavior stops the conduct at the moment but does little to permanently alter the behavior. Reinforcement of the desired behavior is much more effective in bringing about lasting change, which is the goal. For example, instead of scolding each time the student talks out of turn, it is more effective to comment when he raises his hand and waits to be called on. Rewarding desired behavior is used more frequently with younger children than with adolescents, but this needs to change. Studies show and anecdotal evidence proves that no matter the age, positive reinforcement is always more effective than punishment.

## Establishing a positive learning environment

Teachers want students to learn. One way to create an environment in which to accomplish that goal is to establish calming routines and practice them on a daily basis. A warm welcome as each student comes into the room not only sets a positive tone but also gives the teacher an opportunity to gauge mood and attitude and take action when needed. Playing soothing music, turning the lights down low and projecting a brainteaser or some comment related to the day's lesson helps to focus students' attention. Assigning permanent seats prevents students from rushing for a favored place and settles the class more quickly. Taking attendance can be a chore but using the time creatively by asking each student a quick question based the previous day's lesson or the homework assignment gets their attention, makes them think, helps them learn to be prepared and provides a mini-review for everyone.

Once students are settled in their seats and unnecessary items are either confiscated or stowed out of sight, the real work begins. Besides having a well-prepared lesson plan and activities that keep the students interested and involved, there are some things a teacher can do to encourage learning, create a positive environment and maintain classroom control without confrontation. Displaying a sense of humor and refusing to react negatively to an incident will sometimes diffuse a potential problem. Moving around the room, establishing eye contact and starting another activity can redirect an individual's attention as well as divert the rest of the group from the troublesome student. Speaking softly, waiting patiently or staring at the offenders are effective methods to restore order and quiet a noisy classroom. It is essential to maintain control and not yell or threaten. These reactions can escalate the situation and turn the incident into a clash of wills.

## Seating assignments

There is some debate on whether it is better to let students choose their seats in order to give them some control over their environment or to assign them according to the teacher's particular needs. If students make the choice, teachers have the responsibility to make changes if discipline becomes an issue or if instruction is hampered. If teachers make the decision, some accommodation should be made for reasonable requests, if possible.

The physical arrangement of the desks does have an impact on communication and movement. It is important to balance the teacher's need for territorial control and the students' need to feel comfortable. Space limitations may dictate the arrangement. Many teachers and students prefer a semi-circle, one desk deep arrangement: everyone can see and hear each other easily, communication is enhanced and the teacher can move around unimpeded. Each teacher needs to discover the arrangement most effective in his classroom.

## Peaceful classroom environment

There are several things teachers can do to create a peaceful, harmonious classroom. Show genuine interest in the students by respecting all the cultures represented, being aware of, learning and understanding adolescent slang and offering praise and encouragement often. Explain the rules clearly, consider the circumstances before taking action and apply the rules fairly and consistently. Look at situations from the students' perspectives and try to be objective rather than judgmental. A teacher should be willing to admit mistakes; it not only makes him more human but also tells students it is okay to make a mistake as long as one admits it, learns from it and tries not to make it again. Address problems and issues immediately so they do not escalate or appear again. Collaborate with the students, ask for their opinions and offer choices. When students are active participants and believe they are heard, behavior issues are minimized.

## Discipline plan

<u>Basics</u>
A discipline plan is a written description of acceptable behavior which creates a more suitable learning environment. It gives the teacher a framework in which to diagnose problems, assess situations, address issues and make changes as needed. Polls in many cities indicate that lack of discipline is a major concern of both parents and teachers. While violence and vandalism are unfortunately common in schools today, that which most annoys teachers and disrupts learning are seemingly minor problems such as students talking without permission, wandering around the room, refusing to do what they have been told to do and generally goofing off. All these contribute to burn-out because teachers continually have to deal with disorderly conduct and disrespectful behavior. A discipline plan will not stop or prevent unacceptable or disruptive behavior, but it does give the teacher a means to identify and deal with the problems.

Once a discipline plan has been developed, explained to students and parents and implemented in the classroom, it should be evaluated after it has been used for a few weeks. In order to assess the plan effectively, the teacher needs to keep good notes. Each time the plan is used, a brief description of the incident, who was involved, the action which was taken and short and long term consequences, if any, should be recorded. At some predetermined time (e.g., the end of the grading period, the end of the semester) the recorded information should be analyzed. Some questions that should be considered:
- Is it working for everyone? If not, why not?
- Has it been used fairly? Consistently?
- Should counselors, parents or administrators be consulted?
- Does the plan need to be modified?
- Is it time to develop a new plan which recognizes changes and addresses current needs?

<u>Elements</u>
A discipline plan must meet the needs of the teacher, consider the age of the students and address the particular requirements of the class. They can be imposed by the teacher or developed by the teacher with input from the students. Whichever method used, the plan needs to be explained to and understood by both students and parents. Critical elements which should be included in every discipline plan are:
- Rules written as positive statements. Examples include: "Be prepared," "Raise your hand before speaking," and "Respect other people and their property."
- A clearly defined incentive plan that is easy to understand and fair to everyone.
- Positive consequences, which are explained and may vary with each rule.
- Negative consequences, which are the hierarchal steps taken to address unacceptable behavior. The mildest is a verbal warning; the worst is suspension or expulsion with several steps in-between.
- Identifying "limit setting" acts, which are actions (e.g., blinking the lights) that the teacher takes before invoking next step.

## Kounin and Ginott models
The Kounin Model is based upon:
- The ripple effect, i.e., correct one student's behavior and the others will most likely follow.
- The teacher being aware of what is going on in the classroom at all times.
- Making smooth transitions from one activity to the next.
- Keeping students alert and holding them accountable for their work and their behavior.
- Avoiding boredom by using many activities.
- Keeping students aware of their progress.

The Ginott Model is based upon:
- Using sensible messages.
- The teacher modeling expected behavior at all times, in all situations.
- Addressing behavior, not character.
- Requesting cooperation from all of the students.
- Feelings are expressed in words not actions.
- Never using sarcasm.
- Avoiding peer retaliation, through applauding the act, not the student.
- Recognizing that unless the student really wants to change his behavior, his apology is meaningless.

## Glasser and Dreikurs models
The Glasser Model is based upon:
- Students' ability to control their own behavior.
- Helping students to make good choices, which leads to better behavior.
- Not accepting excuses for unacceptable behavior.
- Asking students to analyze unacceptable behavior so that they learn why they did it.
- Fairly enforcing class rules, which are essential.
- Using classroom meetings to diagnose problems and determine solutions.
- Consequences following actions.

The Dreikurs Model is based upon:
- Understanding that discipline is self-control, not punishment.
- Helping students to learn to impose limits on themselves.
- Teachers modeling expected behavior.
- Involving students in developing rules and consequences.
- Recognizing that misbehavior is often for the purpose of gaining peer recognition, and the result of inappropriate goals such as gaining attention, seeking power, or revenge.
- Identifying incorrect goals and not reinforcing them.
- Understanding that all actions, both good and bad, have consequences.

## Necessity
There are basic human tendencies which cause most behavior problems. Even the best written, most equitable and fairly enforced discipline plans cannot completely eliminate misbehavior, especially during adolescence. These are the years during which young people test out behavior and push the limits in order to learn what is acceptable and what is not. This is a normal part of the maturation process. However, adults who interact with adolescents have a responsibility to set parameters and enforce rules because young people crave guidelines and really do understand, appreciate and respect reasonable

limits. To develop a workable discipline plan and help adolescents learn self-control so that they can reach their full potential, teachers should keep in mind some realities of human nature:

- Humans resist doing that which other people try to make them do.
- Humans like to belittle and question authority.
- Humans have different needs, wants and values.
- Humans have different interests, abilities and learning styles.

## Keeping students on-task

Tasks expected to be completed during class need to be clearly explained with questions about the assignment asked and answered before the work is started. Instructions need to be specific, and the teacher needs to ensure that the students understand that which they are required to accomplish, how much time they have in which to complete the task and which, if any, reference materials can be used. The task needs to be completable in the allotted time with the information available. The teacher needs to maintain the appropriate atmosphere so that the students can complete the assignment. He needs to frequently scan the room to see if anyone appears to be having a problem, not working, or bothering someone else. Consultations with individual students should be quiet and private. Praise should be given when earned, reprimands doled out when needed and help provided when requested.

## Getting adolescents' attention

If a teacher does not have the students' attention, there is no point in starting a lesson at all, much less expecting adolescents to retain the information presented. An effective teacher is always well prepared, knows the subject matter thoroughly and dispenses the data in an interesting, engaging manner. He is enthusiastic, maintains eye contact and varies the timber and volume of his voice. He encourages lively class discussions by asking interesting, thought-provoking, open-ended questions, using props when and where appropriate and telling stories relevant to the subject being studied as well as to the students' lives. Adolescents remember information much better, and longer, if it means something to them, answers a question, challenges a preconceived idea, changes their perception or has an impact on their immediate world. Lessons prepared and activities planned with those things in mind are very effective teaching strategies.

## Multiple intelligences

Multiple intelligences is a theory developed in 1983 by Dr. Howard Gardner, a Harvard professor of education. He believes that everyone learns according to one of eight intelligences rather than just in the traditional linguistic and logical manner, which is how most schools are structured to teach. Since not all students learn this way, some children are labeled "slow," "underachievers" or "learning disabled" because they are not allowed and/or encouraged to learn by using their natural talents and abilities. If a teacher learns to recognize the eight intelligences as defined by Dr. Gardner, he can develop lesson plans that reach every one of his students. Adopting and utilizing the theory of multiple intelligences offers a wide variety of teaching tools to enhance lectures and create activities that spur the imagination and expand learning opportunities for all students.

## Major styles of learning

Learning styles are different ways or approaches used to learn. Teachers should be aware of the various ways adolescents learn, so that they can develop multi-faceted lesson plans that capitalize on the students' strengths and compensate for their weaknesses. Some people learn almost exclusively using one method while others use one or two or a combination of all three. However, those who use a combination do have a predominate or preferred style. The three learning styles are visual, auditory and tactile/kinesthetic:

- Visual Learners tend to think in pictures, and therefore diagrams, graphic illustrations, videos and handouts help them. They take detailed notes for later reference.
- Auditory Learners learn through lectures, discussions, talking things out and listening to others. They may not understand written information until they hear it read aloud.
- Tactile/Kinesthetic Learners learn by moving, doing, touching. They need hands-on activities. They may become distracted if made to sit still for long periods of time.

## Spatial and bodily-kinesthetic intelligence

Spatial Intelligence means someone is picture smart. They think in images and need to create mental pictures to remember data. They enjoy reading and writing and have an uncanny ability to read maps and understand charts and graphs. They are adept at creating visual metaphors and analogies and using them to design practical, useful objects. They like puzzles and have an excellent sense of direction. They grow up to be inventors, architects, interior designers and mechanics.

Bodily-kinesthetic Intelligence means someone is body smart. They express themselves using their body and are adept at reading other people's body language. They are move gracefully, have a superior sense of balance and great hand-eye coordination. They process information by interacting in the space around them. They are excellent dancers, actors and mimes and enjoy using their hands to build things. They grow up to be physical education teachers, firefighters, actors and professional athletes.

## Verbal-linguistic and logical-mathematical intelligence

Verbal-Linguistic Intelligence means someone is word smart. They have a way with both written and spoken language. They think in words rather than pictures, understand the syntax and meaning of words, analyze language usage and have a prodigious memory for retaining information. They not only write well but also are usually wonderful public speakers. They enjoy telling stories, explaining anything and everything and winning people over to their point of view. Most have a delightful sense of humor. They grow up to be writers, journalists, teachers and politicians.

Logical-Mathematical Intelligence means someone is number and reasoning smart. They think in logical, progressive patterns and make connections between seemingly unrelated bits of data. They are curious and ask lots of questions. They excel at classifying information, discovering the relationship between abstract concepts and performing complex mathematical problems. They grow up to be scientists, researchers, accountants and computer programmers.

## Interpersonal and intrapersonal intelligence

Interpersonal Intelligence means someone is people smart. They try to see things from the other person's perspective. Most have an uncommon ability to sense feelings, intentions and motivations. They can be manipulators. They are good listeners and relate well to others because they use empathy when offering advice or counseling someone. They work well within groups because they are adept at generating consensus, building trust and diffusing tense situations. They grow up to be counselors, salespeople and politicians.

Intrapersonal Intelligence means someone is self smart. They try to understand their role in life and their relationship to other people. They are aware of their inner feelings and their strengths and weaknesses and try to understand their dreams and desires. They are self-critical. They analyze their motivation for everything as well as their relationship to everyone in their world. They grow up to be researchers, philosophers and theorists.

## Musical and naturalist intelligence

Musical Intelligence means someone is music smart. They think in sounds, rhythms and patterns. They respond to any kind of music, recognize tonal patterns and understand the structure of music. Many are sensitive to the sounds around them such as barking dogs, ringing bells and dripping faucets. They like to sing, whistle and play instruments. They appreciate, criticize and compose music. They grow up to be musicians, composers, singers and disc jockeys.

Naturalist Intelligence means someone is nature smart. They think in relation to how something affects the natural world. They are sensitive to all living things and need to know how people fit into nature's plan. They have the ability to grow and nurture plants and an affinity with and for wild and domestic animals. They are able to recognize and categorize most plant and animal species. They grow up to be scientists, naturalists, conservationists and farmers.

## Language, vocabulary, pronunciation and grammar

The American Heritage College Dictionary defines language as "voice sounds and written symbols representing these sounds, in combinations and patterns, used to express and communicate thoughts and feelings." Vocabulary is "all the words of a language." Pronunciation is a "way of speaking a word, especially a way that is accepted and generally understood." Grammar is the "rules of a language viewed as a mechanism for generating all sentences possible in that language."

Vocabulary (a set of words), pronunciation (how the words are spoken) and grammar (rules governing how to use the words) are all vital elements in learning, understanding and properly using a language. If one or more elements are not learned, learned inadequately, ignored or misused, communication is impaired. The depth of a person's vocabulary and his ability to speak and write effectively is often used as a measurement of his intelligence and frequently reflects the level and quality of his education.

## Dr. Gardner's theory

From a practical point of view, teachers already use Dr. Gardner's theory of multiple intelligences; they simply may not link their approach to his theory. Teachers know, through experience and observation, that students learn in different ways. That is one of the first lessons they learn in the performance of their profession. Good teachers respond by developing lesson plans and activities with that knowledge in mind. They include lectures (verbal-linguistic intelligence) requiring students to think conceptually and link facts together (logical-mathematical intelligence) and use pictures, charts and other props (visual-spatial intelligence and, depending upon the props used, music-rhythmic intelligence) during the presentation. Many lesson plans include hands-on projects as well (bodily-kinesthetic intelligence and, depending upon the subject, naturalist intelligence). Asking thought-provoking questions that encourage lively class discussions (interpersonal intelligence and intrapersonal intelligence) are classroom staples. A well-prepared teacher with an interactive lesson plan that challenges the students to think uses the theory of multiple intelligences every day.

## Components of language

There are four main components of all languages: reading, writing, speaking and hearing. The following definitions are from <u>The American Heritage College Dictionary.</u>

Reading is "the act or activity of rendering text aloud." To Read is "the ability to examine and grasp the meaning of written and printed material in a given language."

Writing is "meaningful letters or characters that constitute readable material." To Write is "to form letters, words or symbols on a surface such as paper with an instrument such as a pen." (People also use typewriters and computer keyboards.)
Speaking is being "capable of speech involving talking, expressing or telling." To Speak is "to convey thoughts, opinions or emotions orally."

Hearing is "the sense by which sound is perceived." To Hear is "to be capable of perceiving sound by the ear."

## Helping students feel competent

In order to help adolescents feel competent, lessons must be personally relevant. When assignments challenge students' imagination with issues that relate to their survival and quality of life and pose questions involving real problems and products, adolescents are motivated to search for solutions. Because school-to-work programs show a direct correlation to future employment possibilities and teach usable, real world skills, they are usually successful. Similar techniques should be used with academic subjects to excite student interest and give them a reason to learn. The process should involve critical and creative thinking. The student should be required to define the task, set manageable and reachable goals and establish specific criteria. In order to complete the assignment, the student should be made to gather information through research, which will generate more ideas and pose additional questions. The student learns to organize, analyze and integrate subject matter into a meaningful whole, which gradually grows into a feeling of competence.

## Helping students feel control

States and school boards mandate subject matter, outline specific objectives, and make curriculum decisions, while schools set the schedules and make classroom assignments. How can teachers make students feel that they themselves are in control of the learning process? As long as they are allowed to make choices about other things in the classroom, adolescents will accept these parameters if they understand certain requirements are not negotiable. A wise teacher lets the students help decide class rules and procedures; choose some activities and assignments; set required group goals; and decide whether to work separately, in pairs, or in small groups. Research indicates that allowing students to select a study buddy or buddies facilitates motivation and fosters cooperation. With the many issues a teacher encounters in the classroom, he or she must continually review the benefits of providing students with appropriate choices and decide what is best given the circumstances.

## Helping students feel connected

The feeling of being a respected member of the group and a valued member of the community helps the adolescent feel connected to something larger than himself and is important to his psychological development. Cooperative learning encourages students to work together and helps them gain an appreciation for the effectiveness of group efforts. Peer mentoring and peer counseling programs provide students a safe venue where they can learn to analyze situations, devise sensible solutions, and develop understanding and compassion for other people. Schools that offer career counseling and establish mentoring programs sponsored by local employers help students at that time, while preparing them for life in the business world later. More and more school districts require students to perform some type of volunteer community service in order to graduate. This requirement exposes the adolescent to real life issues, enlarges his worldview, and helps build a foundation for future civic involvement.

## Student diversity

Cultural identities are strongly embraced by adolescents but they also want to be recognized and treated as unique individuals. Teachers walk a fine line between respecting cultural differences and avoiding overly emphasizing them or disregarding them altogether. Responding to discriminatory comments immediately, using a wide variety of examples, quoting scholars from many cultures and identifying universal problems needing complex solutions can indirectly communicate appreciation of and respect for all cultures. Teachers must take care never to imply any kind of stereotype or make comments that might indicate a cultural bias. They must refrain from asking a student to respond as a member of a particular culture, class or country. Teachers should learn as much as they can about every racial, ethnic and cultural group represented in their classroom. It is also important that teachers respect students' commitments and obligations away from school, their family responsibilities and job pressures.

## Cultural influences

Study after study has shown that a student's culture has a direct impact on learning. Since educational standards are based on white, middle class cultural identification, students who do not fall into that demographic face challenges every day. It's not that these students are incapable of learning; they simply judge that which is important and how they express that importance differently. Sometimes it is difficult for them to understand and relate to curriculum content, teaching methods and social skills required because their culture does things differently, emphasizes different choices and rewards different behavior. Adolescents identify with their culture; they become what they know. If teachers ignore cultural differences, it causes communication issues, inhibits learning and increases the potential for behavior problems. As long as a child has no physical or mental health issues, he is capable of learning. He simply needs that the information presented and examples used to be relevant to his life experiences; otherwise, it does not seem to make sense to him.

## Social environment

The social environment is the set of people and institutions with which one associates and communicates. It has both a direct and indirect influence on behavior by the individuals within the group. It is sometimes defined by specific characteristics such as race, gender, age, culture or behavioral patterns. When defined by behavioral patterns it can lead to unproven assumptions about entire groups of people. In America's diverse society, it is essential that teachers recognize that various social groups exist within a classroom and thus determine the best strategies not only to facilitate the learning of "book" facts, but also to encourage understanding and acceptance between the groups. The learning theory called social cognitivism believes that people learn by observing others, whether they are aware of the process or not.

Creating opportunities for students to interact with diverse social groups in a neutral, non-threatening situation can bring about positive interpersonal growth that could have long-term societal impact outside of the educational environment.

## Socialization

Socialization is the process of learning the written and unwritten rules, acceptable behavioral patterns, and accumulated knowledge of the community in order to function within its culture. It is a gradual process that starts when a person is born and, in one form or another, continues throughout his life. There are many "communities" within a culture: e.g., family, school, neighborhood, military and country. There are six forms of socialization:
- Reverse Socialization: deviation from acceptable behavior patterns.
- Developmental Socialization: the process of learning social skills.
- Primary Socialization: learning the attitudes, values and actions of a culture.
- Secondary Socialization: learning behavior required in a smaller group within the culture.
- Anticipatory Socialization: practicing behavior in preparation for joining a group.
- Resocialization: discarding old behavior and learning new behavior as part of a life transition; e.g., starting school, moving to a new neighborhood or joining the military.

The agents of socialization are the people, groups and institutions that influence the self-esteem, emotions, attitudes, behavior and acceptance of a person within his environment. The first agents are the immediate family (mother, father, siblings) and extended family (grandparents, aunts, uncles, cousins). They influence religious affiliation, political inclinations, educational choices, career aspirations and other life goals. The school's role is explaining societal values, reinforcing acceptable behavior patterns and teaching necessary skills such as reading, writing, reasoning and critical thinking. Peer groups (people who are about the same age) share certain characteristics (attend the same school, live in the same neighborhood) and influence values, attitudes and behavior. The media (radio, television, newspapers, magazines, the Internet) have an impact on attitude, values and one's understanding of the activities of society and international events. Other institutions that influence people include religion, the work place, the neighborhood, and city, state and federal governments.

## Social ineptitude

Social ineptitude is defined as a lack of social skills; in most societies, this term is considered disrespectful. There are medical conditions that may cause a deficiency in social skills such as autism and Asperger syndrome. Someone who believes himself socially inept may have an avoidant personality disorder. A shy person or an overly bold person may observe societal conventions but still exhibit social incompetence; the behavior is simply manifested in different ways. The criteria for social ineptitude are different in different cultures, which makes it difficult to cite specific examples. People trying to integrate into a new environment may unknowingly commit a social faux pas thereby earning the damaging label unfairly. In a culturally diverse classroom, it is critical to create an atmosphere of acceptance so if a student does something inappropriate, the behavior can be quietly and gently corrected without causing humiliation or embarrassment.

## Social skills

Social skills are the tools used to interact and communicate with others. They are learned during the socialization process and are both verbal and non-verbal. These skills are integral to becoming an active and accepted member of any environment. There are general skills needed to complete daily transactions such as being able to ask sensible questions and provide logical answers and knowing how to read and write and understand simple directions. If these skills are missing or poorly executed, it can cause various problems and misunderstandings, some of which could have long-lasting and/or life-changing consequences. In smaller groups, other skills may be needed such as the ability to engage in interesting conversation, present ideas to peers, teach new concepts or actively participate in discussions. Using body language and gestures appropriate to the situation and the message, having the ability to resolve conflicts and being diplomatic when necessary are examples of advanced social skills.

**Preventing problem behavior**

All adolescents engage in risky behavior; it's a normal part of development and most people come out unscathed. For some youths, however, risk-taking becomes problematic and goes beyond the acceptable norm. Red flags that indicate that an adolescent may be heading for serious trouble include starting the behavior at eight or nine years of age, regular instead of occasional incidents, and involvement with peers who participate in the same dangerous activities. This type of behavior can lead to delinquency, crime and violence, alcohol and drug abuse, early pregnancy and sexually transmitted diseases, and poor academic performance and dropping out of school. Factors that can help prevent these problems from developing include a positive family environment, a stable relationship with at least one caring and responsible adult, a strong religious or spiritual foundation, realistic academic expectations, and the ability to handle stress and ask for help when needed. An added influence is the priority which the community gives to the needs of its young people.

**Successful teachers**

While each person's instructional style is unique, successful teachers share certain characteristics. The most important qualities are attitude, and approach and the following contribute to and influence both:
- A sense of humor will relieve tense situations and make class more pleasant for everyone. Students might actually look forward to coming to class and will more likely pay attention when they are present.
- A positive attitude helps cope with most situations both in and out of the classroom.
- Setting realistic expectations and ensuring that students believe they can reach them is a great motivator and helps them achieve a sense of competence.
- Being consistent creates a safe, predictable learning environment. Students do not like situations in which the rules are always changing.
- Being fair means treating all students in the same manner in similar situations.
- Flexibility is critical. Things change and students expect the teacher to be in charge and in control at all times and in all situations.

**Teacher's role**

Teachers are facilitators and coaches whose main function is to present the required educational material in an interesting and hands-on manner. The information given and examples used should reflect the students' present day reality and teach them how they will use the data in the future. Since the primary tasks of adolescence are learning to understand abstract concepts, acquiring and honing problem-solving skills, and developing critical thought processes, it is the instructor's responsibility to prepare lesson plans that not only teach the facts, but also focus on helping students practice these new abilities. Whether the student is college-bound, planning to join the military, or headed to the workforce, he must be able to interact with others both in groups and personally, adapt to new technology and institutional change, and logically think through new situations. It is imperative that teachers create an atmosphere that encourages students to develop and utilize these critical skills.

## Individuals with Disabilities Education Act (IDEA)

Because the National Institutes of Health (NIH) estimates that about fifteen percent (15%) of Americans have some type of learning issue, Congress passed The Individuals with Disabilities Education Act (IDEA), a law including children with learning disabilities. This federal law states that children with physical, psychological and learning disabilities are entitled to a "free and appropriate public education." Every state and territory is mandated to provide educational opportunities for children between the ages of three (3) and twenty-one (21) no matter how severe the learning problems or physical challenges. Research shows that the earlier these children receive help, the more successfully they learn to function in the real world. According to the NIH, eighty percent (80%) of students with a learning disability have trouble reading; sixty-seven percent (67%) will learn to read normally if they receive help by the first grade and seventy-five percent (75%) who don't get help until age nine (9) have problems reading their entire lives.

## Teaching strategies for special needs students

Accommodating special needs students in a mainstream classroom can be a challenge. Here are some helpful hints that create the opportunity to learn no matter what the needs of individual students:
- Write daily objectives on the board or use an overhead projector. Break complex assignments into manageable parts. Require students to copy the information into their notebook for reference.
- Build background knowledge by defining unfamiliar words and outlining historical facts or other pertinent information before introducing new material.
- Use a variety of presentation methods to accommodate different learning styles. Seeing the written words appeals to visual learners; verbal explanations helps auditory learners; taking notes aids tactile learners; and the light of an overhead projector helps all students focus.
- Design evaluation methods to fairly assess every student. Give oral tests. Limit choices by offering only three possible answers on a multiple-choice test; include a list of words with a fill-in-the-blank test.

## Curriculum

The American Heritage College Dictionary defines curriculum as "all the courses of study offered by an educational institution"; the second definition is, "a group of related courses often in a special field of study." The first definition applies to American middle schools and both the first and second applies to contemporary American high schools. Curriculum refers to the ideas, concepts, processes and skills required to meet the standards set by individual state boards of education. Some school districts further refine these standards by listing the concepts and skills that must be learned at each grade level before the student can move to the next grade level. Lesson plans, lectures, hands-on activities, written requirements, special projects, field trips, textbooks and other source materials provide a framework for teachers to teach and students to learn. Curricula are designed to meet goals by articulating specific guidelines and defining major milestones on the road to achieving those goals.

## English curriculum

Based upon the standards of the particular state, the language arts curriculum needs to be specific and provide focus to ensure that teachers teach the skills that students need to learn at the various grade levels. However, as long as the subject matter is covered and basic skills are mastered, the curriculum also needs to allow some choice of source material such as what books and stories to read and which genres to study. In developing English curricula, one should consider that:
- Reading material is assigned to comprehend meaning and interpret content.
- Writing is needed to communicate thoughts and ideas to a variety of audiences using different vehicles (term papers, essays, poems, etc.).
- Speaking is used to share information and persuade others.
- Listening is a good way to learn new data and determine important facts.
- Analyzing and Evaluating literature in a variety of genres (novels, short stories, diaries, memoirs, etc.) in different eras and many cultures is vital to a well-rounded education.

## Language arts curriculum

Because language arts and English programs overlap so many other areas of education, the curriculum is especially important. It must integrate the needs of the various academic disciplines. In middle school, the curriculum needs to build on what was learned in elementary school while preparing students for the demands of high school requirements. In high school, the curriculum must prepare students for college level courses and teach them the advanced skills (reading, writing, speaking, listening) needed to function in the real world, whether they pursue additional educational opportunities or enter the work force immediately after high school. At both levels, the language arts program must be coherent and build upon concepts and skills already learned. Students must be shown how to make the connection between the skills of reading, writing, speaking and listening, and connect what they learn in school to what they experience outside of school.

## Developmentally appropriate English program

Students do not learn if they are not engaged in the process. They will not engage in the process if they are not motivated. So how does a teacher fulfill the curriculum's requirements and at the same time engage the students? A great way to motivate adolescents is to offer them material that is interesting to them, on topics about which they care and material that helps them understand their world better. The choice of literature has to mean something to the students or it is seen as a boring assignment and the message will be forgotten after the exam. To prevent boredom and help students retain key concepts, teachers need to build on previously acquired knowledge and link new data with old information. Create lesson plans and hands-on activities that relate to the students' lives. Encourage student discussion; as students share ideas and ask questions, alternate perspectives are presented, considered and integrated.

## Language arts curriculum

In a well-designed language arts curriculum, both contemporary and historical literature in various genres is read and analyzed. The content should embrace society's diversity, portray women and minorities accurately and without bias, and explore various countries and cultures. The program should be organized around universal themes that reflect the human condition, promote critical thinking and vocabulary enhancement and integrate information from other disciplines. Teachers should emphasize that timeless literature does not exist in a vacuum and can only be truly understood when viewed through the social, economic, and political environment in which they are set. This is the best way to integrate information from other disciplines such as history, social studies and economics into the language arts program. It is important that teachers recognize that students are at different reading and comprehension levels, and as such, the choice of literature, the time spent discussing and reviewing it, and the hands-on activities assigned should take those differences into account.

## General standards

Students do not live in a vacuum. School is just one part of their lives. Home, church, community, and culture all play vital roles in their lives and learning experiences. Recognizing these influences and working with them by incorporating a wide range of print and non-print media across many countries and cultures should be the cornerstone of every language arts program. Teaching grammar and syntax rules as students read a variety of fiction and non-fiction texts helps them learn about the complex world in which they live and prepares them to function as productive citizens in that world. Learning to understand, evaluate, integrate, and share information gleaned from the literature of many eras and a variety of genres helps students appreciate diversity and enhances their knowledge of the world beyond their backyard. The ability to read, write, analyze, and communicate ideas and concepts effectively should be the ultimate goal of every language arts program.

## Active learning

Active learning uses interactive instructional methods and strategies to impart course content. It creates an environment which encourages students to do more than just sit and listen to the teacher talk. Studies have shown that students learn better and retain information longer when they are actively involved in the process. They should be engaged in some activity, e.g., reading, writing, discussing, experimenting or creating. When students are actively involved in the learning process, they are using critical thinking skills, analyzing, synthesizing and evaluating data, solving problems and integrating new information with previously acquired knowledge. Studies have indicated that students prefer active learning to passive listening. Other research comparing lectures alone to active learning methods showed that active learning is comparable in understanding content and superior in developing critical thinking and written communication skills. In light of these findings, it is important for teachers to develop and incorporate active learning into their classroom management strategies.

Incorporating active learning in the classroom does not mean eliminating lectures altogether, but rather, delivering lectures in a more interactive manner. Reading from note cards or the textbook is boring; moving around the room, talking from memory, using positive body language, animated facial expressions and an upbeat tone of voice engages the students. Stopping periodically for a moment or two to allow the students to consolidate their notes gives them an opportunity to reflect on the information. Writing data down helps students retain it longer. Interjecting demonstrations and showing pictures, charts and illustrations are other ways to engage students. Asking open-ended questions encourages lively class discussion. Dividing the class into groups in order to find a solution and presenting it to the class is a great way to develop communication, presentation and other social skills. Writing in-class essays, conducting experiments and working on projects all incorporate active learning in the classroom.

## Class discussions

- It is a mistake to think lively, equitable class discussions occur spontaneously as a result of a well-prepared lecture or hands-on activity. Discussions that encourage learning and teach communication skills take planning, preparation and forethought. Rules need to be developed either by the teacher or with input from the students; they need to be clearly explained, understood and impartially enforced. Here are some questions teachers should consider as they plan discussion activities:The Goal? E.g., to discover new material, explore other perspectives, encourage students to share relevant experiences?

- What Form Of Participation Will Be Used? E.g., one-on-one dialogue, small group project, large class discussion?
- What Kind Of Student Preparation Is Required? E.g., reading assigned selections, researching additional data using outside resources, writing an essay?
- How Will Participation Be Evaluated? E.g., listening skills, individual contributions, ability to interact with others?

## Equitable class discussions

Teachers need to remember that not all students are comfortable speaking in front of a group. Therefore, it is important to recognize that the goal is to foster an environment that encourages students to participate and that no one is inhibited or prevented from participating because of the teaching methods used. Participation is predicated on teacher and student expectations, instructional methods and strategies, and the atmosphere created in the classroom. Students should be told in a variety of ways throughout the year that their presence is needed and valued and that their contributions are important and welcome. The teacher needs to explain the role participation plays during class time, how much importance is attached to active involvement and how it will be evaluated. It is important to develop class rules for discussions, provide frequent feedback and ask for student input to ensure teaching practices are in line with students' perceptions of reasonable opportunities to actively engage.

## Small group discussions

Dividing the class into small groups (five or less) gives students who might not be comfortable speaking in front of the entire class—but will actively participate in a more intimate arena—a forum in which to shine. One potential problem with these group projects, however, is ensuring that every student has an opportunity to participate. There may be some students who by sheer force of their personality overwhelm less demonstrative students. One way to prevent that is for the teacher to assign each student a specific function that must be completed. He will receive a separate grade for his contribution and it will be included in the evaluation of the group project as a whole. It is important for the teacher to join each group to observe how each student interacts with the others in the group. The ability to work as an effective member of a team is an important skill in today's business world.

## Participation in classroom activities

Calling upon a particular student can be both motivating and intimidating for the student depending upon the individual and the situation, and therefore a wise teacher carefully considers how to use the strategy effectively. When a question is asked, a problem posed or a solution required, students need time to think about the information presented and formulate a response. Even if the answer was unexpected or not correct, it is important to mention some aspect that was correct and then explain how the response could have been improved. Encourage questions by telling the class that other students probably need the same information but do not think to raise the issue. At the beginning of the class, require different students to summarize the lesson from the previous day, pose a prepared question from the assigned reading material or describe something they learned in class that they applied to their lives. Acknowledging every contribution encourages additional participation.

## Class discussion problems

Sometimes no matter what a teacher may do, students are still reluctant to participate in class discussions or feel that they are either not being heard or that their opinions are not taken seriously. If this is the case, give some thought to what happens during a discussion. Do a few students monopolize the time by talking too much? Does the discussion stop after a certain student makes a comment or offers a solution? Are there particular types of questions or comments that generate or inhibit responses? Does the question or comment indicate what kind of response is expected, such as a summary, an analysis, a personal experience, a debate or something else? Ask the students how they perceive the situation; listen to what they have to say. Ask a colleague to observe a class discussion and offer a critique, and take notes. If modifications are called for, tell the students about the changes and evaluate the results in a few weeks.

## Sensitive material

In an ideal world, all information can be presented in a value-neutral way. However, some subjects may generate controversy, which is not necessarily a bad thing if both the teacher and students are prepared. The teacher's role is that of "devil's advocate," to ensure that all sides of the issue are presented fairly. Rules need to be developed so that if the discussion veers off course, there is an agreed-upon solution to apply. In this situation, it is best if the students draft the rules with guidance from the teacher. The main focus is to ensure respect for each student, his feelings, opinions and cultural identity. Here are some points that should be included in the rules:
- Give everyone adequate time to talk.
- Listen to all opinions.
- Speak from personal experience.
- Avoid generalizations, blaming, name-calling.
- Question the quality of the argument, not the validity of the belief.
- Focus on learning, not winning.

## In-class writing

In class writing gives students the opportunity to refine their thoughts before they are expected to reveal them. It also generates more thoughtful, in depth discussions. (An added bonus is an improvement in written communication skills.) This technique can be used in various ways. Put a question, quotation or key concept on the board and allocate the first ten minutes of class to write a response. A second method is to lecture for ten or fifteen minutes then give the students time to write specific questions, comments or observations about the topic. At this point, small group discussions can be formed so that students can hear reactions from a few before presenting to the entire group, or the teacher can select random papers to read anonymously as a way to generate discussion. In both scenarios, it is the students' thoughts, ideas and observations that are addressed rather than the teacher's opinions.

## Reading assignments

Developing thoughtful discussion questions is a great way to motivate students to read assigned material, listen during lectures and take better notes. Providing weekly or unit study questions alerts them to key elements that should be learned and helps students prepare for quizzes, tests and final exams as they progress through the semester instead of waiting until the end. Asking students to submit questions or writing them on the board at the beginning of class are ways to discover what they are struggling with, are curious about or just want to discuss. Having key words, phrases or concepts on the board as students enter is another way to generate discussion. Taking a passage from the textbook or an outside source and asking the class to relate it to information from earlier lectures is a good way to encourage critical thinking and helps students integrate previously presented data with the new material.

## Outside resources

Students always respond enthusiastically to references from pop culture, current films, bestselling books and magazines, and contemporary music. Relating the subject to material they already understand, relate to, and rely upon helps students remember key concepts longer and encourages them to find ways to apply it to their daily lives. Magazine articles, video clips, photographs, and illustrations of people and things about which they already know makes it real, not merely abstract academia. These resources can also present alternate viewpoints or expand the subject in a different or unique way that helps students grasp the concept more quickly. Visiting an art or science museum; touring a senior or childcare center; and observing the judge, jury, and attorneys in a courtroom are all ways to bring a lesson alive and make it real and relevant to impressionable adolescents, generating lively discussions back in the classroom.

## Strategic enhancement

In order to grow as a language arts instructor, teachers need to experience similar activities from the other side of the desk in order to understand how their students feel about and react to course requirements. How? Teachers need to be students. It will help them understand how adolescents learn and develop necessary cognitive skills and help them suggest methods to motivate youth to want to achieve. This requires comprehensive knowledge of not only grammar and syntax rules and literary genres and authors, but the social, economic, and political influences of the countries and cultures studied. To accomplish this goal, an array of resources must be available to prepare intellectually stimulating lectures, hands-on activities, special projects and field trips. It is the district, school, and community's responsibility to provide the tools and training necessary for teachers to teach and for students to learn. Teachers must take pride in preparing and presenting material in an interesting, engaging manner.

## Pacing guide

One method that teachers can use in order to plan lessons based upon a state-mandated language arts test is to create a pacing guide at the beginning of the unit, grading period, or semester. Using the test guidelines and/or specific skills required, one may estimate how much time it will take for the students to learn each objective. Using a calendar and working backwards from the test date, decide which activities need to occur every week and then block out the number of days needed to teach each skill. Once adequate time has been allocated, break each skill into manageable tasks and create a chart to ensure that each has been presented. It is important to note each time part of the skill is taught, reinforced, or evaluated. Use a variety of resources, instructional methods, and strategies to present the material so that all of the students have an opportunity to learn using their particular learning styles.

## State-mandated test

Many states require that students pass a language arts achievement test in order to progress to the next grade level and/or graduate. There are many variables that contribute to student success on these tests, but one that has proven to offer a measurable advantage is a well-planned and implemented program that emphasizes reading comprehension and strong writing skills. To accomplish that goal, productive classrooms are safe and harmonious and:
- Have a teacher who understands the test and establishes an environment that focuses upon doing that what it takes to master the skills needed to pass it.

- Every lesson addresses a concept, skill, or process that appears on the test using a variety of resources, methods, and strategies.
- Students are given adequate time to learn the material.
- Students are expected to integrate learned skills and are held accountable for applying them.
- Pre-tests, benchmarks, and post-evaluations are used to assess student progress and teacher effectiveness.

Schools that consistently perform better on state-mandated language arts tests develop a curriculum that integrates the skills required to pass into all phases of the program instead of devoting time to specifically prepare for "the test." Students are taught how to read, understand, analyze, and write about any topic so that they can become functioning, literate members of society, not merely to pass a test. New knowledge is integrated with skills which they already possess is applied in other disciplines. For example, they learn new vocabulary by reading interesting source material, researching words which they do not know, and using the new words in essays which they write. The words become familiar because students use them, not because they memorize them. Administrators, principals, and teachers work together to determine the key skills required to excel on these tests and develop the materials, methods, and strategies to impart the knowledge needed using a meaningful, integrated approach.

## Sample Pacing Guide Chart

### Sample Pacing Guide Chart

| Skill | Task 1 | Task 2 | Task 3 |
|---|---|---|---|
| Reading Comprehension | Speed | Recall of Facts | Answering Questions |
| Time Allocated: | | | |
| Dates Taught: | | | |
| Dates Assessed: | | | |
| Percent of Mastery: | | | |
| | | | |
| Writing Ability | Content Knowledge | Persuasive Argument | Logical Presentation |
| Time Allocated: | | | |
| Dates Taught: | | | |
| Dates Assessed: | | | |
| Percent of Mastery: | | | |

NOTE: may be modified to reflect the particular test requirements and/or the teacher's specific needs.

## Separated-simulated-integrated activities

The objective of using separated-simulated-integrated activities is to enable students to become better readers, writers, and thinkers. Using only one or two does not help students retain and apply the lessons learned; using all three appropriately does. For example, the teacher assigns separated and simulated activities related to the topic to small groups (five or less) and requires each group to present its findings to the entire class. The teacher uses this data to generate a class discussion, pose a complex problem, or assign individual written reports (in most situations, using all three works best); the work product must use most of the information supplied by the groups. This approach teaches effective note-taking and communication skills and requires the ability to speak, listen, analyze, and evaluate data and integrate new information. Keeping a written compilation of new words, ideas, and concepts generated from these activities is an excellent way to create a reference guide and study tool.

Many schools consistently produce highly literate students by teaching English using the separated-simulated-integrated method. Teachers discovered that learning is most effective when students acquire the skills which they need, retain that knowledge, and are able to apply the information outside the language arts classroom. This approach works for every skill from grammar and syntax usage to learning vocabulary and individual facts to organizing a writing assignment. (It is also effective in other classes.) Students study a single item (separate), memorize its meaning, and record the data in a notebook. The second step is to use the information (simulate) within a limited area in the subject under study. Finally, students are required to use the new knowledge to complete a task that is related to the subject but extends beyond the original item (integrate). This approach teaches critical thinking and enhances the ability to apply concepts instead of simply memorizing isolated bits of data.

## Enabling connections

One of education's primary functions is to prepare students to be productive members of society. In order to do that effectively, the knowledge gained in school needs be meaningful and make sense to the students. Therefore, it is imperative that teachers consciously make connections between information learned and skills acquired in one class to their application in other disciplines. Connected data can be used to understand new facts, integrate new information, and apply lessons learned in one area to problems posed in another. The ability to see the relationship between seemingly unrelated topics and events requires critical thinking and advanced reasoning skills. When teachers encourage students to explore the relationship between activities and attitudes in school, at home, and in the neighborhood, students gradually begin to understand that individual actions have far-reaching consequences beyond the immediate environment. Making that critical connection is a major milestone in an adolescent's maturation process.

Teachers need to make deliberate connections between classes and across the curriculum. Planning lectures, hands-on activities, special projects, and field trips that explore universal themes and address national or international issues makes the lesson real and relevant. Assigning a Stephen King novel and searching for a similar theme in one of Shakespeare's plays, then showing the relationship of both to the political situation in a third world country is teaching students how to think critically and creatively and make connections to what is happening in the real world. Welcoming intrusions in the lesson plan and finding activities to make it meaningful, memorable and teachable is the sign of a creative teacher who uses unexpected opportunities to connect school life to real life. Example: during career day, assign students a guest to interview, create a written evaluation of the merits and drawbacks of the guest's profession, and then debate its desirability as a career option.

## Creative thinking

One of the primary purposes for education is to teach students to become critical thinkers. Language arts classes are fertile fields to sow the seeds of original thinking. After learning the information and meeting the goals required by the curriculum and/or the state-mandated test, teachers should plan activities that use the newly acquired skills and knowledge and encourage students to probe deeper into the subject. Exploring texts through different lenses (social, historical, ethical, political, cultural, psychological, personal) is an extremely effective way to get students thinking creatively and to help them move beyond first impressions and obvious interpretations. Asking open-ended questions and responding to students' concerns, ideas, and unique interpretations is another way to probe more deeply, elaborate, and encourage them to move beyond their initial understanding of the topic. Assigning challenging problems, collectively developing solutions, and applying them to contemporary issues makes learning exciting and relevant to the real world.

## Completing an assignment

Teachers have a responsibility to teach students not only the facts about a topic but also how to think about and approach a task and complete the assignment. Instead of focusing upon memorizing the data, creative teachers give students ways to discover the answer through research and reasoning. They incorporate relevant commentary and detailed explanations into the instructions for all assignments. Students learn better, retain data longer, recall it more easily, and integrate it more effectively when they understand the how and the why, not merely the what. Providing guidelines that explain how to approach a task (such as breaking it into smaller, more manageable parts) and supplying written prompts and reminder sheets gives students valuable tools which they can use in their other classes. These reasoning tools can also be used to make choices in areas outside of the academic environment. This is a prime example of making learning relevant to their life.

## Cognitive collaboration

Cognitive collaboration is bringing together and utilizing the personal, cultural, and factual knowledge of everyone in a group to solve a problem, complete a task, or create a new way of thinking. The individuals in the group are all problem-generators and problem-solvers who provide multiple perspectives by which to tackle the assignment. They are expected to work together, bounce ideas off of one another, question and challenge observations and suggestions, and refine their understanding of the subject to reach a consensus. This type of collaborative group approach is highly prized and sought after in the business world. To be effective in a classroom environment, teachers must impress upon students the importance of functioning as a team. The teacher must treat students as members of a dynamic community and understand and respect the social interactions that encourage or inhibit learning. The teacher must be involved and interact with each group, ask questions, pose problems, and challenge students to think creatively.

## Direct teaching

- The idea behind direct teaching is to shift the emphasis from teaching to learning; the focus is on the student acquiring and integrating knowledge, and not the teacher's particular instructional methods. To maximize learning, several questions should be asked when preparing lessons for all students, but are especially critical when special needs students are involved:The main concept? Are the students ready to learn it? Will it require previously learned knowledge to understand and integrate it?
- What resources are needed to prepare required activities? What steps are necessary to explain the information clearly? Are examples and prompts concrete and easily understood?
- How will progress be monitored? Are students on task? Are they working independently or do they need a great deal of assistance? How will feedback be provided?
- Which evaluation methods will be used? Observation? Questions? Demonstrations? Tests?
- If follow-up instruction is needed, how will it be provided? Intervention? Remediation? Reviewing? Repeating?

## Analyzing key concepts

Providing study guides at the beginning of a unit is an excellent way to help students understand the material as it is presented and prepare for an evaluation at the end of the lesson. One effective method is to paraphrase short passages (one to three paragraphs) from textbooks and outside resources (be sure to credit author, editor, publication, etc.). The purpose is to simplify the message without distorting or diluting the meaning. Using appropriate graphs, illustrations and organizers such as concept maps to clarify and show connections between and among key concepts helps students understand the information and gives them a tool, combined with their own notes, to complete projects and study for tests. Using short sentences, underlining new vocabulary and adding commentary all enhance the usefulness of this tool. It doesn't have to be complicated; in fact, the simpler the explanation, the easier it is for all students to comprehend.

## Taxonomy of Personal Engagement

Developed by Morgan and Saxton, questions based on the Taxonomy of Personal Engagement are different from Bloom's Taxonomy, because this approach solicits the thoughts and feelings of the responder. It requires students to use critical thinking skills and make connections to related concepts by tapping into their thoughts, feelings, attitudes, points of view, real life experiences, and value system. In order to utilize this type of inquiry effectively, teachers need to select key concepts and prepare open-ended questions ahead of time. The questions should:
- Pique the Interest and curiosity of the students.
- Be Engaging so that students want to be involved.
- Require a Commitment to help students develop a sense of responsibility.
- Merge new ideas with experiences so that students Internalize and take ownership of new concepts.
- Help students Interpret information and further their desire to communicate new insights.
- Students should evaluate and show a desire and willingness to use the information.

## Purpose of questions

Students ask questions to clarify a particular point or to learn more about a subject. Teachers pose questions to discover how well students understand the material, to encourage critical thinking, and to help them integrate new data with previously acquired knowledge. Good teacher questions are short, direct, open-ended, and have several possible responses. They require more than a simple recitation of factual data and the student should discover something new from his answer. Questions are asked from several perspectives:
- Personal Growth. Does the story portray life as it really is? Is it relevant?
- Cultural Heritage. What are the main ideas and values in the story? Compare them to another story with a similar theme.
- Functional. What would have to be changed to make the story into a film?
- Critical Literacy. How are social, cultural, and minority groups represented?

## Encouraging questions

There are many innovative ways to generate open-ended, thought-provoking questions, but the important thing is to develop an atmosphere that recognizes and appreciates creative thinking and supports and respects all contributions. The following suggestions are a few approaches to consider.

- Allocate a specific time for questions and suggest that students jot them down during the presentation so that they do not forget them, OR:
- Allow questions by the teacher and from the students any time during the presentation.
- Praise the questions (e.g., "What an interesting observation. I hadn't looked at it that way.").
- Have students write down interesting questions. Have the class analyze why they are interesting. Are they "on topic," between topics" or "beyond the topic." This exercise helps student learn to ask probing, thought-provoking questions.
- Play Jeopardy. Give students the answer, have them form the question.

## Creative thinking framework

Most teachers agree that the best questions are born out of genuine curiosity and excitement about the topic. These are the questions that generate lively discussions, encourage additional inquiries, and help all the students learn and integrate new concepts. When students believe the classroom environment is a safe place to explore new ideas and offer alternative viewpoints, they are more comfortable discussing important, and, sometimes, controversial issues, and proposing innovative solutions. When teachers encourage cooperation, collaboration, discussion, debate, negotiation, reflection, and self and peer assessment, students are more willing to share thoughts, feelings, and experiences. Teachers set the tone for this type of classroom environment by:

- Welcoming questions and modeling active listening to all responses.
- Helping students form the right question to get the information they are seeking.
- Restating or paraphrasing the question.
- Giving students time to reflect on and formulate thoughtful responses.

## Sequence chart

- Creating a sequence chart is a small group activity that requires speaking, listening, reading, writing and critical thinking skills. It can be used in middle and high school classes. The teacher asks a question or poses a problem and the group finds the answer or solves the problem by building a logical sequence of events, concepts, or ideas using information from the textbook, outside research material, an incident in the news, or a combination of these sources coupled with previously acquired knowledge. If the students are new to this activity, providing samples of completed sequence charts helps them understand and visualize the concept. The steps used to create a viable, workable chart:The issue or problem.
- Brainstorm ideas, comments, and connections.Potential solutions.
- Condense each response to two or three words.
- Write responses in appropriate boxes on the chart.

## Alpha ladder activity

Dr. Helen McGrath, a psychologist in the Department of Scientific and Developmental Studies in Education at Deakin University in Melbourne, Australia, developed the alpha ladder collaborative activity for middle school students. The game requires speaking, listening and writing skills, and provides a view of students' ability to analyze and describe word function and structure (but not its meaning). The class is divided into teams of five with each person having a specific role: leader, questioner, runner, recorder, and social skills scribe. The performing team has ten minutes to write twenty questions about a word provided by the teacher (e.g., number of syllables, part of speech). As they call out the yes or no questions, the shadowing teams write answers down and give them to the teacher. The performing team gets one point for each unasked question and the shadowing teams get one point for every correct answer plus bonus points for figuring out the word.

## Consensus of key concepts

A consensus is a general agreement of key concepts developed by the whole class. Each student reads the chosen passage and compiles a list of the major ideas. Small groups (three or five) are formed to prioritize the individual lists after discussing, refining and modifying each person's ideas into statements on which the members agree. The lists from all the groups are written on the board. There will probably be several similar statements that can be quickly merged and adopted. The class discusses the remaining statements. Students should be able to justify and defend their viewpoint based on the final list of key concepts. Related activities that could be assigned include: a written description of the thought process used to create their individual list, an evaluation of how well the small group worked as a team, and the method used to reach the class consensus. Self and peer assessments can also be used to evaluate speaking and listening skills.

## Cloze

Preparing poetry or prose for cloze means to delete certain words or phrases and require students to fill in the blanks. Cloze can be used to study parts of speech, grammar rules, or sentence structure, as well as explore the importance of word choice and how it can change the meaning of the message. In order for cloze to be effective, the teacher must choose the words or phrases to be deleted very carefully based upon the lesson objective. If used to explore how word choice influences the meaning, it can generate lively discussions about the connotation, subtle shadings, and interpretations of words. It can lead to students sharing opinions about why the author choose the word or phrase he did and how using another expression changes the entire message. Teachers can use cloze to assess language development, progress in spelling and grammar, and how well students identify context cues and apply critical thinking skills.

## Six thinking hats

Edward de Bono, a psychologist, physician, and pioneer in constructive and creative thinking, developed the six thinking hats to explain the need for and importance of lateral thinking in today's world. Teachers can adapt the strategy by applying it to brainstorming and problem solving activities. It requires students to think about a topic from several perspectives, learn to recognize which "hat" a speaker or writer is wearing when explaining or discussing a subject, and appreciate the variety of thinking required in different learning situations. The approach can be used to review multiple stories, create a character, or devise a plot. The six thinking hats are:
- White: reviews available data.
- Black: looks at the problems.
- Yellow: studies the benefits.
- Red: views the subject with emotions and feelings.
- Green: uses the imagination and lateral thinking.
- Blue: reflects on the necessity to manage the thought processes themselves.

## SCAMPER

SCAMPER is an acronym: Substitute, Combine, Adapt, Modify/magnify/minify, Put to other uses, Eliminate, Reverse/rearrange. This teaching strategy helps students learn to be creative thinkers when they write their own imaginative stories and is a marvelous tool in role-playing activities. The purpose is to teach students to think outside the box, see beyond the obvious, and create new ways of expressing the same ideas. It is most effective after a book or story has been studied and students understand the message, how the characters relate, why they do what they do, and how all the elements work together. Then students are better prepared to apply some or all of SCAMPER and discover how minor as well as major alterations can change, for better or worse, the original story. It is a fun activity and a great way to stimulate students' imaginations and bring a story to life.

## Y chart

A Y chart explores a topic by examining what it looks like, sounds like, and feels like. It can be used to identify and define appropriate behavior, explore ideas and issues, or develop a character profile to use as a class role model. The activity encourages students to think critically about the importance of social skills, recognize emotional intelligence and helps develop problem-solving skills. The Y chart helps students focus on the strengths and weaknesses of the idea, issue, or behavior. The activity can be done by individual students, small groups, or by the class as a whole. If done by individuals or small groups, their findings should be presented to the class and defended, if necessary. If conducted by the whole class, suggestions must be explained and justified. Evaluations can be made based upon students' ability to use analytical and critical thinking skills and progress in the development of social skills.

## Venn diagram

A Venn diagram is a graphic illustration of the similarities and differences between items. Two or more interlocking circles are used to compare and contrast stories, genres, characters, eyewitness accounts, universal themes, key points, and literary devices, to name a few options. It is an effective method to sort information in both fiction and non-fiction texts so that observations can be made, conclusions reached, and lessons learned. The activity can be done by individual students, small groups, or the entire class, but the choices made must be justified and defended before being accepted. A written exploration of the findings is an optional additional activity. Students can be evaluated on their ability to identify and analyze key concepts, integrate new data with previously learned information, how they present and defend their opinions, their willingness to accept alternative viewpoints, their ability to incorporate other views with their own, and their general communicational skills.

## Brain-based learning

The idea of brain-based learning asserts that one learns merely because one exists and that one learns best by being challenged, not threatened. One learns as long as one is born with a brain which functions normally and is not inhibited by discouraging, ignoring or punishing the brain's natural capabilities. The brain is an amazing information processor which can perform several functions simultaneously. Each brain is unique and learns through both focused attention and peripheral perception using both conscious and unconscious processes. The brain has two types of memory: spatial (natural) and rote (memorizing). The brain remembers best when learning is spatial rather than rote.

The three techniques associated with brain-based learning are:
- Orchestrated Immersion, which is learning by complete immersion in the subject.
- Relaxed Alertness, which tries to eliminate the fear of learning while providing challenges to figure out and work through.
- Active Processing, which encourages the student to consolidate and internalize data.

## Implementing a strategic plan

<u>The American Heritage College Dictionary</u> defines strategy as an "important plan of action intended to accomplish a specific goal." It also defines plan as a "program or method worked out beforehand to accomplish an objective." Using these definitions, a strategic classroom plan is a series of lessons, lectures, and activities prepared at the beginning of the grading period, semester, or year that identifies specific goals and sets realistic milestones that must be reached in order to achieve those goals.

Once the goals are identified and milestones set, a well-prepared teacher develops lesson plans and lectures that address each goal and plans activities that enhance the information presented. The data should include all the facts necessary to understand the topic. Activities should be relevant to the students' current life or suggest possible future uses or potential needs. Real world examples should be used to illustrate the importance and usefulness of the subject being studied.

## Affirmation teaching

Affirmation teaching is based on the Socratic approach of asking questions to learn what the student already knows. This method of instruction believes each student is inherently intelligent with a unique potential and possesses many talents to explore. Affirmation is a means of helping the student discover what he knows and, through that knowledge, learn who he is. The teacher guides the student so he can determine his particular talents or attributes and praises his efforts to learn and grow. The effort expended on a task is directly responsible for the student's success or failure. A basic requirement of the affirmation method is that the student learns to reflect on how his effort, or lack thereof, affects his performance and the results of his actions.

Examples of affirmation include:
- "You passed the exam because you studied for it."
- "Your hard work clearly shows in this term paper!"

## Implementing affirmation teaching

The affirmation style of teaching works best in a one-on-one situation. However, the method can be successfully used in a traditional classroom setting if the teacher views the environment with the four dimensions necessary to affirmation teaching.
- The Spiritual Dimension—a caring teacher believes that each and every student will be successful at assigned tasks.
- The Physical Dimension—a safe, secure, and productive environment.
- The Instructional Dimension—appropriate methods and various strategies are used to help students achieve academic success.
- The Managerial Dimension—a calm, orderly, and smooth-running classroom environment is maintained.

Affirmation teachers use both formal and informal means to assess students' progress and do not believe that standardized test results adequately or accurately measure learning. These teachers prepare lesson plans, ask probing questions, offer feedback and summarize students' progress. They teach with enthusiasm, have a positive attitude and have a sense of humor they often use to diffuse tense situations.

## Helpful planning methods

To be competitive and successful in today's global marketplace, a business must have a strategy. This plan identifies goals and the means to achieve them and determines the best use of people and financial resources. Shown are two methods used to develop a business strategy and create a blueprint to realize it. With some minor modification, these methods can be used to devise a classroom plan.

The Situation/Target/Path Process:
- Evaluate the current situation; i.e., the number of students, the average GPA, the level of diversity.The target; i.e., the specific goals
- Develop the path; i.e., the lessons, lectures, and activities, and set attainable milestones
- The Define/Review/Action Approach:The desired goals and objectives.
- Review realistically the issues; i.e., the number of students, the average GPA, the level of diversity.
- Develop specific actions (i.e., lessons, lectures and activities) that address issues and set milestones to reach goals.

## Constructivist teaching

Constructivist teaching is based on the learning theory developed by Jean Piaget and John Dewey. Their belief is that all learning builds on knowledge previously acquired. They also believe that a student learns better and retains the information longer if he is actively involved in the process, rather than passively listening to a teacher talk. Constructivist teaching encourages the student to reflect on the information presented based on his personal experiences. They learn by taking the initiative for their own learning. The following are characteristics of a constructivist classroom:
- The students are actively involved in a democratic setting.
- All the activities are interactive, dynamic and student-centered.
- Most activities are done in groups, which encourages collaboration and the exchange of ideas.
- The focus is on the development of social and communication skills.
- The teacher encourages the students to be responsible and autonomous.

In a constructivist classroom, the teacher's main role is as the facilitator. He or she asks probing and leading questions that help the students come to their own conclusions about the subject material being studied. Because the process of learning is just as important as the knowledge gained, assessment is based not merely upon test results, which only produce specific answers to pointed questions, but weighs other factors as well.

The teacher also considers:
- The student's behavior in class and participation in open discussions
- The student's production and quality of work throughout the course
- The student's point of view and how well he expresses and defends it
- The development of the student's communication and social skills.

All of these factors are important in determining how well the student has mastered the subject matter, as well as how much he has grown as a person.

## Constructivist classroom activities

Constructivist teaching builds on knowledge previously acquired, encourages active learning, and emphasizes working in groups to develop social and communication skills; therefore there are several activities used to achieve the desired goals. Students perform experiments by themselves and then come together as a class to discuss the results. Teachers assign many research projects in which the students need to read about a specific topic, create an appropriate presentation and present the results to the class. Students are taken on field trips so they can see the concepts they are learning in the classroom in a real-world setting. These trips encourage social interaction and end with class discussions about what they saw and how the concepts they studied worked or did not, as the case may be. Class discussions are inclusive and lively and used every day to encourage independent thinking by sharing the students' individual perceptions of the subject matter being studied.

## Constructivist assessment methods

Some common assessment methods used by a constructivist teacher include:
- Pre-Testing, which indicates to the teacher how much knowledge the students already have about a particular subject. This is helpful both in planning lessons, lectures, and activities and in assessing what the students have learned at the end of the course.
- Mind Mapping, in which students categorize the concepts and ideas related to the subject under study.
- Hands-On Activities, in which teachers watch and evaluate how students use various learning tools, noting progress in mastering the material.
- Oral Discussions, in which the teacher presents a "focus" question and monitors the open, free-ranging discussion it generates to determine the students' understanding of the subject.
- Using KWLH Chart, which stands for what we "K"now, what we "W"ant to know, what we have "L"earned and "H"ow we know it. Keeping this chart enables the teacher to gauge the students' progress during the course of study. It also enables the teacher to make adjustments in lesson plans if necessary.

## Learning style theory

The learning style theory of teaching is based upon the assumption that everyone perceives and processes information differently. Each person is capable of learning as long as the educational tools are geared toward his particular learning requirements. The question is not "is this student smart" but rather "how is this student smart." The theory is based upon research that shows heredity, nurture (upbringing), and nature (environment) all influence how an individual student processes information. Some students predominately use one of the following generally recognized methods, while other students use a combination of one or two or some aspects of all four.
- Concrete Perceivers absorb information by doing, acting, sensing, and touching.
- Abstract Perceivers learn through observing, analyzing, and thinking about the data.
- Active Processors learn by using the information immediately.
- Reflective Processors reflect upon and think about the information before they use it.

## Brain-based learning

The idea of brain-based learning asserts that one learns merely because one exists and that one learns best by being challenged, not threatened. One learns as long as one is born with a brain that functions normally and is not inhibited by discouraging, ignoring or punishing the brain's natural capabilities. The brain is an amazing information processor that can perform several functions simultaneously. Each brain is unique and learns through both focused attention and peripheral perception, using both conscious and unconscious processes. The brain has two types of memory: spatial (natural) and rote (memorizing). The brain remembers best when learning is spatial rather than rote. The three techniques associated with brain-based learning are:

- Orchestrated Immersion, which is learning by complete immersion in the subject.
- Relaxed Alertness, which tries to eliminate the fear of learning while providing challenges to figure out and work through.
- Active Processing, which encourages the student to consolidate and internalize data.

## Presenting information to special needs students

Using short lectures with lots of visual and graphic examples, scheduling frequent breaks and telling students several times when to expect the change to another activity are all important strategies to keep the attention of special needs students. It is imperative to know, understand and plan for the different learning styles and levels of comprehension. Make sure that students understand precisely that which is expected at the beginning of every activity and answer all questions before starting the lesson. Limit the number of ideas, concepts and new vocabulary presented at the same time. Provide copies of outlines, study guides and notes from presentations using the overhead projector and other visual or audio media. Highlight key concepts. Instructions need to be given verbally and with written directions that include visual prompts, if possible. Break assignments into manageable parts, monitor the students' progress, and allow adequate time to complete each section before moving to the next.

Providing the opportunity for special needs students to achieve success requires planning for and preparation of the classroom setting. The area needs to be as free as possible from visual and auditory distractions. An inside room without windows and away from a busy corridor is an ideal setting. A separate area for independent study or to use when a behavioral time out is necessary is also helpful. Students should keep all unnecessary items off of desktops; only that which is needed for the immediate task should be allowed. These students need a predictable structure to their days and therefore teachers should develop a detailed checklist in order to help them get organized, stay on task and know which activities are planned and when. It is very important to stick to the established schedule. A supply of extra pens, pencils, paper, books and other resources should be available at all times.

## Teaching strategies for the learning disabled

Students with learning disabilities have problems in one or more areas including language, memory, attention and social adjustments, to name a few. Because of these difficulties, most students with learning disabilities require structure and predictability in their daily routine and need clear rules, specific responsibilities and well-defined assignments. Teachers need to provide outlines, study guides and notes from lectures, presentations and activities. They need to be specific when explaining tasks and break them into manageable steps. Allowing students with learning disabilities to ask questions and read the notes of other students helps ensure they are hearing and recording key information. (This also improves socialization skills.) It is important for teachers to monitor the progress of students with learning disabilities during each stage of an assignment so that help can be provided when needed and adjustments made if necessary.

## Evaluation strategies for special needs students

To obtain an accurate picture of the progress of special needs students, testing, grading and evaluations should be conducted in a slightly different manner. Tests should be given in a quiet place with as few distractions as possible. Accommodations for asking verbal questions and receiving oral answers should be provided. Tests should broken into short sections with visual prompts where possible. Avoid giving timed tests, and give students however much time they require to complete each section before moving to the next one. Schedule monitored breaks between each part. Teachers should grade spelling, organization and presentation separately from content. When evaluating content, highlight key concepts, creativity and original thinking so that the students and their parents recognize the knowledge gained and progress made. Teachers need to find something specific to point out and praise in order to encourage the student for his accomplishment and as an incentive to learn more. Exempt students from district and state mandated tests if permitted.

## Strategies for the physically impaired

Physical impairments include orthopedic damage (limited or restricted use of one or more limbs) and health issues such as asthma and diabetes. Barriers that impede access or restrict participation in school activities  (e.g., narrow sidewalks and heavy doors) need to be addressed. It is important that teachers help students, faculty and other adults understand and accept physically impaired students by modeling correct behavior, learning about special devices or procedures and ensuring safety measures are observed at all times. Teachers need to ask the student whether he needs help, and in what capacity. Students in wheelchairs may or may not have full use of their hands and therefore no one should presume to help unless asked to or directed by a caretaker. Students with physical impairments should be allowed to participate in all school-related activities such as field trips, special events and class projects. If accommodations are necessary, they should be provided.

## Strategies for the orally challenged

Many students with learning disabilities have language difficulties, which means they often struggle with oral comprehension. Since much of the material in class is presented via lecture and other verbal methods (class discussions, small group projects, etc.), teachers must be aware of students who have problems in this area. Using short, simple sentences with lots of visual aids and repeating and rephrasing key words, concepts, and ideas will help students understand the information better. Providing detailed directions, a logical sequence of tasks to be completed, and asking students to paraphrase instructions will help ensure that they understand what is required. Teaching students strategies for learning and remembering, such as mentally rehearsing before speaking, how to focus on key words during lectures and presentations, and creating mnemonics (such as FANBOYS to remember the conjunctions for, and, nor, but, or, yet, so) benefit all students by giving them tools they can use in all of their classes.

## Strategies for the hearing impaired

Hearing impaired students have moderate or full loss of their hearing and may communicate with sign language and reading lips. They may have difficulties with cognitive, motor, speech and social development. However, they are no different from students who can hear in either ability, personality or mental capacity. Seat hearing impaired students in the quietest area of the classroom; background noise is distracting and interferes with most hearing aids. Ensure that they can see speakers in order to be able to read their lips. Teachers should speak directly to the hearing impaired, write key data on the board or use an overhead projector when presenting information to the class. Keep in mind that hearing impaired

- 76 -

students may be unable to hear soft voices and sounds from another area of the room. If technical terms or new words are going to be introduced, give them a list ahead of time. Unfamiliar words are more difficult to understand and lip read without prior preparation.

## Strategies for the visually impaired

Visually impaired students have either partial or full loss of their sight. They may have difficulties with some cognitive or motor skills and social development may be hindered depending upon their experiences outside of the classroom. However, they are no different from sighted students in ability, personality or mental capacity. Frequently, visually impaired students have keen listening ability and use their sense of touch more than others, and thus activities may need to be modified in order to take advantage of these enhanced skills. Providing readers, books in Braille, recorded books and asking fellow students to verbally describe pictures, people and events are ways to help visually impaired students participate fully in the classroom. Encouraging students to help is a powerful lesson in understanding the challenges the visually impaired deal with daily and a positive way to improve the social skills of the visually impaired student.

## Speech impaired

Speech impairments include stuttering, chronic hoarseness and difficulties in determining the right word or expression to use. These impairments can cause problems with pronunciation, enunciation and voice strength; the student may be unable to speak at all and use a speaking machine or rely on body language to aid communication. However, they are no different from other students in ability, personality or mental capacity. Teachers and fellow students should always use normal speech patterns, avoid supplying words and finishing sentences and never appear impatient for a speech-impaired student to complete his thought. Teachers should accept written questions and comments and never require participation in a class discussion or require an answer to a question unless the student initiates the response. Create ways for these students to participate in classroom activities. For example: he could design a display for a bulletin board or write a report for fellow students to read, review and critique.

## Nonverbal aspects of communication

Many students with autistic disorders not only have difficult or abnormal verbal communication skills—that is, trouble understanding figurative/nonliteral spoken language like metaphors, sarcasm, jokes, and colloquial expressions, and trouble expressing emotional and social content—but also have difficulty with nonverbal communication, including tones of voice, facial expressions, body language, and physical gestures. Autistic students have difficulty noticing and interpreting the meaning of these cues. For example, an autistic student might have no idea that another person is smiling and/or that the smile indicates the person is happy or amused, or might not recognize a downturned mouth as a sign of unhappiness. Some autistic individuals can be taught to identify these signals. Autistic students do not understand verbal irony or sarcasm, because what gives the words the opposite or nonliteral meaning is vocal tone, facial expression, and/or gesture. They have corresponding difficulty expressively, having as much trouble telling jokes as understanding them, or saying anything with more or other than a literal meaning.

## Teaching methods that are most effective for meeting educational needs

Students with lower levels of cognitive development will think more concretely. As in Piaget's theory of cognitive development, normally developing children generally understand abstract concepts by adolescence. Severely or profoundly intellectually disabled students typically do not reach this level of cognitive development. They are unlikely even to reach Piaget's earlier stage of Concrete Operations, which entails performing mental operations with concrete objects but not abstractly. (Some with moderate intellectual disabilities can learn this, as with very simple arithmetic.) Therefore, teachers should use simple, concrete language with them. Teachers will also need to give brief, simple instructions, giving only one step at a time. They will need to repeat information and directions many times, at short time intervals. They need to tell students more explicitly what to do. They must give more frequent correction and should remember always to give positive reinforcement, both material and verbal, for every correct response and minor success.

## Receptive language problems

The language development of children with severe or profound intellectual disabilities is tied to their cognitive development. Because they develop more slowly than normal, these children acquire vocabulary words more slowly. They will have smaller vocabularies than their age peers. This slower development of comprehension for words reflects lower levels of cognitive development. The disabled child will understand spoken language at a simpler level reflecting a younger developmental age than the child's chronological age. Such children will comprehend fewer words and simpler ones. It is not just the words but also the concepts they convey. These children are unlikely to be able to understand abstract concepts, such as justice, democracy, and so forth. Some can be taught to interpret simpler abstractions, such as "it hurts my heart" to represent emotional rather than physical injury, or "sick in the head" (an actual quotation from a student) to represent mental rather than physical illness.

## Writing difficulties

Some students have difficulty writing in any genre. Teachers can help students overcome their fear of writing by providing an organized, sequential approach to the task, (e.g., outline, topic sentence, research tools, first draft, editing rules, final draft, learning from instructor's comments) and explaining and sharing examples of each step. At the beginning of the term, work on composing clear, complete sentences (the building blocks of all writing), progress to short, one-page essays and move to longer research and term papers after the students are proficient in the basics. Assigning a written project to a small group and combining confident writers with those who need extra help is another approach. Providing a list of approved topics and samples of well-written papers are other helpful strategies. Grading spelling and grammar separately from content is an effective way to point out mechanical errors without penalizing sound reasoning, creativity and critical thinking skills.

## Reading difficulties

There are specific things a teacher can do to help students who have problems with reading comprehension. Teach them to recognize the five Ws: who, what, when, where, why. Help students learn to identify the key words, ideas, and concepts and show them how to organize the information in a logical sequence. Teach them how to summarize and paraphrase the data and use various graphic organizers to help remember important points. Develop activities that prepare students for new material (e.g., explain unfamiliar vocabulary, idioms, terms) and after the topic is presented, create activities to review and reinforce the data. If a student is having problems reading out aloud, encourage him to read with a partner, read quietly to himself (sub-vocalization), and practice by reading popular magazines and appropriate web sites on the Internet. Allow all the students to read selected passages silently before asking individuals to read aloud to the class.

## Retaining data

Some students have difficulty retaining and retrieving data. They pay attention during lectures, participate in class discussions and group activities, and complete every written assignment, but they have difficulty committing the data to memory and have trouble retrieving it when they need to apply it. There are some strategies teachers can use to help these students improve their retention rate and retrieval skills. Break instructional units into short, manageable, easily understood sections and rephrase, review, and repeat key concepts frequently during the presentation. Prepare outlines, study guides, and vocabulary lists with important data highlighted and show the relationship between the new information and previously acquired knowledge with diagrams, matrices, and maps. Teach students how to visualize important facts and use mnemonics as a memory tool. Use a variety of methods (visual, auditory, tactile) to explain the concepts and provide concrete examples to demonstrate the relevance of the information to the students' lives.

## Grasping new concepts

In spite of compelling lectures, interesting and challenging activities, and inspiring field trips, some students have difficulty understanding new ideas. Sometimes the information is complex and confusing and even the better students have difficulty grasping the key concepts. There are some steps teachers can take to minimize student (and teacher) frustration and maximize learning, no matter what the topic. Plan adequate time to prepare, present, discuss, and review the data. Allow time to repeat specific lessons if necessary. Introduce new vocabulary, explain historical references and implications, and outline the main concepts using flow charts, diagrams, and appropriate organizers at the beginning of the lesson. Present the information in a variety of ways (multiple intelligences) so that students have an opportunity to learn using their particular style. Encourage cooperative learning, assign peer tutors, and connect new data with previously acquired knowledge. Use appropriate assessment tools to evaluate student understanding and integration of the new material.

## Difficulties taking tests

Some students have difficulty taking any kind of test; other students have problems with one or two test styles. This can stem from a variety of sources: fear and anxiety, problems with retention and retrieval, inadequate preparation, and physical impairments, to name a few. While teachers cannot force students to learn, they can use strategies that offer an equal opportunity to demonstrate mastery of the material. During the lectures and classroom activities, teachers can strongly suggest and/or hint at data that might appear on a future test. Teach note-taking skills. The criteria for evaluation need to be explained before the test. The format to be used, how much time will be allotted, and the material being tested should be outlined. In-class reviews and self-questioning should be conducted and ample preparation time allowed. A variety of question formats (essay, multiple choice, matching, fill-in-the-blank) should be used.

## Difficulties with organization

Some of the most useful tools a teacher can give students are good organizational skills. The ability to create order from chaos; find files, folders, and supplies quickly and develop a workable schedule and keep it, are skills he will use in every area of his life, all of his life. There are concrete classroom activities that help students learn this valuable lesson. Require that desktops contain only items relevant to and necessary for the current activity; everything else is stowed out of sight (books for other classes, backpacks, purses, cell phones, etc.). Show students the value of and reasons for calendars, daily/weekly/monthly planners, folders, and notebooks. At the beginning of the each unit, provide a detailed syllabus so that they know what is expected and when. Give students time management pointers and teach them the importance of planning and preparation in order to avoid last minute, frantic attempts to complete an assignment or study for a test.

<u>Difficulties following protocol</u>
Unruly students do more than disrupt classroom routine and steal time and attention: they prevent fellow students from learning. Teachers have a responsibility to help students acquire self-control and self-monitoring skills. Classroom rules need to be developed, established, explained, posted, and enforced fairly and consistently. If one student is expected to follow the rules, all the students are expected to follow the rules. If it is unacceptable today, it is unacceptable tomorrow. These two classroom conditions must be at the top of the list. Requiring every student to sign a copy of the rules and, with their signature agree to observe them, is a concrete way to help students set personal goals and learn what is acceptable behavior in a community, as school is a microcosm of the larger social dynamic. Positive and negative consequences need to be discussed, understood, and agreed upon before an incident occurs and corrective action is needed.

## Indirect vocabulary learning

Indirect vocabulary learning begins at birth. A child hears conversations all around him from his immediate family, people encountered during daily activities, and the voices on radio and television. He is surrounded by words. He learns to recognize and understand those words by how they are used, who is saying them and what is going on around him when he hears them. He learns the meanings of words and adds to his vocabulary:

- Through conversations especially between and with adults. That is one of the reasons adults should be conscious of what they say and how they say it when children are around.
- When adults read to him. Readers can enhance the experience by explaining words, answering questions, and discussing what is happening in the story.
- By reading on his own. Encouraging a child to read is one of the best ways to help him expand his vocabulary and improve his comprehension.

## Problems learning grammar, spelling and vocabulary

The English language has one of the largest vocabularies of any language currently in use. English has adopted, adapted and integrated words, phrases and expressions from many other languages. English uses more idiomatic words and phrases than most other languages and these idioms can be specific to a particular region of the country or a segment of the population. The same word can be used in multiple ways and have different meanings (i.e. to "spell" a word or come sit a "spell") or two words can sound alike but be spelled differently and have different meanings (i.e. wood and would). English often uses articles, such as "the," "a" and "an" while other languages may lack articles altogether or use their versions sparingly. There isn't just one rule to make a positive word into its negative counterpart. For example: unable, inappropriate, dishonest, amoral. All of these differences can make learning the English language a challenge.

## Context clues

Learning new words is important to and part of comprehending and integrating unfamiliar information. When a reader encounters a new word, he can stop and find it in the dictionary or the glossary of terms but sometimes those reference tools aren't readily available or using them at the moment is impractical (e.g., during a test). Furthermore, most readers are usually not willing to take the time. Another way to determine the meaning of a word is by considering the context in which it is being used. These indirect learning hints are called context clues. They include definitions, descriptions, examples, and restatements. Because most words are learned by listening to conversations, people use this tool all the time even if they do it unconsciously. But to be effective when reading, context clues must be used judiciously because the unfamiliar word may have several subtle variations, and therefore the context clues could be misinterpreted.

## Dictionaries

No matter how many vocabulary lists are passed out, reviewed and tested on, there is no way a teacher can teach students every word he may encounter. Therefore it is important to introduce them to the dictionary, the thesaurus, and the glossary of terms found in many books. Students should receive instruction in how to use these reference books and where to find the glossary. They should also be able to dissect a word into its various parts. The root of the word can be from another language (about sixty percent of English was taken from Latin or Greek). The base word is the foundation from which other words are made. The affixes are attached to words at the beginning (prefix) and the end (suffix). Knowing common root and base words and what prefixes and suffixes mean and how they are used helps students decipher the meaning of complex and unfamiliar words.

## Elaboration techniques

Memorizing definitions helps students pass the test but are usually quickly forgotten. For a student to remember a word or a term and add it to his active vocabulary, it should be relevant to him and essential to understanding the material. The words and terms presented at the start of a lesson should reflect key concepts that form the foundation of the material and be used often. Paraphrasing gives the main idea as well as essential details necessary to understand and clarify the core idea. Students should be able to make a connection to information which they already know, relate the term to personal experience or use it to solve a real problem. Discussing examples and/or applications of the word in a different context along with examples of how not to use it help students understand. Requiring a written explanation of new terms is also effective and makes the terms easier to remember.

## Writing development

A student's ability to clearly express his thoughts and ideas in writing is directly related to his reading fluency, which can be directly attributed to his vocabulary. Print awareness includes the realization that those words which he sees in the books and magazines that adults read to him are made with pens, pencils, and the printer attached to the computer on the desk in the den. The child gradually begins to understand that those funny squiggles on the paper tell his favorite stories, give directions for making chocolate chip cookies, and help solve problems such as assembling his new bicycle. When he practices "writing," a child is learning to distinguish the difference between words and pictures, a major step toward reading comprehension. As the child's ability to write improves, his reading fluency improves as well.

## Reading strategies

Students need to be given the tools to learn to read effectively and intelligently. Comprehension improves when students actively think about what they are reading, apply learned knowledge and experiences, and connect new information to the world as they understand it. They should be encouraged to ask questions and create pictures in their mind of what they are reading. When a student visualizes the material, it becomes more personal and real and he is more likely to understand and complete the assignment. When the reader engages in an internal dialogue with the author, he learns more effectively and retains the information longer. Students need to know how to determine the importance of the facts and ideas presented and discriminate between the "must remember" and the "it's interesting but not necessary."

Carefully worded questions and lively class discussions help students learn what to look for as they read, whether they are reading for pleasure or in order to complete an assignment.

## Importance of reading

There are two reasons to read: for pleasure and to learn. Ideally, the two work together. Whatever the motivation, the main purpose is to connect new data with already known information. It does not matter whether one is reading for pleasure or to learn, as ideas are being formed and connections are being made. Students should read to improve comprehension of new material; develop a broad, eclectic background of knowledge; and to expand their vocabulary. It is important to read different media such as books, magazines, newspapers, and carefully screened articles found on the Internet. Teachers can be an integral part of motivating students and exciting them about reading. When assigning material, teachers should explain how the information could impact students' lives now, as well as how they might use it later when they are out of school. Using class discussions to highlight, summarize, review, and critique the material all contribute to a positive reading experience.

## Transaction

Transaction with the text means the reader has a dialogue with the printed material. He is actively engaged in the process; he is participating in the exchange of ideas and information. At the secondary level, there are two types of transactions: the efferent stance and the aesthetic stance. In the efferent stance, the reader is gathering information and uses his background knowledge objectively. The aesthetic stance involves a personal response. The words bring back memories, recall emotions, and retrieve experiences stored in the reader's background knowledge. Proficient readers are able to use the aesthetic stance while gathering information. For example factual data about London might jog memories of a family vacation in the city. English Language Learners will improve their reading skills if the material is responsive to their culture and recognizes their language differences. The goal is for all students to be able to effectively transact with the text.

## Background knowledge

While background knowledge includes word recognition, its primary meaning is information about and understanding of the world and its social and cultural influences. This knowledge foundation comes from being read to as a young child and reading for pleasure away from assigned school tasks. Because most struggling readers do not read unless it is required that they do so, students should be allowed to select topics and media they find interesting and relevant. If a student feels more comfortable reading magazines and newspapers instead of books, he should be encouraged to do so. Any reading contributes to basic background knowledge, expands vocabulary, and improves fluency. Participating in group discussions helps students activate their background knowledge, which helps them integrate the new data with previously acquired information, make connections between the two and make any necessary revisions in understanding. Teachers can help students in this process by conducting "think aloud" sessions, encouraging self-questioning and explaining the relevance of information to their world.

## Listening and speaking skills

The most effective way a teacher can improve students' listening skills is to set a positive example by listening carefully to what each student says to him, what students say to one another, and being attentive during class discussions. Explain how to listen; for example, paraphrasing what someone said to make sure the meaning and intent is clear. Discuss why the message was clear or why it wasn't. Set up different listening situations: one-on-one, small groups, formal speeches, oral reading, student presentations, and class discussions. Rate the effectiveness of each.

One way students learn good speaking skills is by listening to good speakers so teachers should always use proper English when lecturing to the class, interacting with small groups, and during conversations with individual students. Assign a variety of speaking activities such as speeches, skits, debates, and story-telling. Have students take turns leading class discussions, reading aloud, and making formal presentations. Rate the effectiveness of each.

## Integrated language study

Students need to understand that the language process is integral to learning and developing skills in all fields of study, not merely in English. Language is not static or one dimensional. Students need to know that language varies depending upon the audience (parents, peers, professors); has structural rules, patterns, and conventions; and changes over time with continued use. It entails speaking, listening, and writing. It requires the speaker, the listener, and the writer to respond, interpret, assess, and integrate. In today's information age, media and technology play important roles. Besides books, newspapers, radio, and television; the Internet, CDs, DVDs and personal computers also provide information. It is critical students be taught methods to dissect and discriminate the digital data received and learn to scrutinize the sources from which it comes. The classroom should be a place where students feel safe to explore, ask questions, take risks, and develop effective listening, speaking and writing skills.

## Reading and writing skills

A teacher can influence students' reading skills by frequently reading to the class with expression and enthusiasm, sharing his love of reading, and explaining how reading helped him in life. Assigning different genres such as novels, poetry, short stories, essays, editorials, and biographies keeps students from getting bored because they read nothing but textbooks. Allow students to decide what they want to read and lead a class discussion about the topic. Encourage critical thinking by asking probing questions and posing different scenarios.

Teachers can alleviate students' fear of writing by sharing their experiences with the writing process and reading examples of their own written work, assigning essays, reports, and term papers and giving students the tools to complete the task. Giving students the latitude to choose subjects on which to write encourages creativity. Critiquing and editing during the writing process helps the student learn to think critically and assess his own work more accurately.

## Book discussion groups

Book discussion groups usually have no more than five members (selected by the teacher) who meet at a specified time for at least thirty minutes, twice a week, to review content and share feelings about and responses to the story. Appropriate books are chosen based upon students' interests and level of reading comprehension. Teachers should prepare a short synopsis of approved books to help groups make a choice. By reading, listening, and discussing the book, students learn that the same information can be interpreted in a variety of ways because of different perspectives and background knowledge. Once the groups have finished reading the book, they need to decide on, with the teacher's approval, a book-related activity that reflects their understanding of the meanings and messages discovered. Evaluations can be done by checklist or anecdotal records; the activity can be graded for content, creativity, and structure; and students can conduct self and peer assessments.

## Book report

A book share or as it is more commonly known, a book report, is an oral presentation about a book which the student has read. Students are encouraged to read about a topic in which they are interested or one which they want to learn more about. Teachers, librarians, peers and parents are good resources for help in making a suitable choice. It is the student's responsibility to schedule a time for the oral report, read the book, prepare the report and any props he might want to use and deliver the presentation to the class on the agreed-upon date. Preparing an oral book share helps students learn to: speak in front of an audience; plan an organized, sequential discussion of the story; and offer his opinion about the topic. Letting the student choose the book encourages positive feelings about reading while teaching him how to read for meaning and message and describe what he learned to others.

## Book rap

A book rap is similar to a book discussion group except it is conducted between individual students or small groups of readers in different schools, different states, and different countries via email. (It is very popular in Australia.) It introduces the students to various viewpoints as they share interpretations and explore ideas and concepts. It can also can generate lively in-class discussions, provide interesting insights in journals, and suggest material for related writing assignments and potential field trips. A book rap can be used to evaluate reading, speaking, listening, writing, and communication skills; conceptual understanding of the material; and the ability to think critically and respond with logical and persuasive arguments. The teachers involved are able to monitor the discussion because they have access to every email message. It is relatively easy for an information technology department to set up to use at school, or students can work from home.

## Academic controversy

An academic controversy is a type of debate in which students explore multiple aspects of an issue. Students learn by listening to different perspectives, discussing ideas while respecting other opinions, agreeing to disagree when necessary, and reaching a consensus with which everyone can agree. It is a useful approach to compare and contrast universal themes, study interesting characterizations, and review the effectiveness of literary devices. How does it work? A statement is made, such as "Shakespeare is a better playwright than Arthur Miller." The class is divided into groups that take a positive or negative position. They are given time to research and prepare arguments. Each side may not interrupt while the other is speaking. After the initial presentation, the groups switch sides and prepare arguments to support the other view. Students are graded using a checklist and self and peer assessments. They are evaluated on content, cooperation, presentation and speaking, and listening and social skills.

## Debate

A debate is a structured discussion used to present a variety of opinions about a subject. The topic is stated using a declarative sentence, which takes a strong stand on the issue. Teams consist of four or six students equally divided between the affirmative and negative views. Other students keep track of the time (usually three minutes per speaker), act as moderator, and settle disputes (adjudicate). The purpose of a debate is to encourage collaboration, develop research skills, learn to devise logical arguments, and gain an appreciation for the basic democratic principle of listening to opposing opinions as a way to understand all sides of an issue. The debate is judged by the class on its content, how effectively the content is presented and argued and how well the individuals worked as a team. The teacher evaluates the students on their social, speaking, listening and research skills and how well they understand the topic.

## Guided writing program

In a guided writing program, the teacher helps students focus on one aspect of the writing process: structure (punctuation, literary devices, etc.), organization (planning, editing, etc.), selection of the topic, critical thinking, reasoning needed to present logical arguments, or any activity involved in the writing process. The teacher assigns the topic or students choose their own. It can be a work in progress or a new project. The idea is to focus on a particular part of the writing process until the students are comfortable with it and competent using it. The goal is to take the mystery and fear out of the writing process. While students work on the task, the teacher moves around the room answering individual queries and asking probing questions to guide the student in a direction which he may not have considered. The teacher assesses progress by reviewing each attempt and evaluating the final product against pre-established criteria and/or curriculum goals.

## Guided reading program

In a guided reading program, students with similar reading challenges are grouped together. The purpose of the program is to help the students make sense of what they read, understand the particular structure and literary devices used, evaluate the message and connect the new ideas and concepts with previously acquired knowledge. The teacher observes each student as he reads silently, answers questions about the meaning of the text, and reads aloud to the group. With this information, he develops strategies in order to help the students recognize cues to identify and understand the key concepts and utilize previously learned material to analyze what they read. These steps are repeated during each session: silent reading, answering questions, identifying new ideas, reading aloud. Students are evaluated on their progress by a set of predetermined goals. Support, encouragement, and practice are integral to the success of a guided reading program.

## Recount, narrative, procedure, explanation, exposition

A recount is a personal, factual account of an experience or a series of events using the five Ws: who, what, where, when, why. It uses action verbs in the past tense.

A narrative can be a play, fairy tale, myth, cartoon, legend, or adventure story written to entertain, motivate, or teach a moral lesson. The story is about well-rounded characters who find solutions to universal problems and is set in a specific time and place.

A procedure explains how to do something, such as make a cake, conduct an experiment, explain the rules of a game, give directions to set up a computer, assemble a bicycle, etc.

An explanation explores how things work or how something came to be, i.e., its cause and effect relationship. It may also compare and contrast an item, idea, or concept.
An exposition uses arguments to persuade for or against a particular viewpoint. It offers evidence to support one side and refute the other side.

## Reading/writing relationship

Reading and writing are closely related. In order to write, a person must know how to read. A person who enjoys writing is usually a voracious reader. An insatiable reader is usually able to write fairly clearly and effectively. Both utilize background knowledge and experience to comprehend and integrate information. Both need to understand the structure of the language (syntax usage, grammar rules, the sound-symbol system) and bring certain skills to the task such as the ability to search for and define meanings and ideas and respond to the message by sharing it with others. Readers talk or write about the content. Writers need feedback to make sure they are presenting information in an engaging, enlightening way. Frank Smith, PhD. (reporter, editor, novelist, professor at the University of Toronto) said, "Text is a two-sided mirror rather than a window, with writers and readers unable to see through to each other but gazing upon reflections of their own minds."

## Dictogloss

The object of dictogloss is to help students learn to listen better, to discover the meaning of the text when it is read aloud, and develop proof reading and editing skills. The teacher reads a short, cohesive passage to the class. Students write down key words as they listen closely for the main message. The class is divided into small groups (five is optimal) to recreate the passage using each person's notes. The groups need to edit the paper to make sure it says what they intend and must proof read it closely for grammar, spelling, and syntax errors before presenting the final version to the class. The written copy is graded separately from the oral presentation. The students should be prepared to explain and justify any differences or discrepancies with the original passage. Dictogloss helps students learn to identify and define key words, paraphrase the message, work as a team, and share information with the class.

## Choral speaking

Choral speaking is a group activity used to present a variety of texts such as poems, plays, song lyrics, and raps. It is a collaborative activity that helps students understand not only the message but also the lyrical quality of the piece. It is the only way to appreciate the rhythm and rhyme, how it is structured, and how it sounds. Some genres are written to be spoken or performed and a silent reading does not recognize all their possibilities. To capture the students' attention and make them enthusiastic about an activity, teachers need to select a piece that students are familiar with, one which they will find fun or funny, one that addresses an issue in which they are interested or a topic that touches real life. When evaluating, presentation, voice, volume, body language, facial expressions, and eye contact are important because they deliver the message, convey contextual understanding, and keep the audience engaged.

## Imaginative re-creation

Imaginative re-creation is telling the story from another angle. For example: a minor character shares his feelings about the protagonist; the setting is changed to a different era or reflects another culture; a different genre is used, e.g., novel to screenplay. Imagining "what if" deepens awareness of how viewpoint influences meaning and how important structure, form, and literary devices are to conveying the message. It helps students interpret themes; study the importance of the relationship between characters; understand the impact of mood, setting, and emphasis; and how genre dictates approach. Students can be evaluated based upon comprehension and analysis of the content, understanding of the various genres (stage plays, poems, news reports, diaries, narratives, screenplays, etc.) and how they influence the way the story is told, and the reaction of the audience when the re-creation is presented to the class. Reading, writing, and oral interpretation are used with imaginative re-creation.

## Directed reading thinking activity (DRTA)

The purpose of a directed reading thinking activity (DRTA) is to help students learn to read closely, encourage understanding of literary devices, and develop critical thinking skills and the ability to form hypotheses that help interpret and understand the message. This activity helps students learn to make logical predictions and reach reasonable conclusions based on evidentiary clues in the text. It also encourages them to consider modifying their opinions after hearing alternative viewpoints. The story is read in short installments. Students discuss what they know, how and why they know it, and what they think will happen. After the each section, students consider the same questions and additionally confirm previous predictions. Discussions can be in small groups or conducted by the entire class. Evaluations can assess the ability to identify important data, explore new ideas beyond the concepts explicitly discussed in the story, and the effectiveness of the literary devices used.

## Literary sociogram

A literary sociogram is a diagram of how the characters in a story are related. This graphic organizer illustrates students' understanding of and insight into the text, explores their ability to make inferences, and enhances critical thinking skills. It can be especially helpful if the story has a lot of characters, if new characters are continually added, and if the relationship between characters changes as the plot progresses. A literary sociogram can be used to define the relationship of people in an account of a real incident, such as a newspaper article, or a radio, television, or Internet news story. Characters are placed in a circle in which size indicates importance. The protagonist is placed in the center; other characters are situated according to their relationship to him and to each other; e.g., close or peripheral, friend or foe. Relationships are shown with a solid line (substantiated) or a broken line (inferred.)

## Interviewing an author

Interviewing the author is an effective tool to encourage students to read closely, identify key ideas, understand the message, and develop questions based on clues in the text. They need to determine what is fact and what is make-believe, what the author's opinion is about the subject, whether or not the author is biased, whether his bias influences the outcome, whether the reader agrees or disagrees with the author's message, and whether the message changes the reader's mind about the subject. Questions students might ask the author include why did the author used this genre; what is the author trying to say; is the story is based upon a real person, place, event; who is the author's favorite character, and why. After the interview, students prepare an essay on their reaction to the activity. Assessments can be based upon how well the students understand the message, the quality of and thought behind the questions, and the thoroughness of the written evaluation of the interview process.

## Plot profile

A plot profile, or plot line, is a timeline of events and their impact upon and importance to the development of the story. The horizontal axis shows the sequence of events, while the vertical axis indicates its importance to the story. This graphic illustration helps students understand how the story is structured and enhances their analytical and critical thinking skills. The plot profile can show significant events, changes in the relationship of characters, steps the protagonist uses to resolve the conflict, or, for example, it can compare a nineteenth century novel with a contemporary television show. If there are several sub-plots, they can be added using different colors. This helps students appreciate the complexity required to create an interesting book, script, or screenplay and gives them an overview of the entire story and how all elements work together. Students should be prepared to justify their choice of events and why they believe the scenes are pivotal.

## Writing

Writing is the method used to preserve information using letters and words as opposed to drawings, paintings, verbal recordings and moving pictures. The act of writing is distinctly human. No other animal has the dexterity to form the letters or the intelligence to put them into meaningful order. Writing as a noun is the written word; writing as a verb is the act of forming the letters in the word. Writing is composed of penmanship, spelling and talent. Even in a world of computers, handwriting (penmanship) should be legible. A person should be able to form the letters by hand so they are clearly distinguishable. Reading comprehension is dependent on recognizing the words in the text; a poor speller limits his ability to recognize and understand words. Talent is the ability to express thoughts and feelings via the written word. Spelling and grammar can be taught; talent is inborn; it can only be nurtured.

## Reading skills

Reading is the process of understanding written information and ideas. Before the industrial revolution in the late nineteenth and early twentieth centuries, only a small percentage of the population was literate. The skill wasn't deemed necessary for most people. Preventing certain segments of the community from learning to read was also an effective way to keep them from fully participating in society. There are several reasons for reading: memorizing, learning and comprehension, skimming, scanning and proofreading. All have their uses. Proofreading detects errors in grammar and content. Skimming and scanning are used to process large quantities of information quickly when just surface comprehension is needed. Memorizing remembers and stores information for later retrieval. Understanding and comprehension are the main reasons most people read. Some read because they are required to for school or work, some to expand their general knowledge, and some read simply because they enjoy it.

## Reading tests

Reading ability can be tested in several ways depending upon what skill is being measured. Some reading tests use more than one of the components shown below. Different tests or variations of the same test are used to measure children, adolescents and adults. These are the most common reading tests used to determine various reading skills:
- Sight Word Reading: the person is given words of increasing difficulty. Longer, more complicated, less common words are used until he can't pronounce and doesn't understand them.
- Non-Word Reading: the person is given nonsense words to read out loud until they become too difficult or complex to pronounce.
- Reading Comprehension: the person reads a passage (silently or out loud) and answers questions about the content.
- Reading Speed: how fast a person reads the words.
- Reading Accuracy: the person's ability to read words correctly.

## Speaking and hearing

Speaking is used to convey thoughts, ideas and emotions. It helps develop bonds between individuals and enhances social interaction within and between groups. It is important to the preservation of a culture because it is used to explain, educate and pass on tribal traditions. In early human history, before the written word was created, speaking was the only method available to ensure that civilizations continued from one generation to the next. Communication is a bidirectional process that involves a speaker and an active listener, and these two parts must both work for thoughts, ideas and emotions to be conveyed; if no one hears what someone is saying, there is no possibility of communication. After the written word came into use and books became available, speaking and hearing were still important because reading for the common man has only been encouraged for about the past one hundred and fifty years.

## Hearing problems

The ability to speak develops in the first few years. If a child has a hearing problem, speech will be delayed or disabled. He will have trouble communicating and difficulty learning the skills necessary to function independently. (If a child is profoundly hearing impaired [deaf], sign language and Braille are available to enable communication.) The earlier a hearing problem is recognized, diagnosed and treated, the better the chance to avoid life-long problems with speech and hearing issues. Hearing impairment causes difficulty with learning to read which leads to difficulty with the mechanics of writing (penmanship) and the ability to write (express thoughts, ideas and emotions in written words). A person who hears and knows how to speak will not lose his ability to read if he develops a hearing problem later in life. However, if a person never hears well enough to learn to speak, he will rarely be able to read proficiently.

## English Language Learners instructional methods

There are four English Language Learner (ELL) programs that use the student's native language while he is learning English.
- Transitional Bilingual programs use the native language in core academic subjects. The goal, however, is to phase into English–only courses as quickly as possible.
- Developmental Bilingual programs use the native language in core academic subjects throughout elementary school. Sometimes the program extends into middle and high school even after the student has been classified proficient in English.
- In Two-Way Immersion programs, the students are from similar backgrounds with about half of the class speaking the native language and the other half speaking both. Instruction is about evenly split between English and the native language.
- Newcomer programs are usually reserved for recent U.S. arrivals. Instruction is in the native language and students are also helped to acclimate to their new environment.

The four English Language Learner (ELL) programs (transitional bilingual, developmental bilingual, two-way immersion and newcomer) all use the students' native language as part of the instructional design and plan lessons allowing for a slower pace. There is one ELL method in which instead of switching back and forth between the native language and English, it instead uses the native language in a support role only. Students learning English are placed in mainstream classrooms and instruction is entirely in English with a bilingual paraprofessional available to provide assistance. These paraprofessionals translate vocabulary, explain lessons presented in English and clarify confusing assignments. This method is partially based on the theory that interacting on a daily basis with teachers and students whose native language is English also helps the ELL student learn English more quickly and makes acclimating to the new culture easier.

## Continuum of learning theory

The Continuum of Learning theory outlines predictable steps when learning a new language.
- The Silent/Receptive or Preproduction stage can last from a few hours to six months. Students usually don't say much and communicate by using pictures and pointing.
- In the Early Production stage, students use one- and two-word phrases. They indicate understanding with yes or no and who/what/where questions. This stage can last six months.
- The Speech Emergence stage may last a year. Students use short sentences and begin to ask simple questions. Grammatical errors may make communication challenging.

- In the Intermediate Language Proficiency stage students begin to make complex statements, share thoughts and opinions and speak more often. This may last a year or more.
- The Advanced Learning Proficiency stage lasts five to seven years. Students have acquired a substantial vocabulary and are capable of participating fully in classroom activities and discussions.

## Interpersonal communication skills

Basic interpersonal communication skills encompass two different and distinct styles of communication:
- In context-embedded communication, various visual and vocal props are available to help the student understand that which is being said, including pictures and other objects to graphically explain and communicate demonstratively. The speaker's gestures and tone of voice help the listener understand the words being used. Conversations with speakers who use hand gestures and stories with pictures and props help the language learners understand more quickly and easily.
- Context-reduced communication does not have visual clues and cues and therefore the language learner must rely on his competency and fluency in the language. Phone conversations, for example, do not allow the listener to see the speaker and thus hand gestures and facial expressions and other visual aides are missing. Reading a note without pictorial guides may make it difficult for the student to understand the written words.

## English as a second language

The three methods most commonly used to teach English as a Second Language (ESL) are grammar-based, communication-based and content-based. Grammar-based ESL teaches students the rules of English including structure, function and vocabulary. Emphasis is on the why and how of the language. Communication-based ESL teaches students how to use English in every day, realistic situations. This approach emphasizes practical conversational usage. Content-based ESL teaches students grammar and vocabulary and uses written assignments in order to practice these skills. This approach includes using English as the main method of classroom communication between the teacher and the student and amongst students. This method emphasizes an integrated approach to learning English.

## Teaching English language learners

Basics
In general, researchers have been unable to prove conclusively and empirically that any particular strategy for teaching English as a second language is effective in increasing retention, proficiency and fluency. The methods used to collect data are inconsistent and oftentimes studies don't compare information from both control groups and non-control groups. When comparisons are made, they sometimes do not consider the ages and stages of the groups studied. The evidence that does exist comes from anecdotal observations, surveys and case studies. What has been determined is that most successful classroom methods incorporate several approaches and the effectiveness of each depends upon the age of the students and the degree of language proficiency already attained.

Strategies and approaches should be viewed as starting points for teachers in mainstream classrooms to review and consider. Choices should be made based on the students involved and the environment in which the instruction takes place.

There are four key concepts teachers in mainstream classrooms can use to help English Language Learners (ELL) acquire proficiency in both written and spoken English.

- Increase Comprehensibility of the content of lesson plans and activities. Use pictures, props, gestures and voice variations to explain and demonstrate the subject. Build on the language concepts the student already has.
- Encourage Interaction by asking questions and assigning group activities. This provides the student with many opportunities to practice that which he knows and increase his confidence so that he is able to learn more effectively.
- Increase Thinking and Study Skills by asking thought-provoking questions and assigning complex topics for research and writing projects. Establish and expect the same high standards from every student.
- Use The Native Language to increase understanding and comprehension. Translating questions and assignments into the student's native language clarifies instructions and helps him understand that which is expected.

Dialogue Journals
In the Language Experience Approach (also called Dictated Stories), either the teacher or a fellow student transcribes the language learner's words as he verbally relates a personal experience in his native language. The written English version is then used as a reading lesson when the language learner reads the translated story to the class. This tool shows the student how his native language is encoded into English and helps build word recognition while improving fluency. It also educates the other students about a different culture. Dialogue Journals (also called Interactive Journals) help the student learn how to write English. He keeps a journal of his thoughts, feelings and impressions. The purpose is not to evaluate the content but to offer a non-threatening avenue for the teacher to answer questions and correct grammar and spelling errors. It also provides a method for the student to privately communicate with someone who is proficient in English.

Cooperative Learning strategies
Developed by James J. Asher in the 1960s, Total Physical Response (TPR) uses physical activity to reinforce the words and phrases being taught. Depending upon the age and level of language proficiency, students are given a series of simple to complex commands and/or instructions. They are expected to respond appropriately. TPR is a tool that is effective when incorporated with other methods. In 1995 Robert E. Slavin demonstrated that Cooperative Learning is an effective tool no matter what the students' age or level of proficiency. Pairing English language learners (ELL) and students whose native language is English in small group activities is very effective for a number of reasons. As long as a well-structured task is assigned, students learn to work together as a team and the ELL students get to practice conversational skills while watching others' study habits. It also allows English-speaking students to interact with ELL students in a non-threatening setting.

Accessing Prior Knowledge and Cultural Studies
No matter what the age or level of English proficiency, students come to school with knowledge and experience. Building on and Accessing Prior Knowledge encourages them to explore new ideas and learn new concepts. A teacher who asks the student what he already knows about the subject and then lets him decide that which he wants to discover creates a positive environment in which to learn. If a student is interested in a topic, he is usually more excited about and engaged in learning more. The effectiveness of including the student's native culture in the classroom is well documented. English language learners assigned a Culture Study project are encouraged to share information about their cultural history. The assignment requires research, writing, creating visual aids and giving an oral presentation. It may also include interviewing parents, siblings, grandparents and friends.

## Academic Language Scaffolding and Native Language Support

Academic Language Scaffolding is a gradual step-by-step process that builds on the English language learner's knowledge and confidence as he learns to complete tasks independently and communicate more fluently. A teacher using this approach needs to consistently speak using proper English during lectures and while giving instructions, use expressive gestures and informative demonstrations and assign hands-on activities and projects that reinforce the lessons. No matter what other methods are used, Native Language Support should be available to the English Language Learner. Even when the teacher doesn't speak his language and the student is in an English-only classroom, he should have access to someone who speaks his native language. It provides him with the opportunity to have instructions and assignments clarified and encourages active participation in classroom activities. Decorating the classroom with posters and other objects from his native country shows respect for his language and culture.

## Potential problems

Many people study the English language because it is spoken in several countries; in some situations, it is the accepted and preferred language in which international business is conducted. Because there is no cross-cultural standard for English as there is for other languages (i.e. French and Spanish), there are very real differences in pronunciation, vocabulary and grammar depending upon the region and within the same area because of social groups and educational levels. The degree of difficulty learning English can sometimes be attributed to how greatly the student's native language differs from English. For example, a person who speaks French or Spanish might find it easier to learn English than would a person who speaks Chinese or Russian. No matter what the native language or the language being studied, students may have problems with pronunciation, grammar, spelling and vocabulary. Some may learn to speak the new language with some proficiency but have difficulties writing it.

## Cross-cultural understanding

Society is diverse and schools reflect that diversity. Teachers play an important role in helping students understand and learn to appreciate various cultures. Asking English language learners to tell a story, popular in their home country, in their native language and then translating it into English builds confidence. Sharing a favorite object from their homeland and explaining what it is, how it is made and for what purpose it is used encourages an appreciation for other cultures. An effective strategy to address issues that arise between students with different cultural heritages is called Misunderstandings. A student shares an incident that caused a problem. Words said, body language used, social customs encountered and stereotypes perceived are just some of the things that may be involved. As students discuss the situation, ask questions and get answers, they gain insight into the complexities of cultural differences and the importance of accurate cultural awareness and understanding.

## Written and spoken English

Spoken English sounds different depending upon the country of origin, geographic location within the country, the particular idioms used in a region, the educational level of the speaker and his ethnic and cultural heritage. Dialects, accents and slang all influence how a person speaks. Two English speakers from different countries may have difficulty understanding one another because of these variations. A third party listening to the conversation might think they were speaking totally different languages. Written English, on the other hand, is based on a defined set of rules (grammar) so that a person reading a document written in formal English would not be able to determine from which country or region the writer originates. The only indication might be the way a word is spelled (e.g., colour instead of color) or the context in which it is used (lift instead of elevator). These variations, however, would not prevent the reader from understanding the material.

## Pronunciation problems

Variations in consonant and vowel sounds can cause problems and make the pronunciation of English language learners sound stilted, monotone and flat. For example, the "th" combination is relatively rare in other languages so it is hard for some students to pronounce. American English has sixteen different combinations of vowels with sometimes only slight variations in the sound of the spoken word. Many languages have very few vowel sounds which means students can have problems hearing, and consequently, pronouncing these sounds. English allows for clusters of consonants before a vowel if needed, while several other languages do not. Therefore students may try to insert a vowel where there is none. Stressed and unstressed vowels can be very confusing for English language learners. Native English speakers can determine the pronunciation by the word's placement in a sentence; learners sometimes can't distinguish the slight variations. For example: able, enable, unable.

## Improving the experience

A teacher who has English Language Learners in his mainstream classroom, no matter what the subject area may be, can do many things to help ELL students learn and improve their pronunciation and comprehension. Enunciating clearly, speaking in a normal volume and at a normal pace, avoiding idioms and slang, using appropriate gestures, and pointing to pictures and objects are all beneficial. Because many language learners have trouble reading and understanding cursive, it helps to print information and instructions clearly and legibly on the board and also when correcting papers. Making sure objectives and activities are clearly explained and questions are answered before beginning the lesson helps to prevent misunderstandings. Repeating, reviewing, rephrasing, and summarizing frequently and using short sentences helps students organize and integrate data. Praising students when praise is merited is always effective unless the student's cultural heritage considers individual attention inappropriate, in which case a private word is a better approach. Good classroom management and a predictable routine contribute to everyone's success.

## Phonics

Phonics is an analytical approach to reading. Students take words apart to study individual letters and how they come together to make sounds. These letter-sound combinations form syllables. When syllables are combined, they become a word. Learning to decode or "sound-out" letter combinations enables students to visually recognize words they already hear and speak in every day conversation. It gives students the tools to sound-out unfamiliar words they discover as they explore new subjects and helps expand students' vocabulary by giving them a way to pronounce new words. Phonics helps students learn to spell because most words are spelled like they sound. Consonants have a speech-sound relationship, but the few exceptions need to be memorized. Vowels, however, don't always have a predictable speech-sound relationship. They are influenced by the surrounding letters, the stress placed on the particular syllable and the sentence in which the word is found.

## Learning to read

There are positives and negatives to both phonics and the whole language approach to reading. Phonics provides a dependable way for students to "sound out" unfamiliar words, but often requires monotonous repetition, memorization, and completing worksheets, which can often be boring. The whole language approach emphasizes learning the meaning of words in context but does not provide students with a method to decipher new words. Teachers who teach reading or assign oral presentations, whether to native English speakers or English Language Learners, usually eventually use a combination of both approaches even if they are not aware of it. They help stumbling students disassemble words and sound out each syllable (phonics) because sometimes that is the only way the student can figure out how to pronounce the word. They ask students probing, open-ended questions about the context in which the new word appears in order to help them figure out what the word means (whole language).

## Whole language approach

The whole language approach to reading is based upon the constructivist learning theory, which believes that the teacher is a facilitator who instructs by building upon knowledge previously acquired, encourages active learning, and emphasizes working in groups to develop social and communicational skills. Teachers using the whole language approach to reading develop lesson plans that bring together speaking, listening, reading, and writing experiences and create a rich literary environment that emphasizes quality literature and cultural diversity. The meaning and context of the word is more important than its sound. When students connect new data with information they already know in a meaningful manner, they will better understand the new material and be able to use it more effectively. They will integrate the old and new information more quickly, retain it longer, and be able to retrieve it more easily.

## Combining techniques

There are ways to combine the best of both phonics and the whole language approach to reading so that students obtain the benefit of the positives and avoid some of the negatives. Teachers need to provide students with the tools needed to sound-out unfamiliar words and give appropriate phonics lessons as necessary. A teacher can build a classroom library and encourage students to borrow books during quiet reading time and to use phonics when reading aloud. Teachers can read from a variety of fiction and non-fiction literary works, which introduces the students to new words and expands their vocabularies. It is important for teachers who use both approaches in the same classroom to balance phonetic instruction with other activities like lively discussions of favorite stories or dividing the class into groups and assigning a written report on a story everyone reads together.

## Print awareness

Teachers know that good reading skills are essential to learning, no matter what the subject being studied. Students should also be aware of basic information about books and reading: Books are organized on numbered pages and the letters and words are read from left to right and top to bottom. This is different in other cultures and languages. For example, in some Asian cultures, words are represented by a graphic alphabet instead of letters and the Hebrew language is read from right to left. Students should be exposed to a variety of printed material besides books, such as newspapers, magazines, posters, worksheets, review sheets, and calendars, to name a few familiar forms that can be easily offered in the classroom. Ensuring that reading material on interesting subjects is available encourages students to read for pleasure and to gain knowledge, and ultimately improves their vocabulary.

## Print exposure

Print exposure is the amount of time a person spends reading. He can read fiction and non-fiction books, school and local newspapers, entertainment and news magazines, and professional and scientific journals; reading anything has lasting cognitive consequences. Research has shown that reading, not oral language, is the most effective way to increase one's vocabulary at any age. The conversations between adults contain fewer advanced words than a book for preschoolers. Television scripts and radio commentary is the same, even programs devoted to hard news coverage. This is because oral language is very repetitive and people seldom venture out of their verbal comfort zone. Therefore, in order for a student to improve and increase his vocabulary, he needs to read from a wide variety of written sources. Frequent exposure to printed words helps English Language Learners gain confidence in their speaking ability more quickly and easily than ELL students who do not spend time reading.

## Guided oral reading

Guided oral reading is an instructional strategy used to improve verbal reading skills. Its main function is to improve fluency. This approach can be used with students of any age and grade level and will help both native English speakers as well as English Language Learners. This exercise can be used at home, in the classroom with the whole group or in pairs (i.e., a fluent reader with a struggling student); the process is the same each way:

1. A parent, teacher, or peer reads a passage aloud at about eighty (80) to one hundred (100) words per minute. The material needs to be at the student's level of comprehension.
2. The student reads the text silently several times.
3. The student reads the passage aloud. The parent, teacher, or peer offers encouragement and constructive feedback. It usually takes four times before the student is able to read the text without errors.

## Fluency

Fluency is the ability to read and comprehend the written word accurately and quickly. Fluent readers recognize words and expressions and understand their meaning automatically. When reading aloud, their presentation is smooth, expressive, and effortless. They sound natural, as though they were talking instead of reading a prepared text. Fluent readers do not focus on the words; they concentrate on the meaning. They make connections between knowledge they already have and ideas and concepts discovered in the new information. Because of their fluency, they enjoy reading and frequently read for pleasure. Readers who are not fluent read word by word because they have to sound out each word as they move through the text. When they read aloud, their presentation is slow, choppy, and monotonous. Because less fluent readers must concentrate on decoding the words, they usually do not understand the information in the text and have difficulty processing and integrating the new data.

## Direct vocabulary learning

Some words are introduced by direct vocabulary learning. This is the primary way a student learns unfamiliar words that relate to complex concepts that are not a usual part of or relevant to his world. Specific words are taught to help him understand and comprehend new information. A teacher can enhance the experience by:

- Explaining words the student will encounter before he reads the assigned text. This improves comprehension of unfamiliar subject matter.
- Encouraging the student to look for the new words and to use ones just learned. The more a student uses a new word, the more quickly the word becomes a permanent part of his vocabulary.
- Providing the same words in different contexts. This helps students to understand, remember and retrieve new words.
- Defining new words, using them in sentences and relating them to familiar scenes and situations.

## Importance of vocabulary

In order to read, a person must be able to decode the letters, arrange them in a logical sequence and know what each word means. Readers need to recognize how spoken words appear when they see them written. Vocabulary is also vital to comprehending what is read. If readers do not recognize the words which they see in print, they will not understand the ideas and concepts being discussed. Most beginning readers quickly learn words they hear in every day conversations. As they read more and are introduced to unfamiliar subjects, they must expand their vocabularies so that they can comprehend the new content. Research has shown that most vocabulary is learned indirectly through conversations, being read to by someone else and reading on one's own. Complex words, words related to a specific subject and words not relevant to daily life are learned by instruction or direct learning.

## Writing process

Writing is hard work. A well-written paper takes thought and preparation and should not be rushed. The steps in the writing process are:
- Brainstorm by reading and researching different subjects in order to generate ideas. Take notes and highlight important facts. Write down book and article titles, authors, and page numbers.
- Develop an outline of the main topics to be covered. This guide can be general or detailed depending upon the writer's preference.
- Write first version or rough draft to get the ideas on paper. Sometimes this is called the "sloppy copy."
- Revise the rough draft by rewriting awkward sentences, adding and deleting information and improving the introductory and concluding paragraphs.
- Edit revised version. Correct spelling and grammar errors.
- Ask for feedback. Have a parent or peer review and comment.
- Make corrections.
- Print (publish) the final version.
- Learn from the teacher's comments.

## Clarifying table

A clarifying table is a tool to help students separate a topic into smaller, more manageable parts. The purpose is retention and comprehension by taking notes in a systematic way. The core concept is captured, supporting ideas are recognized, clarifying details are reported and connections to previously learned material are made. The steps to teach the clarifying table:
- I Do It: The teacher prepares a completed example and explains the components. It is usually necessary to do this step at least twice.
- We Do It: The teacher, acting as a guide, and the class construct a table together. This step is repeated until the students grasp the concept.
- You all Do It: The students are divided into pairs or small groups to create their own tables. Support comes from each other rather than the teacher.
- You Do It: Each student creates a table by himself for his particular topic.

A clarifying table is a visual device created to capture and organize information.
- Section 1: a definition of the word or term or a summary of the topic.
- Section 2: details that clarify the meaning of the word or term or facts related to the topic.
- Section 3: the major meaning of the word or term, or the core idea of the topic.
- Section 4: the knowledge connections to information already known.
- Section 5: a statement explaining the word or term or an example of the topic.
- Section 6: a statement explaining the incorrect use of a word or term or an example of what the topic is not about.
- Section 7: a sentence using the word or term correctly or a topic sentence that can be used as a basis for a paper.

## Using a clarifying table

Because it is a powerful elaboration tool, a clarifying table can be used to identify core concepts in any subject; develop reading skills; improve note-taking ability during lectures, while researching topics, and in preparation for potential pop quizzes, unit tests, and final exams. The device can be used in many ways in most classrooms. Some ideas:

- Paraphrasing Tool: Students read assigned passages on a particular subject and use the table to take notes for later class discussions and to review when preparing for tests.
- Note-Taking Tool: The students write down key ideas and interesting details during a lecture, which can be reviewed in preparation for pop quizzes, unit tests, and final exams.
- Outline Tool: The students use the table to gather information, organize ideas, and plan the structure of any written assignment including one-page essays, book reports, and research papers.

---

**Sample clarifying table**
Word, Term, Topic

Core Idea or Concept: _____

| Clarifiers | Knowledge Connections |
|---|---|
| 1. | 1. |
| 2. | 2. |
| 3. | 3. |
| 4. | 4. |
| 5. | 5. |
| 6. | 6. |
| **Don't Confuse With** | **Not An Example Of** |
| 1. | 1. |
| 2. | 2. |
| 3. | 3. |

Sample Sentence or Topic Sentence

_____

_____

Note: can be modified depending upon the subject and specific assignment.

---

## Motivating secondary students

By the time students reach secondary school, many feel as though they were failures because they cannot read well, dislike reading for any number of reasons or have a negative view of reading in general. Some had bad experiences in middle school and thus turned away from reading, especially in an academic setting. An effective way to motivate these students is to create a classroom atmosphere of recognition and respect for cultural and language differences (which may account for certain reading issues). Keeping these differences in mind when selecting reading material sends a positive message and encourages the students to read the assignment. Another motivating strategy is to assign reading tasks from sources other than textbooks, such as newspapers, magazines, and trade books. The content is current, reflects the real world, and students can make connections relevant to their lives. Public praise and positive feedback are huge motivators for students struggling to improve their reading skills.

## Linguistic knowledge

Linguistic knowledge is defined as understanding the system: how the language works, what the words mean, and how to use the words properly. The system is composed of several parts. The definitions cited are from <u>The American Heritage College Dictionary</u>.

- Phonology: the sounds of the words and their proper pronunciation.
- Semantics: the meaning of the signs and symbols used to form the words.
  - Morphology: the structure and form of the words including inflection (changing pitch or tone of voice), derivation (adding prefixes and suffixes to change the meaning), and compounds (combining two or more words to form a different word).
  - Word Meaning: the idea or thought conveyed.
- Syntax (grammatical structure): the rules governing the formation of sentences.

In order for students to learn, integrate, and use the language system correctly, they must be given opportunities to read in many genres and from a variety of source material.

## Literature

<u>The American Heritage College Dictionary</u> defines literature as "the body of written works of a language, period, or culture." This is the commonly accepted definition; however, literature can mean different things to different people. Some only consider serious literary works to be literature and would ridicule and refuse to consider any composition that did not meet a strict set of arbitrary criteria. But according to the dictionary definition, any written work is part of a nation's literature and reflects its culture and diversity. Throughout the centuries, different genres have been explored. Early history was preserved in oral literature, by the older generation telling the next generation stories and traditions. The earliest written documents had a religious and/or didactic purpose. The Age of Reason produced nationalistic epics and philosophical treatises. Romanticism focused on popular folk tales. Early nineteenth century literature embraced realism and naturalism, and the twentieth century spawned symbolism and character development.

## Poetry

Poetry is a literary form in which words are written in verse. Sometimes it rhymes and sometimes it does not. Poetry chooses its words carefully, uses imagery, similes, and metaphors and has a defined meter, rhythm, and pattern. Poetry may be the earliest form of literature. Parts of the Bible, Homer's Iliad, and the Indian epics have some poetic characteristics. Cultures with oral traditions frequently use rhythm and rhyme as a memory aid. Therefore, legal texts, genealogical histories and moral treatises may initially have been in poetic form.
There are different types of poetry. For example:

- The haiku has seventeen syllables in three lines of five, seven, and five and is usually about nature.
- A limerick is an irreverent form of poetry, also often about nature, consisting of five lines with a rhyming scheme of AABBA and lines of three, three, two, two, three syllables.
- Sonnets can be various lengths but are always written in iambic pentameter.

## Poetic traditions

The language used in a country, its unique pronunciation and oral traditions and cultural influences sometimes dictate in which form its poetry is written. Some languages prefer short lines of verse, while others are more suited to longer ones. Vocabulary limitations and grammatical requirements may influence the particular poetic conventions used. The vocabulary may have more words that rhyme or the words are longer. A preference may develop because people like the work of a particular poet, in which case his format becomes dominant in that culture. Historically, in most cultures, works written for production in the theater were done in a poetic format. Countries with a poetic history have particular preferences: Persian poetry always rhymes, Greek poetry never does; Italian and French poetry usually rhymes; English and German poetry is written both ways. English blank verse, such as the works of Shakespeare and Milton, are unrhymed iambic pentameter; many were written to be performed on the stage.

## Literary genres

- Autobiography: an account of a person's life and times written by that very person, based upon his own memories.
- Biography: an analysis of a person's life and times written by another.
- Children's Literature: written primarily for children; some may also be read and appreciated by adults. Some literature originally written for adults may, in later years, be deemed appropriate for children as well.
- Diaries and Journals: a log of discrete entries describing the activities of a finite period of time. Some differentiate the two terms by calling a daily log a diary, while a journal is used sporadically or on a random basis.
- Essay: a short, non-fiction, and subjective composition written from the author's perspective.
- Fiction: a story that is invented by the author; may be based upon actual events, but the final version is from the author's imagination.
- Parody: imitation of another work for the purpose of ridicule, irony, or to make fun of the original work.
- Satire: a technique used to criticize a person, event, group, idea, institution, or social practice in a clever manner; sometimes amusing and very often funny.
- Fable: a short story with a moral lesson that uses animals, plants, or inanimate objects, which are given human qualities (anthropomorphized).
- Romance: a style of heroic prose that deals with traditional themes; a term used to differentiate popular literature from scholarly and/or religious works.
- Fantasy: a story that uses magic and the supernatural as elements of plot, theme, or setting. Sometimes this genre overlaps with horror and science fiction.
- Horror: a story written to frighten the reader; it is often gruesome, morbid, or suspenseful. Sometimes this genre overlaps with fantasy and science fiction.
- Science Fiction: a story that usually takes place in the future and speculates on potential scientific possibilities. Sometimes this genre overlaps with fantasy and horror.

## Narrative fiction

Narrative fiction is a form of prose writing that tells a story. Early narrative fiction was not taken seriously because it was not poetry, did not necessarily carry the same grand aesthetic of eloquence and did not adhere to any particular structure except the rules of grammar. Prose offers the freedom to develop a complex plot and tell a compelling tale with lots of details with no structural restrictions. The author can explore a myriad of styles and literary devices within a single work instead of being forced to write within a narrowly defined format.

Contemporary publishing defines narrative fiction by its length:
- A Mini Saga is exactly fifty (50) words.
- Flash Fiction is under one thousand words (1000).
- A Short Story is five hundred (500) to twenty thousand (20,000) words.
- A Novella is twenty thousand (20,000) to fifty thousand words (50,000).
- A Novel is any prose work over fifty thousand (50,000) words.

## Glossary

Assessment
Assessment is the various information (homework, in-class activities, special projects, written assignments, quiz and test results, social and cognitive development, etc.) used to monitor students' progress and make educational decisions.

Compacting
Compacting is a strategy that streamlines the data and adjusts the pace of the presentation of new material to reflect the students' ability to absorb information.

Concept Diagram
Concept Diagram is an organized method of presenting vocabulary; it lists the word and its definition along with specific characteristics.

Concept Map
Concept Map shows the relationship between and among concepts and lists their individual characteristics.

Cooperative Learning
Cooperative Learning is an instructional approach in which students work together in small groups to complete a project. The students have different abilities and learning styles.

Core Competency
Understanding the basics of English, math, science, social studies, and the arts.

Course Competency
Knowledge and understanding of material presented in one field of study.
Curriculum
Defined set of courses required to obtain a diploma.

Disability
Disability is defined by the Americans with Disabilities Act as "a condition that limits some major life activity." The condition can be physical, cognitive, psychological or social.

Environmental Objections and Outcomes
The atmosphere in which learning takes place, i.e., class size, subject content, instructor's expertise, quality and comfort of the classroom.

## Gifted
Gifted is an innate ability or talent in one or more areas such as a specific academic field, visual arts, performing arts, creativity, leadership or athletics along with an inquisitive mind and insatiable curiosity.

## Graphic Organizer
Graphic organizer is a visual presentation of information that shows the relationship between and among the different parts of a topic.

## Memoir
A less structured form of autobiography, told from the subject's perspective, that usually focuses on the person's public activities.

## Mnemonics
Mnemonics is a code to help remember specific data.

## Multiple Intelligences
Multiple intelligences is the concept developed by Howard Gardener that suggests there are eight types of intelligence: verbal-linguistic, logical-mathematical, spatial, bodily-kinesthetic, musical, naturalist, interpersonal, intrapersonal. (For an in-depth discussion, see cards 95, 96, 97, 98, 99, 100.)

## Non-Fiction
A simple, balanced, coherent presentation of truthful facts about a subject as understood from the author's perspective.

## Objective
General statement explaining the general curriculum; specific goals of each course.

## Oral History
A disciplined method of historical documentation gleaned from first person accounts of events as interpreted by the person being interviewed.

## Outcome
Reaching the desired goal, e.g., passing the course, obtaining a diploma.

## Parable
A brief story that imparts a moral lesson by setting the scene, describing an action and giving the consequences. Unlike a fable, a parable does not use anthropomorphized animals, plants or inanimate objects.

## Rubric
An evaluation tool that defines goals and accomplishments and shows a score for each one.

## Self-Questioning
A strategy that encourages students to ask themselves questions to determine how well they understand the material.

## Semantic Mapping
A process that uses word associations to help teach conceptual relationships.

## Slave Narrative

Grew out of the slaves brought to the United States and Caribbean from Africa. These books and pamphlets provided a first person account of their experiences. About one hundred fifty (150) were published. There were also accounts of Americans and Europeans enslaved in North Africa.

## Strategic Plan

A plan detailing where the educational program is going and the how it plans to get there; it consists of the goal, the objective and the strategies.

## Strategies

Actions developed and taken to help the program plan meet its goals and objectives.

## Target Specification

The required knowledge and understanding of each course and the skills mastered by the students before graduation.

# Working in the Professional Environment

## Resources available for professional development and learning

- Professional literature - books and publications are examples of literature that can help a classroom teacher.
- Colleagues - a fellow member of a profession, staff, or academic faculty; an associate
- Professional Associations - an association of practitioners of a given profession, for example NEA, NSTA, etc.
- Professional development activities – sometimes put on by a local or state school board to teach educators the newest trends in education.

## Code of Ethics

Ethical codes are specialized and specific rules of ethics. Such codes exist in most professions to guide interactions between specialists with advanced knowledge, e.g., doctors, lawyers and engineers, and the general public. They are often not part of any more general theory of ethics but accepted as pragmatic necessities. Ethical codes are distinct from moral codes that apply to the education and religion of a whole larger society. Not only are they more specialized, but they are more internally consistent, and typically can be applied without a great deal of interpretation by an ordinary practitioner of the specialty.

## School as a resource to the larger community

Our mission is to work with communities to ensure learner success and stronger communities through family-school-community partnerships. Through schools, individuals value learning; learn how to learn; demonstrate effective communication, thinking and problem solving; enjoy a better quality of life; are fulfilled; experience the joy of learning; and contribute to and benefit from the intergenerational transmission of culture. in supporting the educational role and function of local education agencies (and organizations), families, and communities increase local capacity to improve and ensure learning opportunities for the children and citizens of the community.

## Advocating for learners

Public support for education is fragile. Poverty jeopardizes the well-being and education of our young people and some communities are caught in a downward spiral of cynicism and mistrust. Teachers must necessarily be advocates for education. One might become involved in efforts to change policies, programs, and perceptions to benefit learners; such involvement is crucial for educators today, for when they do not create effective channels of communication with legislators, the media, and community members, their opinions will very likely go unfulfilled legislatively. These consequences can be devastating to children and to learning. The stakes are simply too high for educators not to engage in advocacy efforts. Just as teaching and learning require commitment, energy, and perseverance, so too does advocacy.

## Parental education

As families shrank during the last half of the past century, parental education rose. Among adolescents ages 12-17 in 1940, about 70% had parents who had completed no more than 8 years of school, while only 15% had parents who were high school graduates, and 3% had parents who were college graduates.

Expenditures for education have expanded enormously since then, and the educational attainment figures have been turned on their head. By 2000, only 6% of adolescents ages 12-17 have parents with no more than 8 years of school, while 82% have parents with high school diplomas, including the 21%-29% who have mothers or fathers with 4-year college degrees.

Parental educational attainment is perhaps the most central feature of family circumstances relevant to overall child well-being and development, regardless of race/ethnicity or immigrant origins. Parents who have completed fewer years of schooling may be less able to help their children with schoolwork because of their limited exposure to knowledge taught in the classroom. They also may be less able to foster their children's educational success in other ways because they lack familiarity with how to negotiate educational institutions successfully. Children whose parents have extremely limited education may, therefore, be more likely to benefit from, or to require, specialized educational program initiatives if their needs are to be met by educational institutions.

Parents with limited educational attainment may also be less familiar with how to access successfully social institutions, such as healthcare, with which children and their parents must interact in order to receive needed services. Equally important is that parent educational attainment influences their income levels. Parents with limited education tend to command lower wages in the labor market and are, therefore, constrained in the educational, health, and other resources that they can afford to purchase for their children. For all of these reasons, among children generally, negative educational and employment outcomes have been found for children with low parental educational attainment.

## Meeting with parents

Studies have shown that the more parents are involved in their children's education, the better the students learn and the fewer behavior problems one must handle. Teachers are an integral part of the process. It is up to them to keep parents informed about the academic and social progress of the students. Report cards only provide letter or number grades and are not designed to explore and explain how well the student is learning and progressing in the intangible skills like critical thinking, reasoning ability, study habits, attitude, communication with adults and peers and other social and interactive development. Sending home periodic progress reports is an effective way to keep parents abreast of changes. Meeting with parents regularly to discuss their child's particular progress and being available to answer questions are excellent ways to work together as a team to ensure the student benefits the most from his educational experience.

## Parent/student/teacher agreement

If a teacher should wish to use a formal parent/student/teacher agreement as a way to involve parents, provide students with a written set of expectations and explain their commitment to a successful educational experience, there are several activities that can be included:
- Parent Priorities:
    - Show respect for and support of the student, teacher and the discipline policy.
    - Monitor homework assignments and projects.
    - Attend teacher conferences.
    - Ask about the student's day.
- Student Priorities:
    - Show respect for parents, teachers, peers and school property.
    - Put forth his best effort both in class and at home.
    - Come to class prepared.
    - Talk to his parents about school.

- Teacher Priorities:
  - Show respect for the student, his family and his culture.
  - Help each student strive to reach his potential.
  - Provide fair progress evaluations to students and parents.
  - Enforce rules fairly and consistently.

Many schools use some sort of parent/student/teacher agreement to ensure everyone understands the rules and agrees to abide by them. It can be as simple as requiring parents, students and teachers to sign a copy of the student handbook or it can be a formal contract drafted with specific activities each pledges to perform. Whichever format is used, it should detail each party's responsibilities. This accomplishes several goals:
- Parents are recognized as an important part of the educational experience. They are also made aware of what is expected of them, their children, the teachers and the administration.
- Students are given written expectations, which prevent an "I didn't know" attitude. It encourages respect for himself, his parents, his teachers, his peers and the rules.
- Teachers make a written commitment to students and parents to provide an environment that encourages learning. They list specific, observable behavior which they pledge to perform.

## Levels of parental involvement

Some parents are eager to participate in their child's education, some do so only when required, and others avoid involvement of any kind. All three approaches can be a challenge. Eager parents may bombard the teacher and administration with notes, phone calls, emails and requests for information and meetings. Setting reasonable, well-defined limits may be necessary. Parents who only show up when specifically requested (e.g., semi-annual parent/teacher conferences, meeting with the administration about a behavior problem), might only be going through the motions in order to keep their child enrolled in school. They may be incapable of or don't really care to address any underlying issues; they show up because they are required to do so. Parents who are never available and impossible to contact provide no help or insight and offer no support.

## Parent/teacher conferences

Basics
Parent/teacher conferences can be stressful experiences for both parties. But with a positive attitude and much preparation, they can be pleasant, provide a forum for the exchange of information and improve the educational experience for the students. The first step is for the teacher to be rested. Fatigue can cause an inability to concentrate, unfortunate misunderstandings and inappropriate reactions. If a teacher thinks parents might be difficult to handle, it might be wise to ask an administrator to sit in. The teacher needs to have a plan prepared with discussion points and copies of the student's work available to review. He needs to keep in mind that the parents may have items to discuss as well, and therefore the plan needs to be flexible and allow time for questions. The discussion should focus on the positive and present negative information with a "we can fix it" approach.

In order to avoid wasting everyone's time during a parent/teacher conference, there are several things a teacher can do to set the scene for a productive meeting. Make initial contact early by sending a note or newsletter home briefly outlining plans and objectives for the year and providing contact information (e.g., phone number, email address, days and times available). This tells parents the teacher is willing to talk and/or meet when necessary. When a date for a conference is set, the teacher should be certain to invite both parents. It is the best way to gauge how involved they are, yet individual family circumstances need to be considered (one-parent families, parents' work commitments, et cetera). Schedule twenty to thirty minute conferences; if more time becomes necessary, schedule a follow-up meeting. Develop a flexible agenda and gather necessary paperwork. Verify parent and student names just before the meeting.

## Encouraging parental involvement

Every teacher needs to develop ways in which to involve parents in the education of their children. Some communication methods may be more effective than others depending upon the age of the students, the educational level and time limitations of the parents, and the administrative support and resources available to the teacher. Some schools encourage a parent orientation program at the beginning of the year, in which the teacher informs parents what his expectations are concerning behavior and outlines classroom rules. He presents a broad picture of the material to be covered, projects that will be assigned and homework requirements. If a meeting isn't possible, the same information can be conveyed in a letter sent home just before school starts or during the first week. Besides regularly scheduled parent/teacher conferences, a periodic newsletter, perhaps when report cards are issued, can be sent to update parents.

## Being prepared

Parent/teacher conferences are the best time for candid communication. For the encounter to be productive, both parties need to be prepared to discuss the student's strengths and weaknesses, share any concerns and decide upon the best way to help the student meet required goals and reach his potential. Some topics to consider in preparation for this important meeting:

- The skills and knowledge that should be learned and mastered.
- Required academic standards. Give parents a copy to which to refer during the year, and explain these standards.Projects planned and assignments required to complete academic requirements.The evaluation method, what data is considered and when progress reports are issued.How parents can help. Suggest concrete activities which they can do at home in order to encourage learning and support the teacher's efforts.Programs available for both fast and slow learners.What programs are available to prepare students for life after high school.

## Things to remember

Try to use a table rather than a desk and chairs so that the parents and the teacher meet as equals; this creates a more relaxed environment. Start with a positive statement about the student and then briefly review the objectives of the meeting. The teacher should not do all of the talking; it should be a conversation, not a monologue. Avoid educational jargon. Many parents will not understand it or will interpret it incorrectly. Focus on strengths, give specific examples, provide suggestions for improvement and refer to actions rather than character. For example: "Sam turned in his essay the day after it was due," instead of "Sam is irresponsible." Ask for parents' opinions and listen to their responses. Use body language that shows interest and concern and make eye contact. Do not judge the parents' attitude or behavior, and consider cultural differences. Briefly summarize the discussion and end with a positive comment or observation about the student.

## Conclusion

If either the teacher or the parents feel that there is more to discuss or that a follow-up meeting is necessary for an update on progress made, a time can be scheduled before the parents leave. As soon as possible after the conversation while the details are fresh, the teacher should make notes of the general discussion and record any specific actions that he or the parents agreed to take as well as the parents' attitude and willingness to offer support. Any private information and/or family issues which the parents shared should be kept in the strictest confidence. If a cooperative relationship is to be established, parents need to know that their family business will remain private. It is very important and even required in some states that teachers report any indication of or concerns about possible child abuse or endangerment to the authorities. All teachers and administrators need to be familiar with the pertinent statutes in their state.

## Cooperating with colleagues

To be successful, a teacher must be constantly cooperating with and learning from colleagues. There are a number of ways to do this; one is to set up regular meetings with them. Many teachers are part of a team of teachers who instruct the same group of students, and these meetings will therefore already be in place. If this is not the case, however, teachers should try to set up frequent meetings with colleagues who either teach the same students or the same subject. These meetings should not be the equivalent of teacher's lounge gripe sessions, but instead should be forums in which new teaching methods can be discussed, teaching content can be coordinated, and basic plans of behavior management can be established.

## Peer review programs for teachers

Another way in which a community of teachers can foster professional improvement is through peer review. In a peer review program, teachers observe one another and offer suggestions for improvement. This is especially helpful when it is done among teachers in the same grade level or subject. Another teacher who is fluent in French, for instance, would be a great resource for a non-French-speaking teacher helping new immigrants from West Africa. Of course, in order for this sort of program to work, there needs to be a spirit of collaboration and constructive criticism among the teachers. Unfortunately, school politics and competitiveness often poison the relationships between colleagues, and make it difficult to offer or accept well-meaning suggestions. The best peer review programs establish a specific protocol for criticism and encouragement.

## Mentoring programs for teachers

Mentoring is another professional improvement program that can be extremely valuable to a teacher. In a mentoring program, experienced teachers develop relationships with beginning teachers. The schools that use these programs find that they are able to retain a larger proportion of their beginning teachers. When mentoring programs are not offered, new teachers should ask a veteran teacher to act as a mentor, as a mentor can provide guidance on any aspect of teaching, from classroom management to lesson plans. New teachers get the most out of the relationship if they consciously remain open to constructive criticism. A mentor should observe his or her mentee directly in the teacher's classroom, but the mentee should also keep a list of concerns and questions to bring to private meetings. Teachers who accept advice and are willing to see things from a different perspective will grow immeasurably from the mentoring experience.

## Peer tutoring programs

Another way that teachers can join with their colleagues in order to improve the quality of instruction is through peer tutoring. In a basic peer tutoring program, more advanced students work with the younger students on class work. For instance, the members of a second-grade class might be paired with the members of a fifth-grade class. The older children will still be using many of the concepts that they learned in second grade, thus it will be beneficial for them to explain and demonstrate these concepts. The younger children, meanwhile, will enjoy working with older children and may be more receptive to the material when it comes from a source other than the teacher.

Peer tutoring relationships are especially fruitful when they are between students from similar backgrounds. In a modern class, there may be students from several different linguistic backgrounds. Some students may be the sole representative of their native culture in their grade level. If there are other students in the school with the same origin, however, they may be profitably united through peer tutoring. Also, peer tutoring programs are a great chance for students to develop their social skills; the older children will practice being generous and considerate of someone younger, while the younger children will practice being attentive and receptive to counsel. Of course, only those older students who have a good grasp of the content and are well-behaved should be involved in a peer tutoring program.

## Field trips with other classes

Another way that teachers can band together is by arranging field trips with other teachers, as it is often easier to handle the logistics of a large field trip in cooperation with another teacher. Also, many field trips will have applications to multiple subject areas. For instance, a trip to a local battlefield could have relevance for American history, English, and Social Studies students. A visit to the local natural science museum could be pertinent to content in math, science, and history. It is always a good idea to encourage students to make associations between content areas. Furthermore, a field trip encourages students to mix with other students, forming social connections that improve investment in the academic setting.

## Coordinating subject matter

One of the most positive ways for teachers to work with their fellow teachers is by coordinating subject matter. This strategy is often used in teacher "teams" in elementary and middle school, but it can also be effective in high school. Let us consider a brief example of how teachers can coordinate subject matter with great results. Imagine that you are a sixth-grade teacher. Before the school year begins, you could propose that the sixth grade uses "cities" as a theme. Each teacher can then construct lessons in their instructional domain that connect with this theme. As the teacher, you could look at texts that focus on life in the city. The history teacher could teach students about the rise of the big urban centers during the Industrial Revolution. The math teacher could incorporate some study of the various statistics and charts that are used to describe and learn about cities. If your school is located in or near a large city, you might also take some field trips so students can observe first-hand the things that they have learned.

## Coordinating instructional content

The net effect of coordinating content seems to be that students learn more. Educational research suggests that all knowledge is associative, and people therefore tend to remember those things that they can easily fit into their existing store of information. If a teacher and his colleagues can link diverse disciplines together by looking at the same subject from a number of different perspectives, they can help students develop a well-rounded and coherent way of intellectually exploring the world. This is especially true for students, who will be encountering a dizzying amount of new information at school. If this material is disconnected and seemingly random, students will be more likely to forget it. Thematic content in multiple subjects helps avoid this problem.

## Communicating with colleagues

An instructor should meet with his colleagues at some point during the year so that he can get a general idea of the structure and content of his colleague's classes. During the year, the teacher should stay abreast of that which students are learning in their other classes, and should note associations between disciplines whenever they arise. A teacher should also know when his fellow teachers are assigning major projects or exams, so that he can avoid giving important assignments on the same day. Many schools assign a certain day of the week for tests in each subject; e.g., math tests on Monday, history tests on Tuesday, and so on. If the school does not do this, the teacher should make sure that major projects and examinations are scheduled such that students are not overwhelmed with a flurry of work.

## Relationship with school administration

It is important for the teacher to have a strong relationship with the school administration. The principals and support staff of a school are supposed to be there to make life easier, but they can only do this with cooperation. In order to maintain a happy partnership with the school administration, teachers should remember one guideline of great importance: namely, teachers should always report any significant problems immediately; these problems can include disciplinary matters, personal problems, or conflict with school protocol. In large schools where there is little one-on-one contact between the administration and the faculty, it is common for teachers to let their grievances fester in silence. The result is that what could be a cooperative relationship becomes poisoned by resentment and frustration. Teachers who have complaints or concerns about the way the school is being run, or who need help, should immediately discuss the problem with the principal.

## Meeting with the principal

A teacher should try to avoid only visiting the principal when there is something wrong. A principal, like any person, will develop certain assumptions about a teacher whom they only see in times of crisis. Also, many principals will resent those teachers who they feel are constantly passing their problems onto the administration. Teachers should be referring problems to the principal only as a last resort. It is appropriate to let the principal know about concerns without necessarily asking for help. A teacher should try to check in with the principal periodically when things are going well in class, so that he or she can get a more balanced appreciation of the class' progress. When a teacher maintains a good relationship with the principal throughout the year, he or she will be much more helpful on those occasions of crisis.

## Scheduling an observation by the principal

One great way to cultivate a positive relationship with the principal is to invite him or her to sit in on a class. A teacher should invite the principal on a day when a particularly innovative and exciting lesson is planned. It is a good idea to let the students know ahead of time that the principal will be joining the class, so they need to be on their best behavior. During the observation, the teacher should invite the principal to participate whenever appropriate. Many principals were teachers at one time, and will welcome the opportunity to join in with the activities of the class. After the class, the teacher should ask the principal for his opinion. As in relationships with other teachers, teachers should try to remain open to criticism and accepting of advice. These kinds of observations can be very useful for beginning teachers, who may be unaware of some fundamental mistakes they are making.

## Relationships with teacher aides and assistants

Some teachers are lucky enough to have full- or part-time aides and assistants. When this is the case, the teacher should make sure that the aide is being used appropriately. For the most part, an aide should not be busy doing paperwork during class time. It is certainly useful to have another person to help with grading, but this can be done during the planning period or lunch. While the children are in the classroom, the aide should be another set of eyes and ears. In other words, the aide should circulate around the room while students are working. He can answer any questions students may have about the lesson, and can make sure that students stay on-task. Aides are also useful when some members of the class have fallen behind the others. The aide can assemble those students and give them a brief refresher on the recent material as the teacher instructs the rest of the class.

## Frequent updates to parents

After sending this first letter home, it is also helpful to send home periodic notes letting parents know how the class is proceeding. If one has a small number of students, one may even be able to make personal phone calls to each parent. Another way to stay in contact with many parents is through email; if one finds that all (or even some) of the parents in ones class have internet access, one may send out a short weekly update. Whatever format one chooses, one should try to keep parents informed of upcoming evaluations, field trips, and special events. If possible, one should personalize each message with some specific information about the child; this will convey the impression that one is taking a direct interest in the educational progress of each member of the class. It is important to make an effort to communicate both good news as well as bad. For many parents, the only contact they ever have with the school is when their child has gotten into trouble. One should occasionally make a call or drop a note to praise a student for improved academic performance. Parents will respond very positively to teachers who take the time to praise their children.

## Keeping parents alert to student performance

It is also important to let parents know how their children are faring in class by sending home their grades regularly. Many teachers require students to take home their major tests and have them signed by a parent. Increasingly, teachers are posting student grades on a class website so that parents and students alike can keep track. Whichever method one chooses, one should make sure that one does not wait until the end of the term to let a parent know that their student is in danger of failing. As soon as any student falls behind, it is imperative to alert his parents so that a strategy for improvement can be developed. Do not assume that students will keep their parents informed as to how they are doing in class. Many students will claim to be doing well even if they know that this will be disproved by their final grade. As a teacher, it is ones responsibility to keep parents informed.

## Parent-teacher conferences

Another important part of developing a positive rapport with parents is the parent-teacher conference. Most elementary schools schedule these near the beginning of the year, often at the end of the first grading period. In middle and high school, parent-teacher conferences are not always mandatory, though they are recommended. If one is a beginning teacher, one may approach ones first conferences with some anxiety. It is important to remember, however, that both the teacher and the parent both have the student's success as a goal. It is important to accurately communicate a student's standing within the class. It is also important for both parties to agree on a strategy for maintaining or improving the student's performance subsequent to the conference. Conferences are meant to be punishment for neither the instructor, the parent, nor the student.

## Teacher-parent phone call

When a student is struggling, contacting his parents should not be a last resort. Rather, it should be done soon so that the student's course can be corrected. Many students act out at school because of problems they are having at home; learning about these motivating factors can not only help one understand the behavior, but can lead to possible solutions. In any case, when one calls a parent to communicate bad news, it is important to always maintain a focus on the steps that should be taken for improvement. Do not call a parent simply to gripe. At the end of the call, make plans to talk again in the near future, so that everyone can assess how the strategy for improvement is proceeding. Always treat the parent as part of a team whose aim is the success of the student.

## Open house

Another traditional means of making contact with parents is the open house. Most schools hold an open house at the beginning of the year so that parents can meet the teachers and see the classrooms. Besides being an opportunity to give information about the class, the open house is a chance for the teacher to present himself in a favorable light. The neatness and organization of the room is very important, as is greeting the parents as they enter. One should try to avoid getting bogged down in discussion with any one parent; discussions of individual students should be handled in another setting. The open house is a chance for one to sell oneself and the class. One should demonstrate the structure of one's class as well as present an appeal for help from parents.

## Inviting parents to class

Besides the open house, parents should be invited to school whenever their presence will have a positive impact on learning. For instance, if students are going to be putting on a group or individual presentation, parents should be invited to attend. This is especially important in elementary grades, where the presence of a parent can be extremely comforting and motivating to students. Other instances where parents could be invited to attend school are field days, class parties, and field trips. Too often, students create a rigid separation between their school and home lives. Language differences reinforce this separation. By inviting parents to class, a teacher breaks down the division between the academic and the family life, and encourages the student to incorporate what he is learning into all phases of his life.

## Incorporating parents into instruction

A teacher should try to take advantage of parents' special skills or talents, especially as they relate to different content areas. For instance, if one is teaching a science-related unit and one of the students' parents is a botanist, you should invite him to speak to the class. If one is teaching a unit on Social Studies and discovers that one of the parents works for the federal government, it might be useful to invite him to speak. Whenever possible, one should be striving to make course content relevant to the daily lives of the students. There is no better way to do this than by incorporating their family members into the lesson.

## Consequences of poverty

In general, poverty has been found to have negative developmental consequences for children. Children in impoverished families may be at risk of educational failure because they lack access to adequate nutrition, health care, dental care, or vision care, as well as lacking access to educational resources that parents with higher incomes can afford to purchase for their children. Children whose parents possess less education have parents who are less able to find full-time year-round work, and the work they find pays less well. As a consequence, policymakers and program administrators in areas with large numbers of children in groups with low parental education tend to have children as clients who not only have parents with limited education, but who work more sporadically, and who have limited income to provide for the needs of their children.

## Respectful, reciprocal communication

One simple way to communicate more effectively is to treat the person whom you are addressing respectfully regardless of one's own emotional inclinations. Exhibiting disrespect is almost never helpful, as it immediately places the listener in an adversarial, and probably hostile frame of mind, and encourages them to disregard or dispute anything that is said. This does not mean that one has to agree with everyone and hide any opposition which one may hold to their attitudes, beliefs, values, or positions; it simply means that one should state ones differences in a way that does not belittle another's. For instance, instead of saying "that is a really stupid way of looking at the situation," it is usually more helpful to say "well, I see the situation somewhat differently." Then you can go on to explain how you see it, without ever saying directly that they are "stupid" or even wrong, but simply that it is possible to see things in different ways. Reciprocal communication involves each party receiving equal respect for their ideas and views.

## Inappropriate treatment of students

According to the U.S. Children's Bureau, "More than half (approximately 53%) of all reports alleging maltreatment came from professionals, including educators, law enforcement and justice officials, medical and mental health professionals, social service professionals, and child care providers." David Finkelhor, Director of the Crimes Against Children Research Center and Codirector of the Family Research Laboratory at the University of New Hampshire says, "The key problem is that educators are confused about what child protection does and whether it does any good." Finkelhor, who has been studying child victimization, child maltreatment, and family violence since 1977, adds, "There is the other problem that schools may not support the reporting process."

## Reporting abuse

Teachers are in a unique position to observe and report suspected allegations of child abuse and neglect, but they are in a precarious position for educators - especially neophytes struggling to comprehend various community systems and the vast arena of child abuse reporting laws. Educators should be guided by their school's internal administrative policies for reporting abuse. Sometimes, however, these polices can be confusing. Some schools, for example, encourage educators to report suspected abuse internally before contacting CPS. Nevertheless, state and federal laws mandate educators to report suspected child maltreatment-allowing school administrators to determine if a teacher's suspicions should be reported is unlawful. Because educators are not trained investigators, it is especially important for them to report suspected maltreatment and not assume the responsibility of determining whether a child has been abused.

## Neglect

Neglect is the most common type of reported and substantiated maltreatment. According to the National Child Abuse and Neglect Data System, of the estimated 826,000 victims of child abuse and neglect in 1999, 58.4% - more than 482,000 children - suffered from neglect; 21.3% were physically abused, and 11.3% were victims of sexual abuse. Whereas physical abuse tends to be episodic, neglect is more often chronic and involves inattention to a child's basic needs, such as food, clothing, shelter, medical care, and supervision. When considering the possibility of neglect, educators should look for consistencies and ask themselves such questions as:
- Does the child steal or hoard food consistently?
- Does the child consistently demonstrate disorganized thinking or unattended needs?
- Would observing the family in the context of the community provide any answers?
- Is this culturally acceptable child rearing, a different lifestyle, or true neglect?

## Sexual abuse

According to CAPTA, sexual abuse is the "employment, use, persuasion, inducement, enticement, or coercion of any child to engage in, or assist any other person to engage in, any sexually explicit conduct or simulation of such conduct for the purpose of producing a visual depiction of such conduct." Sexual abuse includes any interactions between a child and adult caretaker in which the child is used for the sexual stimulation of the perpetrator or another person. Sexual abuse may also be committed by a person under the age of 18 when that person is either significantly older than the victim or when the perpetrator is in a position of power or control over the child

## Reporting child abuse

Reporting child abuse involves a complex array of dynamics. Individual subjectivity, personal perceptions, education, training, and life experiences affect everyone involved in the reporting and investigation process. To maintain objectivity, getting as many facts as possible is essential. Before calling, the reporter should have all of the important information, including the child's name, date of birth, address, telephone number, details of the suspected abuse and information about the suspected perpetrator. Are there bruises or marks? Is the child at risk if he returns home? Callers should be clear about what they are reporting. Vague statements of concern limit the screener's ability when determining whether to assign a case for investigation. Educators need enough information to answer basic questions that will be asked if they call CPS.

## Behaviors that would be detrimental for an abuse case

When talking to children about suspected abuse, it's imperative not to ask leading questions or insert information. A case can easily become tainted if anyone involved asks leading questions or fills in statements for a child. The incident must be conveyed in the child's own words. Investigators, attorneys, social workers, psychologists, police detectives, and judges will scrutinize statements for information that could appear tainted if a case goes to court. A recent study published by the American Psychological Association examined how misleading suggestions from parents influenced children's eyewitness reports. Psychologist and coauthor of the study, Debra Ann Poole, says even children as old as 7 or 8 will repeat misinformation. "Apparently," she says, "general instructions to report only what 'really happened' does not always prompt children to make the distinction between events they actually experienced versus events they only heard described by a significant adult."

## Work of Special Education Teachers

Special education teachers work with children and youths who have a variety of disabilities. A small number of special education teachers work with students with intellectual disabilities or autism, primarily teaching them life skills and basic literacy. However, the majority of special education teachers work with children with mild to moderate disabilities, using the general education curriculum, or modifying it, to meet the child's individual needs. Most special education teachers instruct students at the elementary, middle, and secondary school level, although some teachers work with infants and toddlers.

## What a principal needs to know about inclusion

Inclusion is the meaningful participation of students with disabilities in general education classrooms. To practice inclusion successfully the school principal and staff must understand the history, terms, and legal requirements involved as well as have the necessary levels of support and commitment. The word inclusion is not a precise term, and it is often confused with similar concepts such as least restrictive environment (LRE) and mainstreaming. Educating children in the least restrictive environment has been mandated since the 1970s, when it was a major provision of the Education for All Handicapped Children Act. The law states that to the maximum extent appropriate, children with disabilities are educated with children who are nondisabled; and that special classes, separate schooling, or other removal of children from the regular educational environment occurs only if the nature or severity of the disability is such that education in regular classes with the use of supplemental aids and services cannot be achieved satisfactorily.

## Oberti test

Court cases have produced guidelines that can be helpful in determining the best placement for a student. One of these is Oberti v. Board of Education, which specified three considerations for determining placement: (1) the steps taken by the school to try to include the child in the general education classroom; (2) the comparison between the educational benefit the child would receive in a general education classroom, including social and communication benefits, and the benefits the child would receive in a segregated classroom, and (3) possible negative effects inclusion would have on the other children in the general education class.

## Behavioral disorders

Students who have emotional and behavioral disturbances exhibit significant behavioral excesses or deficits. Many labels are used to denote deviant behavior; these labels include: emotionally handicapped or disturbed, behaviorally disordered, socially maladjusted, delinquent, mentally ill, psychotic, and schizophrenic. Each of these terms refers to patterns of behavior that depart significantly from the expectations of others. In recent years, "behavioral disorders" has gained favor over "emotional disturbance" as a more accurate label leading to more objective decision-making and fewer negative connotations.

## Emotionally disturbed childred

Estimates of the number of school-age children and adolescents with emotional or behavioral disorders depend on the definitions and criteria that are used. At some point in their lives, most individuals exhibit behavior that others consider excessive or inappropriate for the circumstances. Thus, frequency, intensity, duration, and context must be considered in making judgments of disturbance. Unlike some other educational disabilities, emotional and behavioral disorders are not necessarily lifelong conditions. Although teachers typically consider 10–20 percent of their students as having emotional or behavioral problems, a conservative estimate of the number whose problems are both severe and chronic is 2-3 percent of the school-age population. Currently, less than one-half that number are formally identified and receive special education services.

## Disordered behavior

There is considerable agreement about general patterns or types of disordered behavior. One researcher suggests two discrete patterns that he calls "externalizers" (aggressive, disruptive, acting out) and "internalizers" (withdrawn, anxious, depressed). He identifies the following four dimensions:
- Conduct disorders (aggression, disobedience, irritability); personality Disorders (withdrawal, anxiety, physical complaints); immaturity (passivity, poor coping, preference for younger playmates); and socialized delinquency (involvement in gang subcultures).

In addition to these, other researchers discuss pervasive developmental disorders (including autism and childhood schizophrenia) and learning disorders (including attention deficit disorders with hyperactivity). Not all behaviorally disordered students experience academic difficulties, but the two factors are often associated.

## Adapting physical education to include students with disabilities

Adapted physical education is an individualized program of developmental activities, exercises, games, rhythms and sports designed to meet the unique physical education needs of individuals with disabilities. Adapted physical education may take place in classes that range from those in regular physical education (i.e., students who are mainstreamed) to those in self contained classrooms. Although an adapted physical education program is individualized, it can be implemented in a group setting. It should be geared to each student's needs, limitations, and abilities. Whenever appropriate, students receiving an adapted physical education program should be included in regular physical education settings. Adapted physical education is an active program of physical activity rather than a sedentary alternative program. It supports the attainment of the benefits of physical activity by meeting the needs of students who might otherwise be relegated to passive experiences associated with physical education. In establishing adapted physical education programs, educators work with parents, students, teachers, administrators, and professionals in various disciplines. Adapted physical education may employ developmental, community-based, or other orientations and may use a variety of teaching styles. It takes place in schools and other agencies responsible for educating individuals.

## Dual exceptionalities

Gifted students with disabling conditions remain a major group of underserved and under-stimulated youth. The focus on accommodations for their disabilities may preclude the recognition and development of their cognitive abilities. It is not unexpected, then, to find a significant discrepancy between the measured academic potential of these students and their actual performance in the classroom. In order for these children to reach their potential, it is imperative that their intellectual strengths be recognized and nurtured, at the same time as their disability is accommodated appropriately.

## Children with one parent

Children with only one parent in the home tend to be somewhat disadvantaged in their educational and economic success. Children in immigrant families are much less likely than children in native-born families to have only one parent in the home, but there is substantial variation across groups. For example, no more than 10% of children live with one parent among children in immigrant families who have origins in India, Australia and New Zealand, Canada, China, and the Eastern and Southern former Soviet bloc, compared to more than 30% for those with origins in the English-speaking Caribbean, Haiti, and the Dominican Republic. Similarly, the proportion with one parent in the home is 17% to 25% for children in native-born families who are white or Asian, compared to about 50% or more for those who are Central American and mainland-origin Puerto Rican. The variation in number of parents in the household appears to be highly associated with level of parental education. For example, among children in immigrant families, only 10% live with one parent in the high education group, while 17% live with one parent in the medium and low education groups. Among children in native-born families, proportions are 18% for children with high education parents versus 49% for children with low education parents. The proportion with one parent rises from 20% at ages 0-2, to 24% at ages 3-8, and then to 25% at ages 9-13, and 26% at ages 14-17.

## Having siblings

The presence of brothers and sisters in the home is a mixed blessing for most children. Siblings provide companionship, but they must share available resources. Insofar as parental time and financial resources are limited, parental resources must be spread more thinly in families with a larger number of siblings than in smaller families. Dependent siblings under age 18 are especially likely to compete for parental time and income. As a result, family size can have important consequences for the number of years of school that a child completes, and hence, for economic attainment during adulthood.

Among families of diverse native-born groups, the proportion with four or more siblings in the home ranges from 9% to 11% for Asians, Central Americans, and whites, to 18% for blacks and American Indians. In contrast, among children in immigrant families, the proportion in large families ranges more widely—from a low of 4% to 5% for children with origins in India and China, to a high of 35% for those with origins in the Pacific Islands (other than Australia and New Zealand).

As was the case with the number of parents, the number of siblings in the home also appears to be highly associated with level of parent education. Those children in families with high parental education are least likely to live with four or more siblings.

## Having grandparents

Relatives, such as grandparents and older siblings, and non-relatives in the home can provide childcare or other important resources for children and families, but they may also act as a drain on family resources. Especially in families with few financial resources, doubling-up with other family or non-family members provides a means of sharing scarce resources, and benefiting from economies of scale in paying for housing, energy, food, and other consumable goods. At the same time, doubling-up can also lead to overcrowded housing conditions with negative consequences for children. Taking grandparents, other relatives, and non-relatives together, many children have someone other than a parent or dependent sibling in the home. However, children in newcomer families are nearly twice as likely as those in native-born families to have such a person in the home. Children in white, non-Hispanic native-born or immigrant-origin families are least likely to live with such other persons. About 9% of all children in the United States have at least one grandparent in the home, and whether or not a child lives with a grandparent is strongly correlated with racial/ethnic and immigrant status. For example, living with grandparents is much less common for white children (3%-8%) than for nonwhite children (12%-22%).

## Overcrowded home

Overcrowded housing has deleterious effects on child health and well-being, including psychological health and behavioral adjustment, as well as the ability to find a place to do homework undisturbed. Nearly 1 in 5 children live in crowded housing conditions (that is, with more than one person per room). But nearly half of children in immigrant families live in overcrowded housing, compared to only 11% of children in native-born families. There is wide variation among groups, however. Among children in native-born families, the proportion in overcrowded housing ranges from 7% for whites to 40% for Native Hawaiian and other Pacific Islanders. Among children in immigrant families, the proportion in overcrowded housing among white groups is about the same as for native-born white groups, while the highest levels of overcrowding are experienced by children in immigrant families from Central America (59%) and Mexico (67%). Overcrowding is strongly correlated with parental education and poverty across racial/ethnic and immigrant generation groups, suggesting the need to double-up with relatives or non-relatives to share resources. This appears to be especially true among immigrant-origin groups.

Moreover, while overcrowding improves slightly for older versus younger age groups, these reductions tend to be smaller among children in immigrant families, despite their initially higher levels.

## School in need of improvement

This is the term No Child Left Behind uses to refer to schools receiving Title I funds that have not met state reading and math goals (AYP) for at least two years. If a child's school is labeled a "school in need of improvement," it receives extra help to improve and the child has the option to transfer to another public school, including a public charter school. Also, your child may be eligible to receive free tutoring and extra help with schoolwork. Contact your child's school district to find out if your child qualifies.

## Caring community

A caring community is the way in which the school interacts with the surrounding neighborhood and town. In such a community, all families are welcome and the immediate area is seen in the spirit of cooperation between the students and their families. The populations of students who attend a school will tend to be diverse, and therefore all families should feel included in the community of the school. Individual students will feel included if they are treated well by the staff and their fellow students and feel that the staff has concern for their well being, and that they are valued. In order for this to work, students must feel that their input and participation is a necessary function of the school and that there is communication between all facets of the school and the community. Family and staff members work together to solve problems and the rights of all students are strictly upheld.

Constructing a caring environment in the classroom from the beginning means that insults and derogatory terms are eliminated so that students feel safe in the environment. Students should treat the teacher with courtesy and respect, and that should be reciprocated. Having interactions between students on a regular basis will increase the level of community in the classroom because students will get to know each other and not use prejudice readily. When appropriate, if the students have the chance to provide their input into that which they study, they will feel motivated to learn and share their knowledge with others. Balancing between teacher-centered and student-centered activities will spread out the activities and make students feel accountable for their own learning. Setting an appropriate way to deal with behavior will also increase the sense of community, in that students feel that they are being dealt with appropriately. This works reciprocally, as well, in that pre-set consequences for actions which are enforced fairly and regularly create a stable environment.

## Zero tolerance

"Zero Tolerance" initially was defined as consistently enforced suspension and expulsion policies in response to weapons, drugs and violent acts in the school setting. Over time, however, zero tolerance has come to refer to school or district-wide policies that mandate predetermined, typically harsh consequences or punishments (such as suspension and expulsion) for a wide degree of rule violation. Most frequently, zero tolerance policies address drug, weapons, violence, smoking and school disruption in efforts to protect all students' safety and maintain a school environment that is conducive to learning. Some teachers and administrators favor zero tolerance policies because they remove difficult students from school; administrators perceive zero tolerance policies as fast-acting interventions that send a clear, consistent message that certain behaviors are not acceptable in the school.

## Education law

One function of government is education, which is administered through the public school system by the Federal Department of Education. The states, however, have primary responsibility for the maintenance and operation of public schools. The Federal Government does maintain a heavy interest, however, in education. The National Institute of Education was created to improve education in the United States. Each state is required by its state constitution to provide a school system whereby children may receive an education, and state legislatures exercise power over schools in any manner consistent with the state's constitution. Many state legislatures delegate power over the school system to a state board of education.

## Compulsory attendance laws

The state of Connecticut enacted a law in 1842 which stated that no child under fifteen could be employed in any business in the state without proof of attendance in school for at least three months out of twelve. The compulsory attendance act of 1852 enacted by the state of Massachusetts included mandatory attendance for children between the ages of eight and fourteen for at least three months out of each year, of these twelve weeks at least six had to be consecutive. The exception to this attendance at a public school included: the child's attendance at another school for the same amount of time, proof that the child had already learned the subjects, poverty, or the physical or mental ability of the child to attend. The penalty for not sending your child to school was a fine not greater than $20.00 and the violators were to be prosecuted by the city. The local school committee did not have the authority to enforce the law and although the law was ineffective, it did keep the importance of school before the public and helped to form public opinion in favor of education. In 1873 the compulsory attendance law was revised. The age limit was reduced to twelve but the annual attendance was increased to twenty weeks per year. Additionally, a semblance of enforcement was established by forming jurisdictions for prosecution and the hiring of truant officers to check absences.

## Homeschooling laws

States that require no notice
No state requirement for parents to initiate any contact.

States with low regulation
The state requires parental notification only.

States with moderate regulation
The state requires parents to send notification, test scores, and/or professional evaluation of student progress.

There are states with high regulation
The state requires parents to send notification or achievement test scores and/or professional evaluation, plus other requirements (e.g. curriculum approval by the state, teacher qualification of parents, or home visits by state officials).

## No Child Left Behind Act

Title 1 of the No Child Left Behind supports programs in schools and school districts to improve the learning of children from low-income families. The U.S. Department of Education provides Title I funds to states to give to school districts based on the number of children from low-income families in each district.

## Individuals with Disabilities Education Act

The Individuals with Disabilities Education Act (IDEA) is the law that guarantees all children with disabilities access to a free and appropriate public education. It addresses the educational needs of children from birth through age 21 and accounts for 13 categories of educational special needs.

## FAPE

FAPE (Free Appropriate Public Education) is requirement coined in order to comply with the federal mandate, Public Law 102-119, known as the Individuals with Disabilities Education Act. More specifically, part B of the act, which mandated that all disabled children receive a free appropriate public education and as such a school district must provide special education and related services at no cost to the child or his parents.

## SED

IDEA defines a serious emotional disturbance (SED) as "a condition exhibiting one or more of the following characteristics over a long period of time and to a marked degree, which adversely affects educational performance:
- An inability to learn which cannot be explained by intellectual, sensory, or health factors.
- An inability to build or maintain satisfactory interpersonal relationships with peers and teachers.
- Inappropriate types of behavior or feelings under normal circumstances.
- A general pervasive mood of unhappiness or depression.
- A tendency to develop physical symptoms or fears associated with personal or school problems." The federal definition includes children who are diagnosed as schizophrenic, but excludes socially maladjusted children "unless it is determined that they are seriously emotionally disturbed." Although autism was formerly included under the SED designation, in 1981 it was transferred to the category of "other health impaired."

## Section 504 of the rehabilitation act

Section 504 of the Rehabilitation Act (regarding nondiscrimination under federal grants and programs) states:
- Sec. 504.(a) No otherwise qualified individual with a disability in the United States, as defined in section 7(20), shall, solely by reason of her or his disability, be excluded from the participation in, be denied the benefits of, or be subjected to discrimination under any program or activity receiving Federal financial assistance or under any program or activity conducted by any Executive agency or by the United States Postal Service. The head of each such agency shall promulgate such regulations as may be necessary to carry out the amendments to this section made by the Rehabilitation, Comprehensive Services, and Developmental Disabilities Act of 1978.

Section 504 protects qualified individuals with disabilities. Under this law, individuals with disabilities are defined as persons with a physical or mental impairment which substantially limits one or more major life activities. People who have a history of, or who are regarded as having a physical or mental impairment that substantially limits one or more major life activities, are also covered. Major life activities include caring for one's self, walking, seeing, hearing, speaking, breathing, working, performing manual tasks, and learning. In addition to meeting the above definition, for purposes of receiving services, education or training, qualified individuals with disabilities are persons who meet normal and

Copyright © Mometrix Media. You have been licensed one copy of this document for personal use only. Any other reproduction or redistribution is strictly prohibited. All rights reserved.

essential eligibility requirements. For purposes of employment, qualified individuals with disabilities are persons who, with reasonable accommodation, can perform the essential functions of the job for which they have applied or have been hired to perform. (Complaints alleging employment discrimination on the basis of disability against a single individual will be referred to the U. S. Equal Employment Opportunity Commission for processing.) Reasonable accommodation means an employer is required to take reasonable steps to accommodate your disability unless it would cause the employer undue hardship.

## Section 504 of the Rehabilitation Services Act

1. People with disabilities have the same rights and must receive the same benefits as people without disabilities when they are applying for jobs or when they are employees.
2. All medical services and instruction available to the public must be available to people with disabilities.
3. They are entitled to participation in any vocational assistance, day care or any other government program on an equal basis as those who do not have disabilities.
4. Selection to college, job-training or post-high school education programs must be based on academic records, not by disability.  For example, someone with a learning disability can take a modified version of the ACT entrance exam.
5. An appropriate elementary and secondary education must be provided for all students with disabilities.

## Purpose of Section 504

Section 504 was enacted to "level the playing field"; to eliminate impediments to full participation by persons with disabilities. In legal terms, the statute was intended to prevent intentional or unintentional discrimination against persons with disabilities, persons who are believed to have disabilities, or family members of persons with disabilities. Though enacted almost 25 years ago, until recently Section 504 has been largely ignored by schools. Given the statute's tempestuous history, this is little short of shocking. Two years after Section 504 was enacted, advocates held highly publicized demonstrations on the doorstep of the then-U.S. Department of Health, Education and Welfare simply to get the Department to adopt implementing regulations. But since then, the statute, regulations and their mandate have been considered by many as the "black hole" of the education law universe.

## Differences between Section 504 and IDEA

There are a number of differences between the two statutes, which have very different, but complementary, objectives. Perhaps the most important is, as has been stated, that Section 504 is intended to establish a "level playing field" (usually by eliminating barriers that exclude persons with disabilities) whereas IDEA is remedial (often requiring the provision of programs and services in addition to those available to persons without disabilities). Thus, Section 504 precludes hurdles to participation, whether physical (e.g., steps that prevent a person in a wheelchair from accessing a building) or programmatic (e.g., excluding a child with hepatitis from a classroom). By distinction, IDEA is similar to an "affirmative action" law: as some have asserted, school children with disabilities who fall within IDEA's coverage are sometimes granted "more" services or additional protections than children without disabilities.  The "more" and "additional" denote another important difference between Section 504 and IDEA. While IDEA requires "more" of schools for children of disabilities, it also provides schools with additional, if insignificant, funding. Section 504 requires that schools not discriminate, and in some cases undertake actions that require additional expenditures, but provides no additional financial support. For this reason, schools often drag their feet in providing needed services to children under Section 504, and are less hesitant to openly discuss the limitations of funding.

## Section 504 and the ADA

The Americans With Disabilities Act (ADA), enacted in 1990, has deep roots in Section 504. In many ways, the ADA is Section 504 "writ large." The primary difference is that while Section 504 applies only to organizations that receive Federal funding, the ADA applies to a much broader universe. However, with respect to education, the ADA's objectives and language are very similar to Section 504, and for this reason both statutes are administered by the Office for Civil Rights and considered essentially identical.

## State assessments in the No Child Left Behind Act

This refers to the tests developed by your state that your child will take every year in grades 3-8 and at least once in high school. Using these tests, the state will be able to compare schools to each other and know which ones need extra help to improve. Parents can contact your child's school or school district to find out more details about your state's tests.

## Adequate Yearly Progress (AYP)

Adequate Yearly Progress is the term which the No Child Left Behind Act uses to explain that a child's school has met state reading and math goals. Your school district's report card will let you know whether or not your child's school has made AYP.

## Americans with Disabilities Act (ADA)

The ADA was passed by Congress in 1990. This act outlines the rights of individuals with disabilities in society in all ways besides education. It states that they should receive nondiscriminatory treatment in jobs, access to businesses and other stores, as well as other services. Due to this law, all businesses must be wheelchair accessible, having a ramp that fits the standards of the law, and making sure that all doors are wide enough and that bathrooms can be maneuvered by someone in a wheelchair. If these rules are not followed, businesses can be subject to large fines until these modifications have been complied with. The ADA also ensures fair treatment when applying for jobs to make sure that there is no unfair discrimination for any person with a disability who is applying to the job.

## Title 20

Title 20 states that denial of equal access is prohibited. More precisely:
- Restriction of limited open forum on basis of religious, political, philosophical, or other speech content is prohibited. It shall be unlawful for any public secondary school which receives Federal financial assistance and which has a limited open forum to deny equal access or a fair opportunity to, or discriminate against, any students who wish to conduct a meeting within that limited open forum on the basis of the religious, political, philosophical, or other content of the speech at such meetings.

## Soler and Peters (1993) as it relates to confidentiality

Confidentiality provisions help protect families from embarrassing disclosures, discrimination against themselves or their children, differential treatment, and threats to family and job security. Confidentiality provisions also may encourage students or families to take advantage of services designed to help them. Many of the legal protections to confidentiality are constitutionally based in the fundamental right "to be let alone". Right-to-privacy protections also are reflected in federal and state statutes, statutory privileges, agency regulations, ethical standards and professional practice standards.

## FERPA

A 1974 federal law, the Family Educational Rights and Privacy Act (FERPA), protects the privacy interests of students in elementary and secondary schools (and their parents) with regard to certain types of education records. FERPA requires that prior consent be obtained from the student (if 18 or older) or the student's parents before certain types of information can be released from school records. FERPA also gives parents and students access to records, along with the right to challenge the accuracy of those records and make necessary modifications. Changes to FERPA most recently were enacted as part of the Improving Schools Act of 1994, resulting in the issuance of final regulations of FERPA by the U.S. Department of Education. These amendments help promote information sharing by educators.

## Child Abuse Prevention and Treatment Act (CAPTA)

The federal Child Abuse Prevention and Treatment Act (CAPTA) provides a foundation for states by identifying a minimum set of acts or behaviors that characterize maltreatment. CAPTA also defines what acts are considered physical abuse, neglect, and sexual abuse. Individual states determine and define what warrants further investigation. Civil laws, or statutes, describe the circumstances and conditions that obligate mandated reporters to report known or suspected cases of abuse, with each state providing definitions. Physical abuse is an intentional injury to a child by the caretaker. It may include but is not limited to burning, beating, kicking, and punching. It is usually the easiest to identify because it often leaves bruises, burns, broken bones, or unexplained injuries. By definition, physical abuse is not accidental, but neither is it necessarily the caretaker's intent to injure the child.

## Lau vs. Nichols

English as a Second Language students (ESL) comprise one of the most hidden failure groups in American schools. Due to their difficulty in understanding, speaking and writing English, they fall further behind in school and increasing numbers drop out altogether. In 1974, a group of Chinese speaking children had a class action suit filed on their behalf in San Francisco. The San Francisco school system allegedly discriminated against the students by not helping with their language problems. The Lau case did not make bilingual education mandatory, but it paved the way for other states to start bilingual programs. The U.S. Office of Civil Rights outlined the Lau Remedies, or ways in which bilingual programs could be instigated, mainly that students should be taught in their native language until they could benefit from receiving instruction on the English language.

## Supplemental Educational Services (SES)

Supplemental Educational Services is the term which the No Child Left Behind Act uses to refer to the tutoring and extra help with schoolwork in subjects such as reading and math that children from low-income families may be eligible to receive. This help is provided free of charge and generally takes place outside the regular school day, such as after school or during the summer.

## Highly Qualified Teacher (HQT)

This is the term which the No Child Left Behind Act uses for a teacher who proves that he or she knows the subjects he or she is teaching, has a college degree, and is state-certified. No Child Left Behind requires that a child be taught by a Highly Qualified Teacher in core academic subjects.

## Equal Education Opportunities Act

There is a strong concern for equality in education. Within states this leads to efforts to assure that each child receives an adequate education, no matter where he or she is situated. The Equal Education Opportunities Act of 1974 provides that no state shall deny equal educational opportunity to an individual on the basis of race, color, sex, or national origin.

## National School Lunch Program

The National School Lunch Program (NSLP) is the oldest and largest of the child nutrition programs operated by the Food and Consumer Service (FCS) of the U.S. Department of Agriculture. Since 1946, the NSLP has made it possible for schools to serve nutritious lunches to students each school day. States receive federal reimbursement and other assistance in establishing, maintaining, and operating the program. To participate in the NSLP, schools and institutions must agree to:

- Operate food service for all students without regard to race, color, national origin, sex, age, or disability.
- Provide free and reduced price lunches to students unable to pay the full price based on income eligibility criteria. Such students must not be identified nor discriminated against in any manner.
- Serve lunches that meet the nutritional standards established by the Secretary of Agriculture.
- Operate the food service on a nonprofit basis

To qualify for federal reimbursement, schools must serve lunches which meet meal pattern requirements specified by the Secretary of Agriculture. The lunch pattern is designed to provide, over a period of time, approximately one-third of a student's Recommended Dietary Allowance for key nutrients and calories. Meals are planned to include foods from the Food Guide Pyramid. While there are different specific requirements for each age group, it is not difficult to plan good tasting, healthy meals that offer the required balance of meats, breads, dairy products and fruits or vegetables - while reducing salt, fat and sugar.

## Basic first-aid tips and supplies

Since it is necessary to act fast when an emergency happens, it is a good idea to think ahead and have a plan in place. If you are in a public place, you may want to begin by shouting for help to see if a doctor is available. Someone should immediately dial 911. Do not attempt any resuscitation techniques unless you are trained. If you have a car and it is appropriate, you should immediately take the victim to the nearest hospital. Furthermore, every home should have some basic first-aid supplies. A good first-aid kit will include bandages, sterile gauze pads, scissors, adhesive tape, calamine lotion, cotton balls, thermometer, ipecac syrup (to induce vomiting), a sharp needle, and safety pins.

## Treating various ailments

### Open wound
When treating an open wound, a person should apply direct pressure to the wounded area after covering it entirely with sterile gauze or a clean cloth. Apply steady pressure for between 5 and 15 minutes. If possible, elevate the wound above the heart to slow bleeding. Placing a plastic bag of ice or cold water on top of the protective gauze will also help to slow the bleeding. If, after 15 minutes, there is no sign that the blood loss is decreasing or the injury appears serious, the victim should see a doctor for further treatment. If bleeding has stopped within 15 minutes, care from a doctor may still be needed. This is the

case if stitches will be required to keep the wound closed or if the victim has not had a tetanus shot within the last 10 years.

## Broken bone

If you think someone may have broken a bone, restrict the person from moving unless there is some immediate danger. First, ensure that the person is breathing normally. If the person is bleeding, apply pressure to the wound before assessing the potentially broken bone. Never try to push a broken bone back into place, especially if it is protruding from the skin. If possible, apply a moist compress to any exposed bone. Moisture prevents drying and may promote better healing. Never try to straighten a fracture, and never allow the victim of a broken bone to walk. Any unstable fractures should be placed in a splint to prevent painful motions.

## Internal bleeding

If you suspect that a person is bleeding internally (for instance, if they cough or vomit up blood or if they pass blood in their waste matter), do not allow the person to take any fluids or medication because these could get in the way if surgery is necessary. Lay the victim flat and cover the victim with a light blanket; then seek medical attention immediately. If a person is experiencing a bloody nose, have them sit down, leaning slightly forward. The victim should spit out any blood in the nose or mouth. Apply light but steady pressure to the area for about 10 minutes and then, if the bleeding continues, pack the nose with gauze. If there is a foreign object lodged in the nose, do not attempt to remove it.

## Choking victim

Never slap a person's back if the person appears to be choking; this can make the situation worse. If the victim is conscious but cannot cough, speak, or breathe, perform the Heimlich maneuver. Begin by standing behind the victim, wrapping your arms around the victim's waist. Make a fist with one hand and place the fist just above the victim's navel. Grab the fist with your other hand and pull upward sharply, trying not to exert too much pressure against the rib cage with your forearms. Repeat this procedure until the victim is either no longer choking or has lost consciousness. This procedure can be performed on oneself, either with one's fist or by pressing sharply against some stationary object, like the back of a chair.

## Unconscious choking victim

If a person is choking and has lost consciousness, lay the person on the ground and perform mouth-to-mouth resuscitation. If this does not seem to work, give the person a few abdominal thrusts, as in the Heimlich maneuver. Repeat this from six to ten times if necessary. Next, try to clear the victim's airway: tilt the head back, use your thumb to depress the tongue, and gently sweep a hooked finger through the back of the throat to remove any objects. Repeat the sequence of abdominal thrusts, probing of the mouth, and mouth-to-mouth resuscitation as many times as necessary. If the victim suddenly is revived but nothing has come out of the mouth, go to the hospital. Hard matter can damage the internal organs as it passes through the body.

## Burns

If a person has been burned by fire, cool the burned area with water as soon as possible. This will help to stop the burn process. Next, remove the victim's garments and jewelry and cover the victim with clean sheets or towels. Once the victim is secure, call for emergency medical assistance. If burns have been caused by chemicals, wash the affected area immediately with cool water. Affected areas should be washed for at least 20 minutes. When the eyes are burned by chemicals, the victim will require immediate medical attention even after the eyes have been washed with cool water for 20 minutes.

## Drowning victim

A person who has drowned can die 4 to 6 minutes after breathing stops. Get the victim out of the water immediately. Place the victim on his or her back and, if not breathing, immediately begin performing mouth-to-mouth resuscitation. Continue this treatment either until the victim begins breathing normally or help arrives. It should be noted that it can take as long as 2 hours for a drowning victim to regain independent breathing. Never leave a victim of drowning alone. Once the victim has begun breathing normally, simply wait nearby until professional help arrives. Resuscitation efforts can be suspended if the individual begins coughing.

## Poisoning

If you feel an individual has been poisoned, you should be prepared to call 911 and the Poison Control Center and tell them the kind and quantity of poison that has been ingested, as well as the symptoms. Do not administer any medications unless you are instructed to do so by a professional. If a poisoned child is conscious, give him or her a little bit of water to dilute the poison. If a victim of poisoning is unconscious, make sure the person is breathing and, if not, perform mouth-to-mouth resuscitation. If the victim is vomiting, make sure they do not choke. Even though vomiting is the easiest way to remove poisons from the body, never try to induce vomiting when an individual has swallowed acid or an alkaline substance.

## Heart attack

An individual may be suffering from a heart attack if he or she has an intense clenching pain in the chest, has shortness of breath, sweats heavily, is nauseous, has an irregular pulse, has pale or bluish skin, and is beset by severe anxiety. If you believe someone may be having a heart attack, immediately call 911. Have the person sit up and loosen any tight clothing. Try to keep the person comfortably warm. If the person is on medication for angina pectoris, help him or her take it. If the person is unconscious and you are trained to perform CPR, then do so after checking for a pulse at the wrist or neck. If there is no pulse, perform CPR along with mouth-to-mouth resuscitation.

## Breathing problems

If an unconscious victim is either not breathing or shows no signs of breath, lay the person on his back on the ground. Loosen any clothing that may be constricting some part of the body. Immediately check the air passages for any foreign objects, and then open the air passage by tilting the head back and lifting the chin up. Pinch the nostrils shut with thumb and index finger, then deliver two deep breaths directly into the victim's mouth. Each of these breaths should last from one to ten seconds. After each, look at the victim's chest to see if it rises. Repeat this process once every five seconds until medical help arrives. If your breaths do not seem to raise the victim's chest, tilt the head back farther and check for signs of choking.

## Meeting physical and medical needs

Those working with students with severe and profound disabilities need to be aware of many details specific to each individual student. For example, some students with severe or profound cerebral palsy can have an extreme bite reflex, as well as being physically unable to feed themselves. The person feeding such students must know not to use plastic spoons that will break in their mouths. Adaptive equipment is available, like metal spoons coated with rubber or similar cushioning material to avoid damage to the student's teeth and the spoon. Some students with CP cannot grasp and manipulate utensils to feed themselves, but can do so with assistive devices, like holders that steady the utensils or automatic "feeding machines" that move the spoon toward the student's mouth and rotate the plate. Some students with neurological damage have visual field defects: their eyesight is normal, but they cannot see the full visual field on one or the other side. Therapists, including speech-language pathologists, can do training to compensate for this.

## Genetic syndrome with specific physical and behavioral symptoms

Some genetic syndromes that cause severe or profound disability also have specific, unusual physical and behavioral symptoms. For example, Prader-Willi syndrome may not only cause intellectual disabilities that may be severe or profound, but also ravenous, uncontrollable hunger in the individual. The resultant overeating, added to common physical characteristics of the syndrome like poor muscle tone and low activity in those who are nonambulatory, leads to overweight or obesity without intensive management. Students with this syndrome are also prone to self-injurious behaviors, particularly when frustrated in their constant attempts to get more food, and especially when they have profound intellectual disability that precludes explaining or reasoning with them. Behavior modification techniques, including replacement behaviors, may be used, but with profound disability, managing the symptoms of Prader-Willi syndrome also requires such measures as locking up food, constant monitoring, and dietary management by a dietitian or nutritionist.

Certain genetic syndromes may cause profound physical and intellectual disabilities, as well as significant and unusual behavioral symptoms. For example, Lesch-Nyhan syndrome, which primarily affects boys, causes varying degrees of intellectual disability, severe or profound for some, as well as physical symptoms like inability to walk. This syndrome includes an inability of the body to produce an enzyme needed to process certain substances like carotenes. Caregivers must be aware not to feed or serve these students carrots, which will turn their skin orange. Due to metabolic insufficiencies, Lesch-Nyhan patients often need gout medications like allopurinol to reduce excessive uric acid in the bloodstream. An unusual symptom of Lesch-Nyhan is self-injurious behaviors like gouging one's mouth with the fingers; rubbing one's nose on the bed to the point of destroying the tissue; and sometimes behaviors injurious to others, like punching or hitting. Some patients need hand restraints. Some can learn to control these symptoms through behavioral training.

## Profound multiple disabilities

Some students with developmental neurological damage and/or defects have multiple disabilities. For example, a student diagnosed with profound intellectual disability and cerebral palsy requires a feeding tube due to inability to chew and swallow normally, let alone use his arms and hands to feed himself. This student also cannot speak. Motor apraxia and dysarthria are conditions often associated with severe or profound cerebral palsy and other neurological damage, causing muscular weakness and inability to coordinate breathing and motor movements to produce speech sounds. His digestive insufficiency requires a slow, constant drip of liquid nourishment. The feeding apparatus is battery-powered, so caregivers must periodically charge the battery, refill the liquid, make sure the tube is not clogged, and so on. Even a student aware enough to know something is amiss must be monitored: if he cannot speak or move much, he can only indicate concern or distress with facial expressions and limited body language.

## Positioning, mobility, and adaptive equipment

Many students with severe or profound neurological damage have multiple disabilities, such as profound intellectual disability, cerebral palsy, and scoliosis, which is abnormal curvature of the spine. When scoliosis is severe enough, the student's body literally cannot be straightened out. The spinal deformity combined with the cerebral palsy often means the student cannot sit up, and can only lie down in a configuration that takes up much space due to twisting of the back. These students require reclining wheelchairs, often custom-made from a body mold. Some have such profound curvatures that a "flatbed" type of chair must be specially constructed for them, often by a physical therapist. This accommodates the student's body shape but can present problems fitting through doorways and other more narrow openings. Students who can grasp a pencil but are always lying supine may be accommodated for testing and other manual activities by someone holding a clipboard with paper above them to make marks, for example.

## Safely lifting and transferring

Just as public safety agencies now require employees to undergo programs of exercise and stretching to increase overall physical fitness, strengthen the back and enhance flexibility, teachers, therapists and caregivers working with severely/profoundly disabled students should also have this kind of training. They should also be trained in proper lift and transfer techniques to avoid injuring the student and/or themselves. To lift, you begin facing the student, with your legs shoulder-width apart, your back straight, head up, and shoulders square. Bend your knees if the student is lower than your arm level. Lift with your palms facing up, keeping your arms straight and locked and the student's body as close to yours as possible. If bending, use your leg strength to straighten to standing position. Do NOT twist while carrying even a very light student! Whenever possible, heavier students should always be lifted by more than one person, as many as are needed/available.

## Positioning and moving an injured student in an emergency situation

In an emergency, if head, neck, or spinal injuries are suspected, you should first check to make sure the student has an airway to breathe. Only if breathing is impeded should you reposition the student's head. Emergency first aid and CPR courses teach how to do this. Otherwise, injured students should be stabilized in the same position in which they were found to prevent further injury. Positioning also involves protecting from hazards. In an accident or weather emergency, use a blanket to protect a student from flying glass and/or debris, electrical sparks, wind, precipitation, and so on, or if blankets are unavailable, whatever is at hand, such as carpeting, coats, or clothing. When it is necessary to make a life-saving emergency move, you should always try to pull the student in the direction of the body's long axis to minimize spinal injury. On the ground, either grasp the student's clothing around the neck or the shoulders and pull; roll the student onto a blanket and pull it; or slide your hands under the student's arms from behind, grasp the student's forearms, and drag.

# Practice Test

## Practice Questions

1. What most makes the study of emotional and social development in LD students relevant?
   a. The stigma of an LD automatically causes emotional and social difficulties
   b. Cognitive deficits affect learning in these as well as academic domains
   c. They are part of a whole person even though LDs do not affect them
   d. Emotional and social deficits are implicated in causing or exacerbating an LD

2. Research has found that in elementary school-age children, working memory:
   a. Increases with age
   b. Decreases with age
   c. Stays stable with age
   d. Fluctuates over time

3. Researchers have found that students with reading disabilities (RD):
   a. Scored lower on working memory tasks that involved sentences only
   b. Scored lower on working memory tasks that required just counting
   c. Scored lower on working memory tasks with sentences and counting
   d. Scored equally on working memory tasks as normal achievers scored

4. Researchers have found that students with arithmetic disabilities:
   a. Have the same general working memory deficits as students with reading disabilities
   b. Have specific deficits in working memory for processing both numbers and language
   c. Have specific deficits in numerical processing, but these are not for working memory
   d. Have working memory deficits specifically for processing numerical information only

5. When researchers compared elementary school students with attention deficit disorder (ADD) to students with reading disabilities (RD), arithmetic disabilities (ARITHD), and normal achievers (NA) on working memory measures, they found that:
   a. Students with ADD performed most comparably to students with RD
   b. Students with ADD performed most similarly to students with ARITHD
   c. Students with ADD performed most comparably with the NA students
   d. Students with ADD performed differently from all these other groups

6. Current neurobiological research finds that dyslexia is related to:
   a. Malformations in certain structures in the brain
   b. Abnormal functioning of structures in the brain
   c. Genes affecting structure and function in the brain
   d. All of these are found to be related to dyslexia

7. The central problem in reading disability (RD) or dyslexia is thought to be:
   a. With processing visual stimuli
   b. With phonological processing
   c. With aural and visual systems
   d. With some unknown variable

8. The left side of which lobe of the brain is most involved with mathematical calculations?
   a. Parietal
   b. Frontal
   c. Occipital
   d. Temporal

9. Current research finds that brain stimulation has which result on numerical abilities?
   a. It can produce improvement that is only temporary
   b. It can produce processing deficits that are permanent
   c. It can produce improvement that is fairly long lived
   d. It can produce no influences upon numerical abilities

10. The current IDEA law defines a specific learning disability as a "disorder in one or more of the basic psychological processes involved in understanding or in using language, spoken or written, which disorder may manifest itself in an imperfect ability to listen, ____, speak, ____, write, ____, or to do mathematical calculations." Which of the following words does not fill in one of these blanks?
    a. Think
    b. Read
    c. Spell
    d. All do

11. The proportion of students who receive special education services for the category of Specific Learning Disabilities among all students receiving special education services:
    a. Is about the same as each of the special education categories
    b. Is a much smaller proportion than students in any other group
    c. Makes up the majority of students receiving special education
    d. Seems to include equal numbers of male and female students

12. Among school-age children, reading disabilities are found in:
    a. 10%
    b. 20%
    c. 30%
    d. 40%

13. Among all persons with learning disabilities, what proportion has reading disorders?
    a. 20%
    b. 40%
    c. 60%
    d. 80%

14. Broca's aphasia is primarily:
    a. An expressive language disorder
    b. A disorder of receptive language
    c. A disorder of both types
    d. A disorder of neither type

15. Wernicke's aphasia is primarily:
   a. An expressive language disorder
   b. A disorder of receptive language
   c. A disorder of neither type
   d. A disorder of both types

16. Among students with specific language impairment (SLI), those with prognoses of the least cognitive, educational, and social difficulties are those whose problems are mostly with:
   a. Syntax
   b. Prosody
   c. Phonology
   d. Semantics

17. One factor that affects a student's motivation to learn is the difficulty of the task involved. Which of the following is not another factor important to motivation?
   a. Ability
   b. Effort
   c. Luck
   d. All are important

18. Students with LD are found to be different from normal learners in four dimensions. One of these is motivation. Which of these is not one of the other three?
   a. Metacognition
   b. Self-efficacy
   c. Self-esteem
   d. Attribution

19. Perry has difficulties with differentiating among printed characters and with getting things in the correct order. These would be classified as:
   a. A perceptual disorder
   b. A reasoning disorder
   c. A memory disorder
   d. None of these

20. You may have noticed it is easier to pick the correct answer from several in a multiple choice question like this one than it is to come up with it for a fill-in-the-blank or short-answer question. Which identifies the correct terminology?
   a. Multiple choices use recall, while blanks use recognition
   b. Multiple choices use recognition, while blanks use recall
   c. Multiple choice and blanks are different types of recall
   d. Multiple choice and blanks are two types of recognition

21. Which of the following is the least common behavioral/social characteristic of students with LDs?
   a. Being rigidly organized
   b. Being behaviorally rigid
   c. Being socially immature
   d. Being easily distractible

22. Emotionally, LD students are more likely to suffer from low self-esteem. Due to unsuccessful scholastic experiences, they are more likely to drop out of school. Which of these is another emotional and social consequence secondary to LD?
    a. Greater risk of substance abuse
    b. Greater risk of criminal actions
    c. Greater risk of suicidal actions
    d. Greater risks of all of these

23. Which of the following is not true about assessment of students for LDs?
    a. A discrepancy between intelligence and achievement scores can indicate LD
    b. A discrepancy of greater severity is a newer criterion than those used earlier
    c. A discrepancy between ability and performance can indicate other disorders
    d. All of these statements are equally true about discrepancies in LD assessment

24. Which of these pairs of tests is most amenable to comparison of aptitude with performance?
    a. WISC and WRAT
    b. WIAT and WRAT
    c. WISC and WIAT
    d. None of these

25. Which of these is not an aspect of intelligence in Sternberg's Triarchic Theory of Intelligence?
    a. Linguistic
    b. Analytic
    c. Creative
    d. Practical

26. Which of the following typically use checklist or questionnaire formats and are not self-reports?
    a. Intelligence testing scales
    b. Performance assessments
    c. Rating scales for behavior
    d. All these fit those criteria

27. Which part of the process for early identification of LDs in preschoolers is not always included?
    a. Developmental screening
    b. Risk and protective factors
    c. Systematic observations
    d. Comprehensive evaluation

28. What component of a psychoeducational evaluation depends most upon interviewing parents?
    a. Achievement tests
    b. Cognitive testing
    c. The case history
    d. Giving feedback

29. Of the following behaviors for which assessment procedures might need to be adapted, which is least likely to be equally attributable to either a disability or a cultural/environmental variation?
    a. A child who makes little or no eye contact with the examiner
    b. A child who gets out of his chair, yells, and hits the examiner
    c. A child who never speaks until the examiner asks a question
    d. A child who will not initiate activity without prior permission

30. Which of these is not an example of assistive technology (AT) that could be used in assessment?
   a. A pencil wrapped with tape
   b. A text-to-speech computer
   c. A word processing program
   d. These are all examples of AT

31. Vanderbilt University researchers developed the Test Accessibility and Modification Inventory (TAMI, Elliott, Beddow, & Kettler, 2008) and accompanying Accessibility Rating Matrix (ARM, 2009) to make standardized tests more accessible to all students including those with disabilities. What is not true about the test modifications facilitated by these tools?
   a. They identify items problematic for disabled students for modifications
   b. They enable the creation of separate tests testing different knowledge
   c. They eliminated achievement gaps between normal and disabled students
   d. They do not modify the knowledge that is assessed to be less in-depth

32. Which of the following is not likely to be included in both oral language achievement and written language achievement testing?
   a. Mechanics
   b. Narratives
   c. Forming sentences
   d. Both include all these

33. The examiner who has evaluated a student for LD has a feedback conference with the student's parents. Which of the following will not take place during this conference?
   a. The examiner will explain the test results and diagnosis
   b. The examiner will answer any of the parents' questions
   c. The examiner will inform parents of an educational plan
   d. The examiner will report recommendations to parents

34. Anya's parents do not speak English. Which is the best strategy for the school to communicate her assessment results to them?
   a. Tell them to Anya and ask her to tell her parents
   b. Arrange for an interpreter to attend the meeting
   c. Send them a report translated into their language
   d. Excuse the parents, and just get their IEP signature

35. Gary and Larry are students who were both assessed at their school. Gary's IQ test score was significantly higher than the norm, but his achievement test score was significantly lower than the norm, revealing a wide gap between the two. Larry's IQ test and achievement test scores were both lower than the norms and were at very similar levels. What is most accurate about both students' eligibility for special education services?
   a. Gary will probably be eligible, and Larry will probably not be eligible
   b. Gary will probably not be eligible, and Larry will probably be eligible
   c. Neither Gary nor Larry is likely to be eligible based on the scores
   d. Both Gary and Larry will probably qualify for services based on data

36. Which is true regarding differences between a student's eligibility for special education under IDEA vs. under Section 504 of the ADA?
    a. IDEA has more procedural criteria regulating schools than Section 504
    b. IDEA covers a longer duration of time for disabilities than Section 504
    c. IDEA requires reevaluation before placement change, but Section 504 does not
    d. These statements are all true about differences between IDEA and ADA

37. Which is not true of IDEA and Section 504 of the ADA regarding students with disabilities?
    a. Due process under both laws is enforced by the U.S. Department of Education, but by two different offices of that department
    b. Both laws require impartial hearings for parents who disagree with the identification, evaluation, or placement of their child
    c. Both laws require students' parents to provide their written informed consent for evaluation and due process procedures
    d. If parents disagree with evaluation, schools pay for independent evaluation under IDEA, but not under Section 504 of the ADA

38. Which of the following is correct regarding provisions for IEPs (individualized education programs) for providing free appropriate public education (FAPE) under IDEA and Section 504 of the ADA?
    a. Only IDEA requires a student qualifying for special education to have an IEP
    b. Both IDEA and Section 504 of ADA require special education students to have IEPs
    c. Both laws require some kind of plan for providing FAPE, but not necessarily an IEP
    d. Both laws apply the same definition of FAPE for students who have disabilities

39. Katie has a central auditory processing disorder. Her IEP includes a goal to follow spoken directions more accurately. The current objective is for her to increase her accuracy from 40% to 60%. Which type of evaluation would apply for her general classroom teacher to keep track of her progress with this objective?
    a. The use of a portfolio assessment
    b. The use of a behavior rating scale
    c. A functional behavior assessment
    d. Structured behavioral observation

40. Which of the following classroom accommodations for LD students is least applicable to a diagnosis of memory deficits?
    a. Carbonless paper for classmates taking notes
    b. Using a computer's word processing program
    c. Presenting information in multiple modalities
    d. Permitting student recording of class lectures

41. Of the following, which is most likely to have an adverse impact on the education of a student with LD?
    a. LDs diagnosed in more than one area
    b. Stigma from special education services
    c. Stigma from inclusion in regular classes
    d. One's teacher and peers expecting less

42. To simplify and generalize, the most accurate characterization of any LD is as:
    a. A problem with intellectual functioning
    b. A problem with one's capacity to learn
    c. A problem with information processing
    d. A problem with a combination of these

43. Of the following examples, which student most likely does not have a learning disability?
    a. Sean, who has difficulties with reading any printed material
    b. Susan, who can read but has trouble understanding reading
    c. Rebecca, who finds it difficult to plan and manage her time
    d. Each of these students most likely has a learning disability

44. Which of the following is not true about students with visual perception LDs?
    a. They have a higher rate of visual impairments than other students
    b. They are likely to miss words, sentences, or paragraphs in reading
    c. They can misinterpret facial expressions that transmit information
    d. They can have trouble differentiating among visually similar letters

45. Samantha easily becomes lost, even in places where she has been before. She gets mixed up about left and right and has trouble judging distances. Even when she is given directions, she has difficulty following them correctly. Samantha's LD is characterized by:
    a. Motor coordination deficits
    b. Spatial perception problems
    c. Executive functioning deficit
    d. Difficulties with sequencing

46. Students with LD characterized by deficits in memory typically have:
    a. More difficulty with short-term than long-term memory
    b. More difficulty with long-term than short-term memory
    c. Equal difficulties with short-term and long-term memory
    d. No clear pattern of difficulty with either type of memory

47. Amy finds it problematic to take notes simultaneously while listening to her teacher. This is most associated with:
    a. Visual motor coordination
    b. Writing disorder/dysgraphia
    c. Auditory motor coordination
    d. A reading disorder or dyslexia

48. In general, which is most accurate about class seating for students with learning disabilities?
    a. All students with LDs should be seated in the front row of classrooms
    b. Only students with visual perception or reading LDs should sit in front
    c. Class seating depends on the type of LD and on the individual student
    d. LDs are not sensory by nature, so seating arrangements do not matter

49. Which of the following is not a recommended accommodation for LD students when taking tests?
    a. Giving extra time for students to complete tests
    b. Permitting use of calculators to take a math test
    c. Providing separate quieter rooms for test-taking
    d. All of these are recommended accommodations

50. For a class with many LD students, how best should the teacher communicate class expectations and assignments?
    a. Printed on paper
    b. Printed and oral
    c. Spoken out loud
    d. All methods work equally well

51. Ms. Winslow has a class with many LD students. She consistently calls her students' attention to features in their textbooks such as boldface headings, illustrations, tables, charts, indexes, and chapter summaries. Which is most accurate regarding this practice?
    a. Doing this helps her students to organize what they read and learn
    b. She does this because none of her students ever reads a textbook
    c. It enhances her presentation but does not really facilitate learning
    d. This helps her LD students but is a waste of time for other students

52. Which of the following is the best presentation of study questions to help LD students to prepare for taking a test?
    a. They should cover the content of the test without replicating its format
    b. They should give questions similar to the test, but no answer examples
    c. They should give examples of good answers without explanation
    d. They should show content, format, questions, good answers, and why

53. In the normal acquisition of receptive language skills, which of these can a child do first?
    a. Identify pictures of familiar things in a picture book
    b. Follow simple commands like "Bring me the book"
    c. Use pronouns, for example, "I," "me," and "you"
    d. Listen to stories and understand parts of them

54. In the normal sequence of acquiring expressive language skills, which does a child develop last?
    a. Producing all of the vowel sounds correctly
    b. Producing sentences with grammar errors
    c. Producing all of the consonants accurately
    d. Producing speech with about 75% intelligibility

55. Which of the following assistive technologies is most indicated for a student who has difficulties with memory retrieval?
    a. Voice recognition software
    b. Word prediction software
    c. Speech output software
    d. Spell checker software

56. Which of the following is not true about the universal design approach to instruction?
    a. It benefits LD students only with the required adaptations
    b. It provides various methods of presenting subject content
    c. It affords flexibility among different instructional strategies
    d. It allows different ways of demonstrating content mastery

57. According to research-based practices for teaching children to recognize individual phonemes corresponding to letters, in which order should they be addressed?
    a. Alphabetically, from A to Z
    b. Consonants before vowels
    c. Vowels before consonants
    d. All at once, not in isolation

58. Researchers find that literacy instruction for students who are English language learners (ELL) and also have LDs is most effective when it fosters high engagement levels for students. Which of these is not another research finding about literacy instruction for ELLs with LDs?
    a. It activates the higher-order cognitive functions in such students
    b. It allows these students greater opportunities to give responses
    c. It offers more practice and support in cooperative learning groups
    d. It need not be culturally responsive if teaching practices are valid

59. Which of the following is not a way to teach children phonological awareness?
The jump-rope game "A my name is Alice and I live in Alabama and I sell Apples; B my name is Betty and I live in Boston and I sell Buttons...."
    a. Playing the "I Spy" game while shopping, first looking for an "A" in the surroundings, then for a "B," etc., going through the alphabet
    b. Singing "The Name Game" song "Shirley, Shirley, Bo birley, Banana fanna fo Firley,
    c. Fee fie mo Mirley, Shirley!" etc.
    d. Reading Dr. Seuss books to and with children, e.g., Green Eggs and Ham, The Foot Book, Great Day for Up, and others

60. Researchers have found that to create a culturally responsive environment for enhancing reading comprehension, teachers should concentrate their endeavors on several elements, including teaching approaches and resource management. Which of the following is not another important element?
    a. Positive classroom interactions
    b. Curriculum and materials
    c. Counseling and parent outreach
    d. These are all needed elements

61. In addition to speed, which of the following is not a component of reading fluency?
    a. Suitable intonations when reading aloud
    b. Lack of obvious effort when reading
    c. Accuracy of word decoding
    d. These are all components

62. Which of these is not correct about students who have difficulties with reading fluency?
    a. The more effortful reading is, the more comprehension is likely to deteriorate
    b. These students take longer, but they ultimately understand more deeply
    c. These students lose motivation and practice if reading is unduly hard
    d. These students fall behind more in high school than in primary school

63. Regarding teaching strategies to improve reading fluency, teachers can encourage students to read independently by providing books with suitable difficulty levels that students find interesting. Which is true about these additional strategies?
    a. Timed exercises should be avoided for creating undue pressure
    b. Repetition is a very effective technique to build reading fluency
    c. Readers' theatre is good for showing progress but not making it
    d. Reading in pairs assists reading comprehension but not fluency

64. What is incorrect about strategies for teaching reading skills to LD students?
    a. Using both visual and auditory input greatly increases comprehension
    b. Using both visual and auditory input greatly increases reading speed
    c. Using both visual and auditory input distracts and confuses students
    d. Using both visual and auditory input works better than either alone

65. Which of these is true about books on tape, reading services, and typing services?
    a. These adaptations are only for blind or visually impaired students
    b. These adaptations help LDs in visual processing but not other LDs
    c. These adaptations actually obstruct reading skills for LD students
    d. These adaptations are helpful with reading for many LD students

66. What is not a characteristic of a writing disorder?
    a. Poor organizational skills
    b. Weak phonological skills
    c. Inadequate vocabulary
    d. Weak planning abilities

67. Which assistive technology is least applicable to difficulties with writing?
    a. A computer's keyboard
    b. Speech-to-text software
    c. Text-to-speech software
    d. Using graphic organizers

68. What is true about materials to teach writing skills designed for students learning English as a second language (ESL) when applied with ESL students who also have LDs?
    a. ESL textbooks do not afford enough practice of new material for ESL/LDs
    b. The amount of material presented in an ESL lesson is appropriate for LDs
    c. Graphics in ESL textbooks are just as visually appealing to LD students
    d. The pace of instructional presentation with ESL-only is similar for ESL/LDs

69. According to research findings, which of these is not a recommendation for improving LD students' writing skills?
    a. Teaching students to set specific, attainable goals for writing
    b. Teaching students strategies for planning, editing, and revising
    c. Teaching students to avoid using writing for content learning
    d. Teaching students how to use PC word processing programs

70. Which of the following LDs is least likely to cause a student difficulty with math?
    a. These all cause math difficulties
    b. Language processing difficulties
    c. Visual-spatial relation problems
    d. Sequencing or memory deficits

71. Which of these is a recommended teaching strategy for students with dyscalculia?
    a. Students should be discouraged from using estimates to begin solving math problems
    b. Teachers should present new material by moving from abstract to concrete examples
    c. Teachers should offer alternative explanations for math facts instead of rote learning
    d. Students should not have to use graph paper if they have trouble organizing on paper

72. Recommended by educational researchers, curriculum materials based on teaching approaches that build on LD students' existing knowledge to learn basic arithmetic facts include all except:
    a. Providing longer practice sessions to allow students sufficient processing time
    b. Smaller groups of fewer facts to learn at once, then mixing groups for practice
    c. Raising motivation and attention with interactive games for intensive practice
    d. Distributed practice that makes use of more frequent, shorter sessions

73. Which of the following assistive technology (AT) devices would be most helpful to an LD student who has trouble aligning math problems on paper with a pencil?
    a. A paper-based computer pen like Livescribe's Pulse Smartpen
    b. Electronic math worksheets, such as MathPad Plus or MathTalk
    c. Independent Living Aids, MaxiAids, or AbleData talking calculators
    d. Any one of these AT devices would be equally helpful for this

74. Which of these instructional strategies is mostly likely to enhance an LD student's social skills across different environmental contexts?
    a. Assigning the student to be a peer tutor for another student
    b. Assigning the student to be leader of a small group exercise
    c. Letting the student practice by role-playing various situations
    d. Cooperative designed practice with another teacher

75. Research finds that which of these is most important to effective social skills training for LD students?
    a. Modeling
    b. Coaching
    c. Reinforcement
    d. All of these are equally important

76. Which of these is the best example of integrating social skills development into academic curricula for LD students?
    a. Schedule a specific day and time each week for practicing social skills in class
    b. Assign a collaborative learning group, evaluating academic and social success
    c. Assign students homework to practice learned social skills in the community
    d. These are all equally good examples of integrating social skills into academics

77. In a school-wide positive behavioral intervention and support (PBIS) program such as that used in Michigan, which of the following is specifically a component of a Tier Three intervention?
  a. Functional behavior assessment
  b. Consistent consequences
  c. A simple behavior plan
  d. Positive expectations

78. Which of the following is not a component of crisis intervention?
  a. Coping skills
  b. Problem solving
  c. Review and planning
  d. These are all components

79. As a general behavioral rule, which of these interventions is most effective?
  a. Positive reinforcement
  b. Negative reinforcement
  c. Positive punishment
  d. Negative punishment

80. Federal law dictates that schools must determine whether a problem behavior by a student with a disability is a function of that disability to decide whether standard disciplinary action is indicated. For example, a teen with LDs curses in school; whether this is a manifestation of his disabilities or not is not obvious. Which of these is not a valid criterion for ruling out disability as leading to problem behavior?
  a. The student's placement and IEP are appropriate; the IEP is implemented as written; if there is a BIP, it is appropriate
  b. The student's disability did not impede his understanding of standard disciplinary consequences for the behavior
  c. The student has engaged in the same behavior previously and has experienced the standard disciplinary measures for it
  d. The student's disability did not interfere with his ability to control the problem behavior under consideration

81. Which is not a good representation of what independent living means for persons with LDs?
  a. Having the right to choose where and with whom they live
  b. Living independently of any kind of support, services, or care
  c. Having control over what kinds of help or support are available
  d. Greater involvement in decisions for equal resource access

82. Which is least accurate about integrating life skills into school curricula for LD students relative to current technological advances?
  a. Many parents did not grow up with today's technology and cannot teach their children life skills impacted by technology
  b. Educators should adjust curricula to reflect changes brought by technology, like network security, identity theft, and jobs
  c. Because of the impact of today's technology on society, none of the traditional school subjects is relevant to students today
  d. The more society moves from paper to electronics, the more schools should make PC classes optional, not required, including safety

83. According to research, which has been the most often used instructional strategy for teaching life skills to students with LDs and other disabilities?
    a. Task analysis
    b. Computer-assisted
    c. Prompting
    d. Modeling

84. Of the following, which group does not represent areas included in teaching life skills?
    a. Banking, budgeting, shopping, and purchasing
    b. Safety, first aid, and mobility (like crossing streets)
    c. Housekeeping skills and leisure activities skills
    d. These groups are all parts of teaching life skills

85. Dr. Murray Bowen's Family Systems Theory posits four basic relationship patterns. One of these is "Impairment of one or more children." Which is not a characteristic of this pattern?
    a. Excessive parental worry about the child
    b. Having an overly idealized view of the child
    c. Less reaction by the child to parental focus
    d. Having an overly negative view of the child

86. To help educators and other professionals work with the families of children with disabilities, researchers have proposed aspects of family systems and dynamics to consider. For example, one is the way family members interact on a daily basis. Which is not another one of these aspects?
    a. What resources are available to a given family
    b. The nature and severity of the child's disability
    c. The various individual needs of family members
    d. Changes over time that affect family members

87. Which of the following has not been reported by families as a result of having children with disabilities?
    a. Experiencing more stress in the family
    b. An improvement in family dynamics
    c. Focusing on the child's positive attributes
    d. All of these have been reported by families

88. A special education teacher arrives at a new school to find that most of the general education classroom teachers know little or nothing about LDs. Which is the most appropriate strategy to address this?
    a. Schedule time to instruct each teacher individually
    b. Schedule inservice training for all general teachers
    c. Ask those who know a little to share with the rest
    d. These are all strategies that are equally indicated

89. For which LD students would you recruit the participation of the school's occupational therapist?
    a. Students who have difficulty with processing language
    b. Students who have difficulty with spatial relationships
    c. Students who have deficits in fine motor coordination
    d. Students who have deficits in gross motor coordination

90. What is not correct about the duties of a special education paraprofessional in a public school?
    a. The only school staff they work with are special education staff
    b. They give guidance to individual special-needs students in class
    c. They are likely to work with small groups of students in classes
    d. They record observational data on special education students

91. Which of the following is a more important responsibility for a teacher's aide or assistant in public schools?
    a. Being able to focus on responding to individual students
    b. Being aware of what is going on in the entire classroom
    c. Both of these are equally important responsibilities.
    d. Neither one of these is an important responsibility.

92. What is not accurate about the services to schools of volunteers in general?
    a. Volunteers can save schools a great deal of money over the school year
    b. Volunteers contribute relatively little time in hours over the school year
    c. Volunteers' hours spent in the school are rarely recorded by the school
    d. Volunteers' contributions can inspire others to follow suit and volunteer

93. School volunteers have responded to surveys that positive reinforcement, e.g., being acknowledged and thanked for their contributions, is an important motivational factor. They also expressed wishes for which of the following?
    a. Businesslike job descriptions, including required hours
    b. Clearer, printed instructions and provision of training
    c. A school volunteer coordinator to help with problems
    d. They expressed wishes for schools to provide all of these

94. Which of the following is largely a separate entity from the others?
    a. Public Law # 94-142
    b. Rehabilitation Act, Section 504
    c. Education for all Handicapped Children Act (EHA)
    d. The Individuals with Disabilities Education Act (IDEA)

95. Which federal law affecting special education students was passed first?
    a. The Americans with Disabilities Act (ADA)
    b. Individuals with Disabilities Education Act (IDEA)
    c. Elementary and Secondary Education Act (ESEA)
    d. The Assistive Technology Act, Public Law #108-364

96. When the parents of a student with an LD disagree with how their child was diagnosed, evaluated, and/or placed educationally, what is not true about due process procedures provided under IDEA?
    a. The parents must be given impartial court hearings if they disagree
    b. Parents must be notified of placement changes but not necessarily in advance
    c. Current placement and IEP remain in effect until there is resolution
    d. The parents have to give their written consent to request a hearing

97. Which of these is not a way that provisions under Section 504 of the Rehabilitation Act differ from those under IDEA for due process proceedings regarding special education students?
    a. Section 504 does not require an impartial hearing for parents disputing placement
    b. Section 504 does not require parental consent as IDEA does to formalize disputes
    c. Section 504 does not require placement and IEPs to "stay put" during procedures
    d. Section 504 does not require an impartial appointee to select the hearing officers

98. Professional development for special education teachers includes all but which of these?
    a. Improvement of teachers' knowledge of academic subjects
    b. Participating in workshops that take one day or a short time
    c. Improvement of teachers' skills for classroom management
    d. Learning more research-based effective teaching strategies

99. In the National Association of Special Education Teachers (NASET)'s Code of Ethics, which of the following is not included in one of its principles?
    a. Collaboration of teachers with the students' parents
    b. Collaboration of teachers with community members
    c. Knowing the impact of cultural diversity on individuals
    d. All of these are included in the NASET Code of Ethics

100. According to the Code of Ethics of the National Association of Special Education Teachers (NASET), which of the following is not true?
    a. NASET's members should incorporate academic, social, physical, and psychological aspects of education
    b. Special education teachers are role models for their students and others; hence, this is addressed
    c. Metacognition is a higher cognitive function, but this Code of Ethics does not include it in its principles
    d. One of the ethical principles of the NASET's Code of Ethics involves the application of learning to real life

# Answers and Explanations

1. B: Studying emotional and social development in LD students is most relevant because (b) cognitive deficits affect learning in emotional and social domains as well as in academic domains. Difficulties in cognitive processing can interfere with all kinds of learning. Emotional or social difficulties are not automatically caused by stigma, and having an LD need not automatically stigmatize a student (a). Understanding emotional and social development is part of understanding the whole person, but it is not true that LD does not affect these developmental areas (c). Emotional and social deficits are not implicated in causing LDs (d).

2. A: Research has found that in elementary school-age children, working memory (a) increases with age. In the age group of 7 to 13 years, working memory is found to improve significantly as children get older. Working memory in this age group does not (b) decrease with age. It does not (c) stay the same but makes gains. It does not (d) fluctuate over time but grows in capacity with maturation.

3. C: Researchers have found that students with RDs (c) scored lower than normal achievers on tasks that tested their working memories with respect to both sentences and counting. Their scores did not suffer comparatively only with sentence tasks (a) or only with counting tasks (b). While one might expect RDs to affect working memory for sentences, it was also found to affect working memory for numbers, so the researchers concluded that a general deficit in working memory was implicated in reading disabilities. Answer (d) that RD students scored the same as normal achievers on working memory tasks is therefore incorrect.

4. D: Researchers have found that students with arithmetic disabilities (d) have working memory deficits specifically for processing numerical information only. They have not found that these students (a) have the same general working memory deficits as students with reading disabilities. Students with RDs seem to have such general deficits in working memory which affect their processing of both language and numbers, while students with arithmetic disabilities have not been found to (b) have specific deficits in working memory for processing both numbers and language. They were found to have neither general nor specific WM deficits for both areas, but specific WM deficits for numbers only. These specific deficits in numerical processing were for working memory (c).

5. C: Researchers found that when comparing working memory in students with ADD to that in students with RDs, with ARITHD, and in NA students, the attention-deficit students (c) performed most like the normal achievers tested. They thus concluded that working memory may not depend significantly on attentional factors. ADD students did not compare most to RD students (a), who demonstrated general deficits in working memory affecting both linguistic and numerical tasks. ADD students did not perform most like students with ARITHD (b), who evidenced specific numerical deficits in working memory but not linguistic ones. Because (c) is correct, answer (d), that ADD students performed differently from all these other groups, is incorrect.

6. D: Current (November/December 2010) neurobiological research finds that dyslexia is related to (d) all of these: malformations in certain structures in the brain (a) responsible for processes involved in reading, abnormal functioning of these structures (b) when reading, and genes that affect structure and function in the brain (c). These genes affect the formation of neurons (nerve cells), their axons (extensions that send signals to other neurons' dendrites), the hippocampus (the structure in the cerebral cortex that is central to forming memories and learning), and the neocortex (which makes up the majority

- 143 -

of the cerebrum and is linked with higher intelligence). When most of these genes lose function, this causes malformations in these brain structures and also their abnormal functioning.

7. B: The central problem in reading disability (RD) or dyslexia is thought to be (b) with phonological processing. While reading printed or written language involves processing visual stimuli (a) as well, language is commonly learned through hearing (exclusive of deaf learners, whose lack of the usual auditory basis for language learning explains their reading challenges). Thus researchers believe phonological processing deficits to be more central to dyslexic difficulties than both aural and visual systems (c) for cognitive processing. Because this is the current thinking of neurobiological researchers, they do not primarily cite (d) some as yet unknown variable as being involved in dyslexia.

8. A: Neuroimaging studies find that the left side of the (a) parietal lobe, located behind the frontal lobe at the back of the top of the brain, is most involved with mathematical calculations. The frontal (b) lobe is involved with speech, emotions, and executive functions such as solving problems, making decisions, and planning. The occipital (c) lobe is at the back of the brain and is responsible for the processing of information received through the sense of vision. The temporal (d) lobe is below the frontal and parietal lobes and is involved with aspects of speech, memory, perceiving and identifying auditory stimuli (sounds), and other functions. Damage in the parietal-temporal area can cause deficits in digit span and verbal memory.

9. C: Current research finds that noninvasive stimulation of the parietal lobe (c) can produce long-lasting improvement in numerical abilities, rather than just temporary (a). For example, Cohen et al (2010) found that transcranial direct-current stimulation (TDCS) that affected release of brain chemicals improved both automatic processing of numbers and mapping of numbers in space, which are significant measures of numerical competence. The researchers found that they could either improve or impair these abilities depending on the type of stimulation; however, they did not judge deficits thus caused to be permanent (b). They found improvements thus caused to last at least six months after a six-day training using TDCS during numerical learning. Therefore answer (d), no influences on numerical abilities, is incorrect.

10. D: All do (d). IDEA's definition of specific learning disability is a "disorder in one or more of the basic psychological processes involved in understanding or in using language, spoken or written, which disorder may manifest itself in an imperfect ability to listen, think (a), speak, read (b), write, spell (c), or to do mathematical calculations." Therefore there is not one of these words that does not fill in the blanks correctly.

11. C: Among all students receiving special education services, those with specific learning disabilities (c) constitute the majority, i.e., more than half of those receiving special education services. Therefore the proportion of LD students receiving special education is not (a) the same as each of the other categories, and it is not (b) a much smaller proportion than students in other groups. Also, this group does not include equal numbers of male and female students (d); boys seem to be diagnosed with LD more often than girls are.

12. B: Reading disabilities are identified in (b) 20% of school-age children. Ten percent (a) is only half the percentage of school-age children who are diagnosed with reading disabilities, while 30% (c) overstates this proportion by half, and 40% (d) is double the actual figure.

13. D: Eighty percent (d) of all people with learning disabilities have reading disorders, making this the most common of the learning disabilities. Twenty percent (a) is only one-fourth the actual proportion of

reading disorders among learning disabilities. Forty percent (b) is one-half the actual percentage, while 60% (c) is three-fourths of the true figure.

14. A: Broca's aphasia is primarily (a) an expressive language disorder. It causes difficulty with facets of expressive language, including processes involving recall of specific words, constructing sentences with correct syntax, and other aspects of speaking and writing. It is not a disorder of receptive language (b), which affects comprehension rather than production, or of both types (c). Since (a) is correct, answer (d), neither type, is incorrect.

15. B: Wernicke's aphasia is primarily (b) a disorder or receptive language. It causes difficulties with understanding what other people are saying and with reading comprehension. It is not (a) an expressive language disorder, which causes difficulties with the processing required for speaking and writing language correctly. Individuals with Wernicke's aphasia are likely to be expressively fluent, at least initially. In the long term, their speech tends to become less logical, relevant, and appropriate due to not understanding others' verbal input and feedback, while their speech production still remains fluent. Since only (a) is correct, answers (c), neither, and (d), both types, are both incorrect.

16. C: Students with SLI have the best prognosis if their problems are mostly with (c) phonology, i.e., speech sounds. They may have trouble recognizing, discriminating among, sequencing, and/or producing speech sounds correctly. Students having problems with syntax (a), i.e., sentence structure (including verb tenses, persons, and other grammatical constructions) and word order; with prosody (b), i.e., the rhythms and intonation patterns of speech; and with semantics (d), i.e., the meanings of words and their uses in context, all have difficulties with linguistic processing, which yield poorer cognitive, educational, and social prognoses compared to those for SLI students with only phonological or articulation difficulties.

17. D: These all are (d) important factors affecting student motivation. The student's ability (a) to complete a task will influence the student's degree of willingness to attempt it. However, effort (b) also plays a key part: A student with lesser ability who makes greater effort may do better than a student with greater ability making little or no effort. Luck (c) is an additional factor, and although it is random, students who experience better initial outcomes, even through luck, are more motivated to repeat or continue tasks than those with worse initial luck.

18. C: Self-esteem (c) is not one of the four dimensions wherein LD students differ from normal learners. Self-esteem is a broader, more global term describing one's overall feelings about the self. Self-efficacy (b) is a more specific term describing one's sense of competence to achieve certain tasks, such as learning. Students with LD by definition have impairment in some aspect(s) of learning, so their self-efficacy for learning is likely to be lower; thus it is one of the four areas of difference in LD students. Metacognition (a)—one's own awareness and understanding of one's cognition, or how one thinks and learns—is also an area of difference. Normal learners develop metacognition more readily than LD learners, and strengthening metacognition can improve learning in LD students. Attribution (d) is the other dimension: Students' perceptions of why they succeed or fail, or the factors to which they attribute these outcomes, influence their feelings, motivation, performance, and expectations for future outcomes.

19. A: Differentiating among printed characters is visual discrimination, and getting things in the right order is sequencing. These are both functions that can be impaired in (a) a perceptual disorder. Reasoning disorders (b) would not have these characteristics, but would involve difficulties with making decisions, solving problems, forming concepts, making comparisons, doing calculations, and metacognitive processes. Memory disorders (c) involve difficulties with storage, retrieval, recall,

recognition, organization, classification, and interpretation of information. Because (a) is correct, answer (d), none of these, is incorrect.

20. B: The correct terminology is (b): Questions with multiple choices use recognition, meaning that if you know the correct choice, you can recognize it among several other options, while blanks use recall, meaning you must recall or retrieve the correct answer from your memory without seeing it. This is why multiple-choice questions are generally easier: The correct answer is provided and you need only recognize it. Recalling the answer from memory requires more cognitive effort and processing. Answer (a) is the opposite of the correct choice. Multiple choice and fill-in-the-blank or short-answer questions are not different types of recall (c) or two types of recognition (d).

21. A: Being rigidly organized (a) is the least common characteristic of LD students. LD students tend to have difficulty with organizing and planning. However, they also tend to be rigid (b), not in organization, but in a lack of flexibility to adapt to unexpected or different situations or demands. Social immaturity (c) is another common characteristic of students with LDs. Since cognitive deficits affect social and emotional as well as academic learning, LD students are likely to be behind normally learning peers in social development as well as in school subjects. An additional characteristic of LD students is that their attention is easily distracted (d), interrupting and diverting focus on a subject or activity.

22. D: Greater risks of all of these (d) are secondary to having LDs. Individuals with LDs are at higher risk of abusing substances (a) as self-medication for the frustration, depression, anxiety, feelings of low self-worth, social isolation, and loneliness they often experience as a result of difficulties with learning and achieving in school. They are at higher risk of engaging in criminal activity (b), which is acting-out behavior in reaction against a system with which they are unable to comply successfully. Because of the depression, low self-esteem, and social isolation they often experience, LD children also have higher risks of attempting or committing suicide (c).

23. B: It is not true that (b) a more severe discrepancy is a newer criterion. In the past, educators were directed to look for a "severe" discrepancy between ability and achievement, but this has changed over time as educators realized that using this criterion for identifying LD did not contribute to meeting students' needs. Currently, a discrepancy between intelligence and achievement scores is still considered a sign of possible LD (a). However, such a discrepancy can also indicate other disorders (c). For example, emotional and behavioral disorders can interfere with the performance of students with high IQs. Undiagnosed vision and hearing impairments can do the same, so more specific testing is needed to determine the reason for the discrepancy. Since (b) is not true, answer (d), all of these, is incorrect.

24. C: The WISC and the WIAT (c) are most amenable to direct comparisons of ability and achievement. The WISC, or Wechsler Intelligence Scales for Children (WISC-IV), is for assessing intelligence with subscales for various dimensions (verbal, numerical, spatial, memory, etc.), while the WIAT, or Wechsler Individual Achievement Test, allows norm-referencing for the student's age/grade level. Both authored by David Wechsler and co-normed, they are thus most compatible for comparing intellectual ability with school achievement. The WRAT (Wide Range Achievement Test) noted in (a) and (b), assesses reading recognition, spelling, and mathematical computation. It can identify error patterns to inform instructional plans, but is not as easy to compare with the Wechsler IQ test as the Wechsler achievement test is. As (c) is correct, answer (d), none of these, is incorrect.

25. A: Linguistic (a) is not one of Sternberg's three aspects of intelligence in his Triarchic Theory of Intelligence (note: Sternberg also has a Triarchic Theory of Love). Linguistic intelligence is one of Howard Gardner's types of intelligence in his Theory of Multiple Intelligences. (Gardner originally defined seven types, later adding two more for a total of nine.) Sternberg's three aspects of intelligence are analytic (b),

for breaking down, comparing and contrasting, and evaluating; creative (c), for creating in the areas of art, science, writing, advertising, etc.; and practical (d), for applying ability and tacit knowledge to solving problems in everyday life.

26. C: Rating scales for behavior (c) typically use checklists or questionnaires to identify various behaviors or behavioral characteristics. Behavior rating scales are normally not self-reports; they are completed by a child's parents, caregivers, and teachers based on their observations of the child's usual behavior at home, in school, or other settings. Intelligence testing scales (a) typically do not use checklists or questionnaires but various performance measures, such as repeating series of digits just heard (working memory), answering questions on concepts or situations (comprehension), defining words (vocabulary), assembling blocks to match a design (perceptual reasoning), etc. While an administrator either asks the questions or gives instructions for completing some scales, the child being tested gives the responses. Performance assessments (b) are evaluations made based on a student's work products. The educator evaluates them, but the products are produced by the student being evaluated. Since only (c) is correct, answer (d), all these, is incorrect.

27. D: Comprehensive evaluation (d) is only conducted if it is indicated by the results of the other components. Developmental screenings (a) are the first step. These are not used to diagnose, place, or plan for a child's education. Preschoolers are screened to assess whether further evaluations are needed, and if so, in which developmental areas. Assessment of risk and protective factors (b) identifies prenatal, genetic, and environmental variables, as well as developmental delays and differences in behavior and attention that put children at higher risk of future learning disabilities. It also makes note of protective factors such as the mother's education, high quality care, and redundancy of supports that mitigate future learning disabilities. Professionals make systematic observations (c) of a child's competencies and behaviors over a period of time to evaluate developmental normalcy and/or need for additional assessment.

28. C: The case history (c) is the part of the psychoeducational evaluation that depends most upon interviewing the child's parents. While the evaluator will also consult medical records, school records, etc., to develop the case history, the parents are invaluable sources of detailed and comprehensive information on their child's developmental, behavioral, and health history from a lifetime, daily perspective. Achievement tests (a) are typically administered by classroom teachers or other school personnel. Cognitive testing (b) is usually administered by a psychologist or educational specialist. Giving feedback (d) also involves the parents, but in a conference rather than an interview. The evaluator shares test results, observational findings and related information with parents and they discuss them, as opposed to asking parents questions in an interview to gather information for the case history.

29. B: The least likely to be equally attributable to disability or cultural/environmental differences is (b) a child who gets out of his chair, yells, and hits the examiner. This behavior would need assessment to determine if it is a true behavior disorder or is attributable to environmental factors, such as parental modeling of these behaviors, lack of parental intervention or discipline, chaotic family life, or improper methods. Regardless, these behaviors are highly unlikely to be caused by cultural differences. A child's avoiding eye contact (a) could be equally attributable to a social or emotional disability or to a cultural background that finds children's eye contact with adults inappropriate or disrespectful. A child who never speaks until the examiner asks a question (c) could equally be suspected of shyness, social withdrawal, lack of comprehension of spoken language, or an environmental upbringing that dictates "never speaking unless spoken to" by an adult first. Similarly, a child who will not initiate activity without prior permission (d) could indicate passivity, lack of motivation, lack of confidence, or cultural or environmental training that specifies always getting adult permission before beginning activities.

30. D: These are all examples of AT (d) that could be used in assessment. Not all AT need be "high-tech." A pencil wrapped with tape (a) could assist a student who has difficulty grasping writing implements in completing a written questionnaire. A text-to-speech-enabled computer (b) could assist students whose speech is impaired or absent, who have difficulty with verbal interactions, or have visual impairments, in responding to test questions or items. A computer's word processing program (c) can assist students with dysgraphia (writing disability), as well as problems with spelling, vocabulary, syntax, processing, and so on in responding to test items.

31. B: It is not true that the TAMI and ARM enable the creation of separate tests that evaluate different knowledge (b). Instead, these tools identify which items present problems for students with disabilities and need modification (a). In researching these tools, their authors gave both the original standardized test questions and the modified versions to students both with and without disabilities. They found that by modifying the items predicted to cause problems for students with disabilities, they were able to eliminate the gap in achievement between normally achieving students and those with disabilities (c). It is true that these tools do not change the knowledge being tested to be less in-depth (d); the authors sought to make tests more accessible while assuring they measured knowledge in the same depth as the originals.

32. A: Mechanics (a) are likely to be included in written language achievement testing, but not in oral language achievement testing. Spelling and punctuation cannot be assessed in speech, and other mechanics are never as correct in speech as in writing, even by those without any learning disabilities. Narratives (b) are likely to be included in both types of testing as they demonstrate the ability to sequence events chronologically; to retain and retrieve information; to express that information in language; to recognize narrative elements such as characters, actions, and settings; and to tell a story. While elements such as themes and styles are more applicable to written language, oral narratives are valid (and predate written narratives historically) for assessing the aforementioned abilities. If a student has difficulties or irregularities specifically with forming sentences (c), rather than with either oral or written expression, this is equally likely to show up in spoken or written language when sentence formation is tested.

33. C: In the feedback conference, the examiner will not (c) inform the parents of an educational plan. The examiner will explain the results of tests, observational findings, and the child's diagnosis (a) based on those results and findings; will answer any questions the parents have (b) about this information; and will report to the parents the educational recommendations (d) for their child based on the evaluation and diagnosis during the feedback conference. The parents, child, and involved school personnel will then have an IEP meeting to discuss the recommendations further and develop an individualized education plan (IEP) with goals and objectives designed to fulfill those recommendations for facilitating the child's educational progress. Specific IEP planning is not done during the feedback interview, however. Also, parents should never simply be informed by educators of the IEP. Rather, they and their child should be members of the team that develops the IEP.

34. B: The best strategy is to (b) arrange for an interpreter to attend the meeting with them. This could be a relative or family friend who speaks both languages. If such an individual cannot be identified, community resources can be investigated. Anya should not be asked to relay the information to her parents (a). This is unfair to the student, since she may not be able to remember or explain all the information. Because she is a student, not a professional educator, she should not be expected to be able to explain it. Sending the parents a written report, even translated into their native language (c), is inadequate, since it denies the opportunity for having a face-to-face meeting with all involved personnel, asking questions, providing valuable input, and discussing issues and options. Excusing the parents from

meeting and just requesting their signature(s) on the IEP (d) excludes them from the IEP process, in which parents and family, as well as students, should be encouraged to participate.

35. D: Assuming they meet the other criteria, based on their test scores (d) both students will probably qualify for special education services. The wide gap between Gary's IQ and achievement scores is considered a discrepancy, a classic sign of possible LD. Students with LD are typically not intellectually impaired, but have specific learning problems that interfere with their academic performance. Larry's scores indicate that he may have some form of cognitive impairment, which could result from mild intellectual disabilities, an autistic disorder, etc., because there is no discrepancy between his scores for ability and for performance. (He should still be tested for LD, to rule it out or in case he also has a mild LD.) Therefore, answers (a) and (b), that either student will probably be eligible and the other ineligible, are incorrect as both probably will be eligible; so answer (c), that neither will probably qualify, is incorrect.

36. A: The only true choice here is (a): IDEA (Individuals with Disabilities Education Act) has more criteria for the procedures schools must follow, such as time limits, official paperwork, and parents' involvement. Section 504 of the ADA (Americans with Disabilities Act) has fewer federal regulations, so students may receive less accommodation and tracking: With fewer regulations, compliance is monitored and enforced less. IDEA does not cover a longer duration of services (b); Section 504 does. IDEA provides for special education up to age 21, while Section 504 of ADA protects the rights of persons with disabilities for life. IDEA does not require reevaluation before making significant changes in placement, but Section 504 does—the opposite of the answer given in (c). Therefore answer (d), these statements are all true, is incorrect.

37. C: It is not true that (c) both IDEA and Section 504 of the ADA require written parental informed consent for evaluations and for hearings and other due process procedures: IDEA requires written informed consent of the parents for these, but Section 504 of the ADA does not; it only requires that the parents be notified of evaluations or due process procedures. It is true that both laws' due process provisions are enforced by the U.S. Department of Education, but by different department offices (a): Under IDEA, they are enforced by the Office of Special Education, while under Section 504 of the ADA they are enforced by the Office of Civil Rights. It is true that if parents agree with a school's identification, evaluation, or placement of their child, both laws require the parents be provided with impartial hearings (b). It is also true that if parents disagree with their child's initial evaluation, IDEA provides for an independent evaluation at the school's expense, but Section 504 of the ADA does not make this provision (d).

38. A: The only correct choice is that (a) only IDEA requires a student qualifying for special education services to have an IEP. Section 504 of the ADA requires that there be some kind of educational plan, but does not specify that it be an IEP. Therefore answer (b) that both laws require IEPs for special education, is incorrect, and answer (c) is incorrect about both laws, only applying correctly to Section 504. Answer (d) is incorrect as both laws do not apply the same definition of FAPE: Specifically, the word "appropriate" (in "free appropriate public education") is defined by IDEA as providing "educational benefit" for students with disabilities, while Section 504 of the ADA defines "appropriate" as comparable education to that provided to students without disabilities.

39. D: Structured behavioral observation (d) would apply. The teacher would observe Katie's specific behaviors whenever she gives Katie spoken directions. She might use a very simple data sheet where she checks Yes/No or Correct/Incorrect for each instance to show whether Katie followed the directions correctly or not. A portfolio assessment (a) would not be used to keep track of this particular objective. A portfolio is a collection of work a student has produced over time. An IEP goal to improve written

expression from the beginning to the end of a semester, for example, might be monitored via portfolio assessment. Behavior rating scales (b) are typically questionnaires or checklists to assess a student's various behaviors. While these are available for all sorts of behaviors, they are most often used for evaluating maladaptive behaviors. A behavior rating scale would not be used to measure number or proportion of correct responses. A functional behavior assessment (c) is used to determine the function, or purpose, served by maladaptive behaviors by investigating when, where, with whom, how often, and in what situations they occur, as well as their antecedent and consequent events or situations.

40. B: While all of these are helpful accommodations for LD students, the one least applicable to memory deficits is (b) using a computer's word processing program. This more directly applies to deficits in spelling, grammar, syntax, sentence formation, and organization, as word processing software programs have features that automatically check these and can assist in correcting them as the student chooses. Carbonless paper for classmates taking notes (a) will help a student with memory deficits: The classmate only has to take notes once, but a copy is made for the LD student who has difficulty with auditory memory and/or poor note-taking skills. Presenting information in multiple modalities (c) provides redundancy to aid students in remembering; plus, if the student has difficulty remembering in one modality, one or more others are likely to be easier. Permitting students to record class lectures (d) helps those with difficulty retaining information.

41. D: The factor most likely to have an adverse impact on the LD student's education is (d) the student's teachers, peers, and others expecting less of the student because of the LD diagnosis. Being diagnosed with LDs in more than one area (a) of learning does present more challenges to the student and more complex educational plans, but with proper instructional programming, the student's education need not suffer adverse effects. Receiving special education services does not necessarily cause sufficient stigma (b) to have an adverse impact on the student's education. (In fact, in some schools, peers regard students receiving special education as privileged by this additional attention.) Inclusion in regular classes also does not create adverse educational effects through stigma (c); the reverse is more often true, hence the federal laws providing for inclusive educations for students with disabilities.

42. C: The most accurate simplified generalization of any LD is as (c) a problem with information processing. All LDs signify deficits in acquiring, organizing, storing, and using information. LDs do not represent (a) a problem with intellectual functioning; students with LD typically have intellectual capacities at or above their age and grade levels. Similarly, despite the term "learning disability," they do not signify (b) a problem with the capacity to learn. They have the ability, but difficulties with the perception and integration of the material interfere with applying it. LD students must find, and educators must assist them in finding, alternative ways of learning. Therefore answer (d), a combination of these, is incorrect.

43. D: Each of these students most likely has a learning disability (d). Sean's difficulties with reading (a) characterize the most common LD—reading disability or dyslexia. Susan's ability to read coupled with difficulty understanding what she reads (b) is characteristic of reading comprehension problems also common in LDs, which can be due to problems with connecting new concepts to those stored in the memory or with forming mental images, either of which can hinder understanding and/or remembering new ideas. Rebecca's difficulties with planning and time management (c) relate to weakness in the brain's executive functioning, also a symptom of some LDs.

44. A: It is not true that students with visual perception LDs (a) have a higher rate of visual impairments than other students. Difficulties with visual perception occur in the brain areas that interpret visual signals, not with the sensory ability of eyesight. Students with visual perception problems can have perfect vision. This LD makes students likely to miss words, sentences, or entire paragraphs when they

are reading (b). Students with this type of LD can also misunderstand others' facial expressions that communicate such things (c) as disbelief, approval, boredom, or indicating that a conversation is over. Another common effect of a visual perception LD is having difficulty telling apart similar-looking letters (d), numbers, characters, or symbols. Perceiving letters backwards or distorted also frequently occurs with this type of LD.

45. B: Samantha's LD is characterized by (b) spatial perception problems. Spatial perception allows us to orient ourselves in space, tell left from right, judge how far something is, follow directional instructions, etc. Motor coordination deficits (a) cause clumsiness, such as bumping into things or people, when they affect gross motor coordination, and difficulty manipulating small objects, including writing implements, when they affect fine motor coordination. Executive functioning deficits (c) cause difficulties with planning, organizing, managing time, making decisions, solving problems, using self-regulation, and other tasks involving management and coordination of various cognitive processes. Difficulties with sequencing (d) are likely to cause trouble with the correct order of letters in spelling, of numbers in math, and of class notes in general; with prioritizing; with following step-by-step directions; with the structure of readings or lectures; or with relationships of concepts within a hierarchy.

46. A: Students with LDs characterized by memory problems typically have (a) more difficulty with short-term memory than with long-term memory. This appears related to problems with retrieval more than with storage. (LD students with reading disabilities may also have difficulty storing new information if they have deficits in linking old knowledge to new.) Therefore, answer (b) is backwards. Answer (c) is incorrect as the difficulties are not equal with both types of memory, but more with short-term than long-term, meaning that answer (d), no clear pattern, is also incorrect.

47. C: Problems with taking notes while listening is most associated with (c) auditory motor coordination. Auditory motor coordination also allows us to follow spoken instructions. Writing down what one is listening to relies on this ability. Visual motor coordination (a) is more related to the ability to copy printed or written information. It also relates to writing itself, though not specifically writing what one is hearing, as well as typing or cutting out patterns, which all require coordinating manual motor activities with vision rather than audition (hearing). A writing disorder, or dysgraphia (b), is likely to interfere with writing complete sentences that are grammatically correct. (If neural networks for hand movement and/or immediate memory are affected, a writing disorder can also affect note-taking, but deficits in vocabulary and grammar have less impact on taking lecture notes than on original writing.) A reading disorder or dyslexia (d) affects reading, not writing.

48. A: In general, the most accurate statement is that (a) all students with LDs should be seated in the front row of the classroom. This does not apply only to students with visual perception or reading LDs (b). While many classroom accommodations should be tailored to the individual LD student (c), classroom seating in general should give LD students the best possible access to the teacher, blackboard, overhead projection, and other learning aids to keep from compounding their problems with perception, interpretation, integration, etc., by adding problems with access to the instruction. Although LDs are not sensory by nature (d) like impaired vision or hearing, this does not make seating irrelevant. Students can concentrate more on working around their individual LDs to learn when they do not have to concentrate harder on accessing the material.

49. D: All of these are recommended accommodations (d). Giving extra time to complete tests (a) is indicated as students with LDs have difficulties processing information, so it can take them much longer than normally achieving students to do the same tasks. Time-and-a-half to twice the usual time is often recommended. Permitting calculators for math tests (b) is indicated for students with dyscalculia as well as other LDs: Difficulty performing calculations (adding, subtracting, multiplying, dividing, etc.) should

- 151 -

not be allowed to prevent them from demonstrating their understanding of mathematical concepts learned, their ability to apply the correct formula or process to a problem. Also, providing separate quieter rooms for (individually proctored) test-taking (c) helps students with auditory processing disorders, for example, who are more distracted than others by background noises.

50. B: For LD students, teachers should communicate class expectations and assignments in both (b) printed and oral forms. This is something that is helpful for all students, including normal achievers, but it is especially important for LD students. If they have trouble processing information in one modality, the other may be easier, and if they have problems with both, the redundancy can help them process more of it. For these reasons, presenting this information only on paper (a) or only spoken aloud (c) is not as effective as using both modalities. Thus answer (d) that all methods work equally well, is incorrect.

51. A: The most accurate choice is (a): Doing this helps Ms. Winslow's students to organize what they read and learn from the textbooks. While many of us are familiar with students never reading their textbooks (b), this is not Ms. Winslow's main reason for her practice. The textbook items listed in the question as being features she regularly points out to her students are all specifically organizational devices. Thus answer (c) is incorrect: This practice may or may not enhance her presentation, but it does facilitate learning. Answer (d)—that this helps LD students but is a waste of time for other students—is also incorrect, since all students can benefit from being reminded to use these features in their textbooks as aids to effective learning.

52. D: Study questions for tests should (d) show the content the test will cover, replicate the format the test will have, supply questions that exemplify the kinds that will be on the test, provide examples of good answers to the questions, and also explain why those answers are good ones. They should not cover the content without replicating the format (a), since LD students can be confused by having the same content presented in a different format, and so may not process it the same way or have difficulty processing an unfamiliar format. Not giving examples of good answers to questions (b) does not provide enough guidance for LD students (and often other students as well). Giving examples of good answers is more helpful, but not explaining why they are good (c) does not help LD students learn general principles of critical thinking.

53. B: Of the choices offered here, a child who is normally acquiring receptive language skills will first be able to (b) follow simple commands like "Bring me the book" around the age of 15 months (they can normally follow a "Bring me" command accompanied by a gesture at around 12 months). They can identify pictures of things familiar to them in a book (a) around the age of 18 months. Using pronouns (c) is not an example of acquiring receptive language skills but of expressive language skills (using "I," "me," and "you" emerges around the age of three years). Children can normally listen to stories and understand some parts of them (d) around the age of two years.

54. C: The last or latest development among the choices here in expressive language skills is (c) producing all consonant sounds accurately, which is normally achieved around the age of five years. Children normally can produce all of the vowel sounds correctly (a) around the age of four years. Speaking in complete sentences, albeit with grammatical errors (b), is a skill that normally emerges around the age of three years. Normally developing children usually can speak with about 75% of it being intelligible (d) to others around the age of two years. (About 90% intelligible speech is normally achieved around the age of three years.)

55. B: Word prediction software (b) would be most indicated of the choices for a student having difficulty retrieving words stored in his/her memory. When the student struggles to recall a word, these programs can predict the next word to type based on spelling, syntax, and frequent or recent use. Voice recognition

software (a) would be more appropriate for a student having difficulty with writing or typing, who can dictate spoken information that the software program then types. Speech output software (c) would be more helpful to students having difficulty reading text, by scanning it and reading it aloud with a synthesized voice, and those having difficulty with expressive language, who can type communications and have the voice synthesizer speak them. Spell checker software (d) helps students with sequencing disorders that affect spelling, visual perception disorders that can cause incorrect choices among similar-looking letters, and similar difficulties.

56. A: It is not true that the universal design (UD) approach (a) can only benefit LD students with the required adaptations. Adaptations are needed for some disabilities, but according to Ron Mace at the National Center for Universal Design at North Carolina State University, "Universal design is the design of products and environments to be usable by all people, to the greatest extent possible, without the need for adaptation or specialized design." UD does provide various methods of presenting content (b), so LD students unable to use one method can find another one more suited to their strengths. UD affords teachers more flexibility in the instructional strategies (c) they use, so they can select those more accessible and beneficial to individual LD students. UD also allows LD students different ways of demonstrating their mastery of content (d) so that disabilities in some forms of expression do not stop them from showing in other ways what they have learned.

57. C: Research-based practices include (c) teaching vowels before consonants because it is impossible to make words without vowels, and because children develop correct production of all vowel sounds sooner (about a year earlier) than of all consonant sounds. Therefore, teaching consonants before vowels (b) is incorrect. Going from A to Z (a) is the best way to learn the alphabet, but it is not the most logical way to learn the different speech sounds represented by different letters. Research finds that, just we do not expect children to learn all the letters in the alphabet at once, we cannot expect them to learn all the speech sounds (phonemes) at once; therefore, answer (d) is incorrect. It is more effective to teach one phoneme at a time, and also to teach one limited set of related individual phonemes within a time period.

58. D: Research has not found that literacy instruction for ELLs with LDs (d) need not be culturally responsive if teaching practices are valid. Research has found, to the contrary, that the most effective literacy instruction for this population is both culturally responsive and uses teaching practices that have been validated. Research has also found that the most effective literacy instruction for ELLs with LDs (a) activates their higher-order cognitive functions; (b) allows them greater opportunities to give responses; and (c) offers more chances to practice English language skills and receive peer support through the use of cooperative learning groups.

59. B: Playing "I Spy" looking for each letter in the alphabet (b) is not a way to teach phonological awareness, although it is a way to teach children alphabet knowledge. The jump-rope game "A my name is Alice" (a) is a way to teach phonological awareness by demonstrating similarities in initial word sounds within sentence patterns and using rhythm. Singing Shirley Ellis's song "The Name Game" (c) teaches phonological awareness by demonstrating similarities and differences in initial word sounds, discrimination among sounds, practicing rhymes, using repetition, and making it fun with the use of nonsense syllables and music. Reading Dr. Seuss books to and with children (d) teaches phonological awareness, as the author made extensive use of rhyming and repetition, reinforcing these with humor, imaginary creatures and names, and wonderful illustrations.

60. D: These are all needed elements (d). By promoting positive classroom interactions (a), teachers can improve students' confidence, willingness to participate, and engagement in instruction. By paying attention to the curriculum and materials they use (b), teachers can facilitate learning by making it more meaningful to students. For example, they can provide reading material with which students can identify

personally through themes they recognize, validating their cultural identity. Counseling (c) provides students with the opportunity to express wants, needs, and feelings, even as it allows teachers to help students cope with these, gain insights, and adjust to environmental differences. Parent outreach (also c) gets families involved in students' education and provides teachers with valuable information about students' learning problems, learning styles, strengths, interests, and strategies that have and have not worked at home and/or in previous schools.

61. D: These are all components (d) of reading fluency. When reading aloud, the student has to use appropriate vocal intonations (a), giving expression suitable to the material to meet the definition of fluency. Whether reading aloud or silently, the student's reading should seem effortless (b) to be fluent. Students who read fast but make errors are not fluent readers, as decoding words accurately (c) must accompany speed to be considered fluent reading.

62. B: It is not correct that (b) students with reading fluency difficulties ultimately understand more deeply, while taking longer to read text. They are actually likely to understand less of the material, because the more effort it takes them to read, the more their reading comprehension is likely to suffer (a). Students with reading fluency problems not only lose comprehension with labored reading, they also lose motivation to read when it is so difficult, and less motivation leads to less practice (c). In addition, high school demands a much higher volume of reading than elementary school, so students who cannot read quickly, easily, and accurately cannot keep up and eventually fall behind (d).

63. B: The only true choice is (b): Repetition is very effective for building reading fluency. The teacher can have the student read a passage aloud repeatedly until s/he achieves the desired fluency, and then progress to a harder selection. Timing this exercise also promotes fluency, which includes speed as well as accuracy; therefore (a) is incorrect: Timed exercises should not be avoided in remediating fluency problems. Teachers can also use timing by giving students "speed drills" for individual words. A non-timed exercise can be having a student repeatedly read a familiar book out loud, giving feedback and direction as needed. Another technique is a readers' theatre; it is not true that this is good for showing progress but not making progress (c). The practice and feedback component of this exercise aids with improvement, even as it showcases progress in fluency. It is not true that reading in pairs increases comprehension but not fluency (d); partner/paired reading promotes both.

64. C: It is incorrect that using both visual and auditory input (c) distracts or confuses LD students. The information is reinforced for them when presented in both sensory modalities. Special educators find that students' reading comprehension can improve dramatically when spoken language is presented along with printed language (a). They also find that students with reading LDs, who typically read slowly and laboriously, can increase their reading speed just as dramatically when the auditory version is added to the visual (b). Therefore, it is correct that using visual and auditory input together is more effective than either sensory modality alone (d).

65. D: Only (d) is true: Books on tape, reading services, and typing services, while developed for the blind and visually impaired, also help a great many students with LDs, and are thus not useful only for those with visual impairments (a). They do not benefit only students with visual processing LDs (b), but, as mentioned above, can help students with all kinds of LDs. They do not interfere with LD students' reading skills (c). LDs are complex, involving multiple areas, structures, and functions of the brain. Even students who are able to read visual material benefit with the addition of auditory presentation to visual presentation.

66. B: Weak phonological skills (b) are characteristic of reading disorders. Phonological processing is necessary to being able to decode printed/written language (for hearing students) but is not classified as

a sign of a writing disorder. Poor organizational skills (a) are common in writing disorders, making it hard for students to arrange their written thoughts in logical order. An inadequate vocabulary (c) is another characteristic of a writing disorder; students who know fewer words have fewer choices for composing written language to express their ideas or knowledge. Weak planning abilities (d) are also identified in writing disorders. Like organization, planning is needed to execute written composition.

67. C: The technology least applicable to difficulties with writing is (c) text-to-speech software, which applies more to difficulties with speaking. Students having problems with oral expression can type text, and the software converts it to synthesized speech. A computer's keyboard (a) is applicable to students who have difficulties with writing, but not with typing. It does not apply to students having equal trouble typing or writing, but is more applicable to longhand writing difficulties for students who can type than (c) is. Using graphic organizers (d) is applicable because writing disorders commonly include problems with planning and organization, and graphic organizers facilitate these functions.

68. A: It is true that (a) ESL textbooks do not afford enough practice of new material for ESL/LD students. Students with LDs often need a great deal more practice than normally achieving students to learn new material, including learning a new language. It is not true that the amount of material presented in ESL lessons is appropriate for LD students (b). Typically, lessons for ESL students without LDs present too much material at once for students with LDs to handle. Textbooks for ESL-only students tend to use graphics that make them more visually interesting to engage students; however, these can be visually overwhelming and confusing to students with LDs, so it is not true that they are equally appealing to them (c). The instructional presentation for ESL students with LDs should not be similar to that for ESL-only students (d). Rather, it should be considerably slower for students with LDs to enable them to keep up with it. ESL-only lessons and texts tend to offer too much material, and too quickly, for ESL-and-LD students.

69. C: Research has found that using writing as a tool for learning academic content is helpful to normally achieving and LD students, so (c), teaching students to avoid this is not a recommendation. Based on their findings, researchers recommend (a) teaching students to set specific goals that they can attain for what they will write. They advise teachers to instruct them in strategies for planning what they will write, editing what they have written, and making indicated revisions (b). Researchers also recommend that teachers give LD students instruction in using PC word processing programs (d), which can make many aspects of writing much easier for them.

70. A: These all cause math difficulties (a). While they are LDs in different areas, each can lead to different types of math-related learning problems. Students who have difficulty processing language (b) can have difficulty understanding math vocabulary; solving basic addition, subtraction, multiplication, and division problems; retaining facts, such as times tables; and applying their skills and knowledge to solve math problems. Students with difficulty with visual-spatial relationships (c) can understand the mathematical facts necessary, but they have trouble setting them down on paper in an organized way. They may also have trouble understanding text in a book or writing on a blackboard related to math problems. Students with sequencing or memory deficits (d) will have trouble getting steps in the right order for solving complex problems, and find it difficult to remember facts, rules, formulas, equations, etc.

71. C: It is recommended that (c) teachers should offer alternative explanations for math facts instead of rote learning. For example, instead of simply having students keep trying to memorize the times tables, a teacher can explain that if 3 x 2 = 6, and 4 is twice as much as 2, then 3 x 4 is twice as much as 3 x 2, so 3 x 4 = 12 because twice as much as 6 = 12. Students should not be discouraged from using estimates (a); experts recommend that teachers encourage students with dyscalculia to practice their estimating skills as a way to initiate the solution of math problems. It is not recommended for teachers to move from

abstract to concrete examples when presenting new material (b); educators advise they begin with concrete examples, which are more accessible, and progress as warranted to more abstract problems. Recommendations do not state that students should not have to use graph paper if organizing things on paper is hard for them (d); experts actually advise giving them graph paper to facilitate this process.

72. A: While LD students can take much longer to process information than normal achievers, educational researchers do not recommend (a) providing longer practice sessions for LD students to learn basic arithmetic facts. They have found it more effective to give more practice, but in smaller amounts, within shorter sessions scheduled more often, as with distributed practice (d). For example, they find 15-minute sessions twice a day more effective than 1-hour sessions every other day. Educational research also finds that presenting smaller groups of fewer facts for students to learn at one time, then when they have learned these, giving them practice by mixing the groups learned (b) helps LD students to master basic arithmetic. Playing interactive arithmetic games that afford intensive practice for students while also motivating them and holding their attention (c) by being fun is another expert recommendation.

73. B: For the LD student who has trouble aligning math problems on paper with a pencil, the most helpful AT device listed here would be (b) electronic math worksheets. These PC software programs allow the user to work math problems onscreen instead of on paper. The software lines numbers up correctly for students with perceptual and/or organizational deficits. The paper-based computer pen (a) allows the simultaneous recording of a teacher's lesson and writing of lesson notes. Students also may then touch this pen to any part of their written words or drawings, and it will play back the corresponding part of the recorded lesson. This is helpful for students having difficulty with listening, memory, writing, and reading. Talking calculators (c) use speech synthesizers. The auditory feedback they provide can help students monitor whether they pressed the correct keys, and confirm they are correctly reading and copying the answer onto paper. Since (b) is the best choice, answer (d), any one of these, is incorrect.

74. C: Letting the student practice by role-playing various situations (c) is most likely to enhance social skills across different environmental contexts, such as family, community, and business, instead of just school. Assigning the student to be a peer tutor for another student (a) is an excellent way to strengthen social skills and build self-confidence, but not necessarily across different settings. The student might get these benefits in the context of the specific academic subject or even of school, but not generalize them to other areas, particularly as LD students often have difficulty with generalization. Assigning the student to be leader of a small group activity (b) will also enhance social skills and self-esteem, but again, not necessarily across settings. Cooperative designed practice with another teacher (d) is an effective technique for improving social skills, but this option also does not afford as much generalization as role-playing different contexts.

75. D: All of these are (d) equally important to social skills training for LD students. Research has found that the most effective social skills training incorporates a combination of modeling (a) by teachers for students to emulate; coaching (b) to give students feedback on their performance and progress, indicated correction, and guidance in navigating social situations; and reinforcement (c) to reward and perpetuate students' progress in learning appropriate social behaviors.

76. B: The best example is (b): Assigning a collaborative learning group and evaluating their successes with both the academic content and their social interactions within the group integrates social skills development into academic curricula. Scheduling a specific day and time each week for practicing social skills in class (a) is a good practice, per se, but it does not integrate social skills development into the academic curriculum as much as social interaction in a group learning activity. Assigning the students homework to practice social skills they have learned in the community (c) is a valuable exercise for helping students both generalize their knowledge to other settings and apply their learning in the real

world. However, it does not integrate social skills development into academic subjects as much as the collaborative learning group. Therefore, answer (d), these are all equally good examples, is incorrect.

77. A: In the Michigan Department of Education's model, functional behavior assessment (a) is specific to Tier Three, which involves the most intensive support. The FBA analyzes problem behaviors to determine their purpose, which informs the subsequent intervention. Consistent consequences (b) for misbehavior that are predictable and regularly enforced by all school staff (and are not necessarily punishments) are introduced in Tier One interventions, which are universal for all students. These are continued through all tiers, but are not specific only to Tier Three. A simple behavior plan (c) is introduced in Tier Two for less severe problem behaviors, if needed. It differs from an individualized behavior plan that would require an FBA and be introduced in Tier Three. Positive expectations (d) for behavior are introduced in Tier One, taught to all students, and continued through all tiers; they are also not specific to Tier Three.

78. D: These are all components (d) of crisis intervention. The professional doing the crisis intervention helps the student, teacher, or other individual to explore the coping skills s/he already possesses and how to apply them in the current crisis. The person may also learn some new coping strategies. Coping strategies may include exercising, using relaxation techniques, keeping a journal, seeking social support, spending time with people who provide comfort and nurture, etc. Problem-solving (b) is another component of crisis intervention. The professional helps the person understand the problem, what changes s/he wants, consider various solution alternatives, weigh pros and cons of alternatives, choosing a solution, creating a plan to try the solution, and assessing the results. At the end of the intervention, the professional will review the changes the person has achieved, reinforce effective coping strategies, and help plan (c) for future possible crises.

79. A: Positive reinforcement (a) is most effective, as a general rule. "Positive" is defined as beginning a stimulus in behaviorism; "negative" is defined as ending a stimulus; reinforcement is something that increases the probability of the individual repeating a behavior; and punishment is something that decreases the probability of repeating a behavior. Thus, positive reinforcement—presenting something a student likes—as a consequence of (i.e., immediately following) a desired behavior strengthens the student's likelihood of repeating that behavior. Skinnerian behaviorists find this the most powerful consequence. Negative reinforcement (b) is taking away something the student does not like, increasing the likelihood of repeating a desirable behavior. Ending detention for good behavior is an example. Positive punishment (c) is introducing something the student does not like, decreasing likelihood of repeating an undesired behavior. Giving detention for disrupting class is an example. Negative punishment (d) is ending something the student likes, decreasing likelihood of repeating undesired behavior. Taking away a privilege for hitting a classmate is an example. All these techniques are effective when applied appropriately to the situation, but positive reinforcement for desirable behaviors is still most powerful.

80. C: The student having engaged in the same behavior and experienced the standard disciplinary measures for it (c) is not a valid criterion for determining that a problem behavior is not a manifestation of the student's disability. Yell (2000) describes three criteria the school team can use which, if met, rule out problem behavior as a manifestation of disability: (a) The student has been placed appropriately in the school system for his age, grade level, special needs, strengths, etc.; the student's IEP is appropriate and implemented correctly; and the student's BIP, if already written, is appropriate; (b) The student's disability did not make him unable to understand the standard disciplinary measures for his behavior; and (d) The student's disability did not make him unable to control the behavior in question.

81. B: Living independently of any kind of support, services, or care (b) is not a good representation of what independent living means for persons with LD. Aspects of better representations include having the

right to choose where and with whom they live (a); having control over what kinds of help and support, including equipment, are available (c); and being more involved in the decisions made to ensure them equal access to resources (d) and services. For example, people with LDs may need additional support for transportation to keep appointments, run errands, and/or to be able to communicate when out in the community, as well as in education, employment, and healthcare. When public agencies provide support, LD individuals should not just have needs met, but have choices in how they are met.

82. C: The least accurate statement is (c): Despite the impact of technology on society, the traditional school subjects are not irrelevant. They still apply, but some people believe curricula should be updated to reflect needs brought by technology, like registering for classes, filling out applications, banking, online security, and protecting against identity theft (b). Because many parents of today's LD students did not grow up with today's technology, they cannot teach their children life skills related to this technology (a). Many schools offer PC classes, but they are usually optional; it has been suggested that to keep up with advances, these classes should be mandatory, should address students' technology needs and advantages in today's society, and should include not just the basics, but also security issues (d).

83. A: According to a meta-analysis by the National Secondary Transition Technical Assistance Center (NSTTAC), the most often used instructional strategy for teaching life skills to students with LDs and other disabilities was (a) task analysis, which breaks tasks down into smaller, more attainable steps. Computer-assisted instruction (b); prompting (c) using both least-to-most and most-to-least formats; and modeling (d), both live and on video, were also instructional strategies used.

84. D: These groups are all parts of teaching life skills (d). Intervention studies involving teaching life skills to students with LDs and other disabilities have included skills in (a) banking, budgeting, shopping, and purchasing; (b) safety, first aid, and mobility, like safely crossing the street; (c) housekeeping skills, like cleaning and doing laundry; skills for engaging in leisure activities; and skills for cooking and for conducting one's personal self-care activities.

85. C: Less reaction by the child to the parents' focus on the child (c) is not a characteristic of this family pattern according to Dr. Bowen's theory. In fact, the opposite is true: Bowen states that the more the parents focus overly on a child with some impairment, the more the child reciprocally focuses on the parents, their expectations, their needs, and their attitudes, and reacts more to these than his or her siblings do. Bowen finds that this reactivity of the child can impede his or her school performance, social relationships, and health. Excessive worry about the child by one or both parents (a) is characteristic of this pattern. Having either an overly idealized view of the child (b) or an overly negative view of the child (d) is also symptomatic of this family relationship pattern.

86. B: The nature and severity of the child's disability (b) is certainly a factor that must be considered, but it is not itself an aspect of family systems or family dynamics. Aspects of family systems and dynamics that professionals should consider to work more effectively with families of children with disabilities include (a) what resources an individual family has at its disposal, (c) the different individual needs of various members of each family, and (d) changes that occur over time and have impacts on the members of the family.

87. D: All of these have been reported by families (d). While some families do report experiencing more stress in the family (a) as a result of having a child with a disability, they also report that having a child with a disability can improve their family dynamics (b) out of the additional effort and family interaction the disability demands. Families also find they respond to a disability by focusing more on the child's positive attributes (c), rather than taking them for granted as they might with a normally achieving child.

88. B: The most appropriate strategy is to (b) schedule inservice training for all general education classroom teachers. This is the most efficient way for the special education teacher to inform all general education teachers of methods and materials for assessing and remediating LDs. Scheduling time to instruct each teacher individually (a) is much more time-consuming for all involved and does not afford the training benefits of asking and having questions answered and sharing input in a group with the information available to all parties. Asking those who know a little about LDs to share with the rest (c) cannot hurt, but it is no substitute for the kind of training an educated and experienced special education teacher can provide. Therefore answer (d), these are all equally indicated, is incorrect.

89. C: You would be most likely to recruit the OT for (c) students who have deficits in fine motor coordination, such as grasping pens, pencils, spoons, or forks; using a computer mouse; and other activities involving manipulating small objects and using the hands and fingers. For students who have difficulty with processing language (a), you would be more likely to recruit the speech-language pathologist. For students who have difficulty with spatial relationships (b), an orientation and mobility specialist is more likely to help. For students who have deficits in gross motor coordination (d), you would want to recruit a physical therapist, who works with using the arms, legs, and body, and with strength and balance.

90. A: It is not correct that special education paraprofessionals only work with special education school staff (a). They may work with any members of the general school staff, if indicated. Special education paraprofessionals also give positive guidance to individual special-needs students in the classroom (b), work with small groups of students in the classroom (c), and record data based on their observations of the behaviors of special education students (d) to support the teacher with this information.

91. C: Both of these are equally important responsibilities (c) for a teacher's aide or teacher's assistant in public schools. Teacher's assistants should be able to focus on individual students and respond to their needs (a) while still being aware of what is going on in the entire classroom (b), since they are often called upon to assist with classroom management, as well as providing more one-on-one interactions with students than the teacher alone can give. Therefore, answer (d), neither one of these, is incorrect.

92. B: It is not accurate that in general, (b) volunteers contribute relatively little time in hours. While it is true that schools rarely record the numbers of hours contributed by volunteers (c), when they do, the amounts of time are impressive. For example, one principal of a small school with 285 elementary-grade students did this by developing a register of volunteers. He found that 75 families totaled 140 hours per week of volunteer work, which equaled 5,600 volunteer hours per school year. An educator/researcher calculated that compared to assistants paid $20.00 per hour, those volunteers saved $112,000 in a school year, so it is true that (a) volunteers can save schools a great deal of money. It has also been pointed out that volunteers can inspire others to follow their examples (d). An educator illustrates this with the story of a parent volunteer who painted a mural, inspiring other artistic parents to paint additional murals, until the school's halls were covered with beautiful, educational paintings.

93. D: They expressed wishes for schools to provide all of these (d) to volunteers. When surveyed, parents and others who volunteer at schools responded that they would like schools to be more businesslike in working with volunteers by providing written job descriptions that include the hours required (a) of them by the schools. They indicated the need for schools to provide clearer, printed or written instructions and training (b) to volunteers. They also expressed a wish for each school to have a volunteer coordinator whom they could contact for help when they encountered problems (c).

94. B: The law that is largely a separate entity is (b) Section 504 of the Rehabilitation Act. This law, passed in 1973, guarantees equal civil rights for persons with disabilities within activities, programs, and

institutions, including schools receiving federal funds. A student need not have an educational disability to receive a "504 plan." Public Law # 94-142 (a), passed in 1975, was the first name for this law giving children with disabilities the right to a free, appropriate public education (FAPE), including special education as needed, and providing for federal funding to meet its requirements. The non-numerical name for Public Law # 94-142 was the Education for All Handicapped Children Act (EHA) (c). EHA was reauthorized in 1986 to include infants and toddlers with disabilities and individual family service plans (IFSPs) and numbered Public Law #99-457. This law was amended in 1997. Due to major changes in focus, it was renamed the Individuals with Disabilities Education Act (IDEA) (d), and reauthorized in 2004 as Public Law # 108-446, still called IDEA.

95. A: The federal law passed earliest of these was (a) the Americans with Disabilities Act (ADA), in 1990. It prohibits discrimination against people with disabilities in jobs, public services, transportation, public accommodations, telecommunications, and miscellaneous provisions. Most schools are included under public accommodations. The Individuals with Disabilities Education Act (IDEA) (b) was enacted in 1997, focusing on equal educational opportunities, transitions, and self-sufficiency for students with disabilities and expanding special education categories. The Elementary and Secondary Education Act (ESEA) (c), more popularly known as No Child Left Behind, was passed in 2001. Its emphasis is on accountability for educational performance of all students, including those with disabilities. The (d) Assistive Technology Act (ATA), or PL #108-364, was passed in 2004, providing loans for buying AT devices and supporting projects for transitions from school to employment.

96. B: It is not true that (b) parents need not be notified in advance of changes in their child's placement. Although Section 504 of the Rehabilitation Act merely stipulates that parents be notified, IDEA includes the additional requirement that parents must be notified of any changes in placement at least 10 days in advance. IDEA also provides that parents must be given an impartial hearing if they disagree (a) with their child's identification, evaluation, or placement. According to IDEA, the student's current placement and IEP will remain in effect until all due process proceedings have been resolved (c). This law also requires parents to give written consent to request a hearing (d) if they disagree with how their child was diagnosed, tested, or placed.

97. A: It is incorrect that (a) Section 504 does not require impartial hearings for parents disputing the school's practices in identifying, evaluating, or placing their child in special education. This law does require they receive impartial hearings, as does IDEA. It is correct that Section 504 differs from IDEA by not requiring parental consent for a hearing to formalize a dispute (b), whereas IDEA does. It is correct that unlike IDEA, which has a "stay-put" provision that the student's current placement and IEP continue to be implemented until all due process proceedings are resolved, Section 504 has no such "stay-put" provision (c). While IDEA provides that an impartial appointee selects the hearing officer (or administrative law judge), Section 504 does not (d); under Section 504 provisions, the school usually appoints the hearing officer.

98. B: Professional development for special education teachers does not include (b) participating in workshops that take one day or a short time. According to the National Association of Special Education Teachers (NASET), one facet of the definition of professional development is pursuing "activities that...are sustained, intensive, and classroom-focused and are not one-day or short-term workshops." This is congruent with the idea of lifelong professional growth and with the definition of professional development under Title IX, Section 9101(34) of the Elementary and Secondary Education Act (ESEA), the No Child Left Behind law. NASET's definition of professional development does include activities that improve teachers' knowledge of academic subjects (a), that improve their skills for classroom management (c), and that teach them more about research-based effective teaching strategies (d).

99. D: All of these are included in NASET's Code of Ethics (d). Principle 5 of this code's six principles states, "NASET members collaborate with parents of children with special needs and community, building trust and respecting confidentiality." The principle's description indicates (a) collaboration of teachers with the students' parents, and #5-B further states, "NASET members partner with parents of children with special needs and other members of the community to enhance programs for children with special needs." The title also indicates (b) collaboration of teachers with community members, and #5-A further specifies, "NASET members cooperate with community agencies in using resources and building comprehensive services in support of children with special needs." Knowing the impact of cultural diversity on individuals (c) is addressed in #5-C, which states, "NASET members understand how cultural diversity, family dynamics, gender, and community shape the lives of the individuals with whom they collaborate."

100. C: It is not true that (c) metacognition is not included in the NASET Code of Ethics' principles. Under Principle 1, #1-C states, "NASET members help children with special needs to value their own identity, learn more about their disabilities, and help them reflect on their own learning and connect it to their life experience." Reflecting on one's own learning is metacognition. It is also true that NASET's code enjoins its members to incorporate academic, social, physical, and psychological aspects of education (a). Under Principle 1, #1-A states, "NASET members promote growth in all students through the integration of academic, psychological, physical, and social learning." It is true that this code addresses special education teachers' being role models (b); under Principle 6, #6-C states, "NASET members recognize that they are role models for children, youth and the public." Likewise, it is true that one of this code's ethical principles involves application of learning to real life (d); as quoted above, #1-C states that members help students with special needs not only reflect upon their learning, but also "connect it to their life experience."

# Secret Key #1 - Time is Your Greatest Enemy

## Pace Yourself

Wear a watch. At the beginning of the test, check the time (or start a chronometer on your watch to count the minutes), and check the time after every few questions to make sure you are "on schedule."

If you are forced to speed up, do it efficiently. Usually one or more answer choices can be eliminated without too much difficulty. Above all, don't panic. Don't speed up and just begin guessing at random choices. By pacing yourself, and continually monitoring your progress against your watch, you will always know exactly how far ahead or behind you are with your available time. If you find that you are one minute behind on the test, don't skip one question without spending any time on it, just to catch back up. Take 15 fewer seconds on the next four questions, and after four questions you'll have caught back up. Once you catch back up, you can continue working each problem at your normal pace.

Furthermore, don't dwell on the problems that you were rushed on. If a problem was taking up too much time and you made a hurried guess, it must be difficult. The difficult questions are the ones you are most likely to miss anyway, so it isn't a big loss. It is better to end with more time than you need than to run out of time.

Lastly, sometimes it is beneficial to slow down if you are constantly getting ahead of time. You are always more likely to catch a careless mistake by working more slowly than quickly, and among very high-scoring test takers (those who are likely to have lots of time left over), careless errors affect the score more than mastery of material.

# Secret Key #2 - Guessing is not Guesswork

You probably know that guessing is a good idea. Unlike other standardized tests, there is no penalty for getting a wrong answer. Even if you have no idea about a question, you still have a 20-25% chance of getting it right.

Most test takers do not understand the impact that proper guessing can have on their score. Unless you score extremely high, guessing will significantly contribute to your final score.

## Monkeys Take the Test

What most test takers don't realize is that to insure that 20-25% chance, you have to guess randomly. If you put 20 monkeys in a room to take this test, assuming they answered once per question and behaved themselves, on average they would get 20-25% of the questions correct. Put 20 test takers in the room, and the average will be much lower among guessed questions. Why?

1. The test writers intentionally write deceptive answer choices that "look" right. A test taker has no idea about a question, so he picks the "best looking" answer, which is often wrong. The monkey has no idea what looks good and what doesn't, so it will consistently be right about 20-25% of the time.

2. Test takers will eliminate answer choices from the guessing pool based on a hunch or intuition. Simple but correct answers often get excluded, leaving a 0% chance of being correct. The monkey has no clue, and often gets lucky with the best choice.

This is why the process of elimination endorsed by most test courses is flawed and detrimental to your performance. Test takers don't guess; they make an ignorant stab in the dark that is usually worse than random.

# $5 Challenge

Let me introduce one of the most valuable ideas of this course—the $5 challenge:

*You only mark your "best guess" if you are willing to bet $5 on it.*
*You only eliminate choices from guessing if you are willing to bet $5 on it.*

Why $5? Five dollars is an amount of money that is small yet not insignificant, and can really add up fast (20 questions could cost you $100). Likewise, each answer choice on one question of the test will have a small impact on your overall score, but it can really add up to a lot of points in the end.

The process of elimination IS valuable. The following shows your chance of guessing it right:

| If you eliminate wrong answer choices until only this many remain: | Chance of getting it correct: |
|---|---|
| 1 | 100% |
| 2 | 50% |
| 3 | 33% |

However, if you accidentally eliminate the right answer or go on a hunch for an incorrect answer, your chances drop dramatically—to 0%. By guessing among all the answer choices, you are GUARANTEED to have a shot at the right answer.

That's why the $5 test is so valuable. If you give up the advantage and safety of a pure guess, it had better be worth the risk.

What we still haven't covered is how to be sure that whatever guess you make is truly random. Here's the easiest way:

*Always pick the first answer choice among those remaining.*

Such a technique means that you have decided, **before you see a single test question**, exactly how you are going to guess, and since the order of choices tells you nothing about which one is correct, this guessing technique is perfectly random.

This section is not meant to scare you away from making educated guesses or eliminating choices; you just need to define when a choice is worth eliminating. The $5 test, along with a pre-defined random guessing strategy, is the best way to make sure you reap all of the benefits of guessing.

# Secret Key #3 - Practice Smarter, Not Harder

Many test takers delay the test preparation process because they dread the awful amounts of practice time they think necessary to succeed on the test. We have refined an effective method that will take you only a fraction of the time.

There are a number of "obstacles" in the path to success. Among these are answering questions, finishing in time, and mastering test-taking strategies. All must be executed on the day of the test at peak performance, or your score will suffer. The test is a mental marathon that has a large impact on your future.

Just like a marathon runner, it is important to work your way up to the full challenge. So first you just worry about questions, and then time, and finally strategy:

## Success Strategy

1. Find a good source for practice tests.
2. If you are willing to make a larger time investment, consider using more than one study guide. Often the different approaches of multiple authors will help you "get" difficult concepts.
3. Take a practice test with no time constraints, with all study helps, "open book." Take your time with questions and focus on applying strategies.
4. Take a practice test with time constraints, with all guides, "open book."
5. Take a final practice test without open material and with time limits.

If you have time to take more practice tests, just repeat step 5. By gradually exposing yourself to the full rigors of the test environment, you will condition your mind to the stress of test day and maximize your success.

# Secret Key #4 - Prepare, Don't Procrastinate

Let me state an obvious fact: if you take the test three times, you will probably get three different scores. This is due to the way you feel on test day, the level of preparedness you have, and the version of the test you see. Despite the test writers' claims to the contrary, some versions of the test WILL be easier for you than others.

Since your future depends so much on your score, you should maximize your chances of success. In order to maximize the likelihood of success, you've got to prepare in advance. This means taking practice tests and spending time learning the information and test taking strategies you will need to succeed.

Never go take the actual test as a "practice" test, expecting that you can just take it again if you need to. Take all the practice tests you can on your own, but when you go to take the official test, be prepared, be focused, and do your best the first time!

# Secret Key #5 - Test Yourself

Everyone knows that time is money. There is no need to spend too much of your time or too little of your time preparing for the test. You should only spend as much of your precious time preparing as is necessary for you to get the score you need.

Once you have taken a practice test under real conditions of time constraints, then you will know if you are ready for the test or not.

If you have scored extremely high the first time that you take the practice test, then there is not much point in spending countless hours studying. You are already there.

Benchmark your abilities by retaking practice tests and seeing how much you have improved. Once you consistently score high enough to guarantee success, then you are ready.

If you have scored well below where you need, then knuckle down and begin studying in earnest. Check your improvement regularly through the use of practice tests under real conditions. Above all, don't worry, panic, or give up. The key is perseverance!

Then, when you go to take the test, remain confident and remember how well you did on the practice tests. If you can score high enough on a practice test, then you can do the same on the real thing.

# General Strategies

The most important thing you can do is to ignore your fears and jump into the test immediately. Do not be overwhelmed by any strange-sounding terms. You have to jump into the test like jumping into a pool—all at once is the easiest way.

## Make Predictions

As you read and understand the question, try to guess what the answer will be. Remember that several of the answer choices are wrong, and once you begin reading them, your mind will immediately become cluttered with answer choices designed to throw you off. Your mind is typically the most focused immediately after you have read the question and digested its contents. If you can, try to predict what the correct answer will be. You may be surprised at what you can predict.

Quickly scan the choices and see if your prediction is in the listed answer choices. If it is, then you can be quite confident that you have the right answer. It still won't hurt to check the other answer choices, but most of the time, you've got it!

## Answer the Question

It may seem obvious to only pick answer choices that answer the question, but the test writers can create some excellent answer choices that are wrong. Don't pick an answer just because it sounds right, or you believe it to be true. It MUST answer the question. Once you've made your selection, always go back and check it against the question and make sure that you didn't misread the question and that the answer choice does answer the question posed.

## Benchmark

After you read the first answer choice, decide if you think it sounds correct or not. If it doesn't, move on to the next answer choice. If it does, mentally mark that answer choice. This doesn't mean that you've definitely selected it as your answer choice, it just means that it's the best you've seen thus far. Go ahead and read the next choice. If the next choice is worse than the one you've already selected, keep going to the next answer choice. If the next choice is better than the choice you've already selected, mentally mark the new answer choice as your best guess.

The first answer choice that you select becomes your standard. Every other answer choice must be benchmarked against that standard. That choice is correct until proven otherwise by another answer choice beating it out. Once you've decided that no other answer choice seems as good, do one final check to ensure that your answer choice answers the question posed.

## Valid Information

Don't discount any of the information provided in the question. Every piece of information may be necessary to determine the correct answer. None of the information in the question is there to throw you off (while the answer choices will certainly have information to throw you off). If two seemingly unrelated topics are discussed, don't ignore either. You can be confident there is a relationship, or it wouldn't be included in the question, and you are probably going to have to determine what is that relationship to find the answer.

## Avoid "Fact Traps"

Don't get distracted by a choice that is factually true. Your search is for the answer that answers the question. Stay focused and don't fall for an answer that is true but irrelevant. Always go back to the question and make sure you're choosing an answer that actually answers the question and is not just a true statement. An answer can be factually correct, but it MUST answer the question asked. Additionally, two answers can both be seemingly correct, so be sure to read all of the answer choices, and make sure that you get the one that BEST answers the question.

## Milk the Question

Some of the questions may throw you completely off. They might deal with a subject you have not been exposed to, or one that you haven't reviewed in years. While your lack of knowledge about the subject will be a hindrance, the question itself can give you many clues that will help you find the correct answer. Read the question carefully and look for clues. Watch particularly for adjectives and nouns describing difficult terms or words that you don't recognize. Regardless of whether you completely understand a word or not, replacing it with a synonym, either provided or one you more familiar with, may help you to understand what the questions are asking. Rather than wracking your mind about specific detailed information concerning a difficult term or word, try to use mental substitutes that are easier to understand.

## The Trap of Familiarity

Don't just choose a word because you recognize it. On difficult questions, you may not recognize a number of words in the answer choices. The test writers don't put "make-believe" words on the test, so don't think that just because you only recognize all the words in one answer choice that that answer choice must be correct. If you only recognize words in one answer choice, then focus on that one. Is it correct? Try your best to determine if it is correct. If it is, that's great. If not, eliminate it. Each word and answer choice you eliminate increases your chances of getting the question correct, even if you then have to guess among the unfamiliar choices.

## Eliminate Answers

Eliminate choices as soon as you realize they are wrong. But be careful! Make sure you consider all of the possible answer choices. Just because one appears right, doesn't mean that the next one won't be even better! The test writers will usually put more than one good answer choice for every question, so read all of them. Don't worry if you are stuck between two that seem right. By getting down to just two remaining possible choices, your odds are now 50/50. Rather than wasting too much time, play the odds. You are guessing, but guessing wisely because you've been able to knock out some of the answer choices that you know are wrong. If you are eliminating choices and realize that the last answer choice you are left with is also obviously wrong, don't panic. Start over and consider each choice again. There may easily be something that you missed the first time and will realize on the second pass.

## Tough Questions

If you are stumped on a problem or it appears too hard or too difficult, don't waste time. Move on! Remember though, if you can quickly check for obviously incorrect answer choices, your chances of guessing correctly are greatly improved. Before you completely give up, at least try to knock out a couple of possible answers. Eliminate what you can and then guess at the remaining answer choices before moving on.

## Brainstorm

If you get stuck on a difficult question, spend a few seconds quickly brainstorming. Run through the complete list of possible answer choices. Look at each choice and ask yourself, "Could this answer the question satisfactorily?" Go through each answer choice and consider it independently of the others. By systematically going through all possibilities, you may find something that you would otherwise overlook. Remember though that when you get stuck, it's important to try to keep moving.

## Read Carefully

Understand the problem. Read the question and answer choices carefully. Don't miss the question because you misread the terms. You have plenty of time to read each question thoroughly and make sure you understand what is being asked. Yet a happy medium must be attained, so don't waste too much time. You must read carefully, but efficiently.

## Face Value

When in doubt, use common sense. Always accept the situation in the problem at face value. Don't read too much into it. These problems will not require you to make huge leaps of logic. The test writers aren't trying to throw you off with a cheap trick. If you have to go beyond creativity and make a leap of logic in order to have an answer choice answer the question, then you should look at the other answer choices. Don't overcomplicate the problem by creating theoretical relationships or explanations that will warp time or space. These are normal problems rooted in reality. It's just that the applicable relationship or explanation may not be readily apparent and you have to figure things out. Use your common sense to interpret anything that isn't clear.

## Prefixes

If you're having trouble with a word in the question or answer choices, try dissecting it. Take advantage of every clue that the word might include. Prefixes and suffixes can be a huge help. Usually they allow you to determine a basic meaning. Pre- means before, post- means after, pro - is positive, de- is negative. From these prefixes and suffixes, you can get an idea of the general meaning of the word and try to put it into context. Beware though of any traps. Just because con- is the opposite of pro-, doesn't necessarily mean congress is the opposite of progress!

## Hedge Phrases

Watch out for critical hedge phrases, led off with words such as "likely," "may," "can," "sometimes," "often," "almost," "mostly," "usually," "generally," "rarely," and "sometimes." Question writers insert these hedge phrases to cover every possibility. Often an answer choice will be wrong simply because it leaves no room for exception. Unless the situation calls for them, avoid answer choices that have definitive words like "exactly," and "always."

## Switchback Words

Stay alert for "switchbacks." These are the words and phrases frequently used to alert you to shifts in thought. The most common switchback word is "but." Others include "although," "however," "nevertheless," "on the other hand," "even though," "while," "in spite of," "despite," and "regardless of."

## New Information

Correct answer choices will rarely have completely new information included. Answer choices typically are straightforward reflections of the material asked about and will directly relate to the question. If a new piece of information is included in an answer choice that doesn't even seem to relate to the topic being asked about, then that answer choice is likely incorrect. All of the information needed to answer the question is usually provided for you in the question. You should not have to make guesses that are unsupported or choose answer choices that require unknown information that cannot be reasoned from what is given.

## Time Management

On technical questions, don't get lost on the technical terms. Don't spend too much time on any one question. If you don't know what a term means, then odds are you aren't going to get much further since you don't have a dictionary. You should be able to immediately recognize whether or not you know a term. If you don't, work with the other clues that you have—the other answer choices and terms provided—but don't waste too much time trying to figure out a difficult term that you don't know.

## Contextual Clues

Look for contextual clues. An answer can be right but not the correct answer. The contextual clues will help you find the answer that is most right and is correct. Understand the context in which a phrase or statement is made. This will help you make important distinctions.

## Don't Panic

Panicking will not answer any questions for you; therefore, it isn't helpful. When you first see the question, if your mind goes blank, take a deep breath. Force yourself to mechanically go through the steps of solving the problem using the strategies you've learned.

## Pace Yourself

Don't get clock fever. It's easy to be overwhelmed when you're looking at a page full of questions, your mind is full of random thoughts and feeling confused, and the clock is ticking down faster than you would like. Calm down and maintain the pace that you have set for yourself. As long as you are on track by monitoring your pace, you are guaranteed to have enough time for yourself. When you get to the last few minutes of the test, it may seem like you won't have enough time left, but if you only have as many questions as you should have left at that point, then you're right on track!

## Answer Selection

The best way to pick an answer choice is to eliminate all of those that are wrong, until only one is left and confirm that is the correct answer. Sometimes though, an answer choice may immediately look right. Be careful! Take a second to make sure that the other choices are not equally obvious. Don't make a hasty mistake. There are only two times that you should stop before checking other answers. First is when you are positive that the answer choice you have selected is correct. Second is when time is almost out and you have to make a quick guess!

## Check Your Work

Since you will probably not know every term listed and the answer to every question, it is important that you get credit for the ones that you do know. Don't miss any questions through careless mistakes. If at all possible, try to take a second to look back over your answer selection and make sure you've selected the correct answer choice and haven't made a costly careless mistake (such as marking an answer choice that you didn't mean to mark). The time it takes for this quick double check should more than pay for itself in caught mistakes.

## Beware of Directly Quoted Answers

Sometimes an answer choice will repeat word for word a portion of the question or reference section. However, beware of such exact duplication. It may be a trap! More than likely, the correct choice will paraphrase or summarize a point, rather than being exactly the same wording.

## Slang

Scientific sounding answers are better than slang ones. An answer choice that begins "To compare the outcomes..." is much more likely to be correct than one that begins "Because some people insisted..."

## Extreme Statements

Avoid wild answers that throw out highly controversial ideas that are proclaimed as established fact. An answer choice that states the "process should used in certain situations, if..." is much more likely to be correct than one that states the "process should be discontinued completely." The first is a calm rational statement and doesn't even make a definitive, uncompromising stance, using a hedge word "if" to provide wiggle room, whereas the second choice is a radical idea and far more extreme.

## Answer Choice Families

When you have two or more answer choices that are direct opposites or parallels, one of them is usually the correct answer. For instance, if one answer choice states "x increases" and another answer choice states "x decreases" or "y increases," then those two or three answer choices are very similar in construction and fall into the same family of answer choices. A family of answer choices consists of two or three answer choices, very similar in construction, but often with directly opposite meanings. Usually the correct answer choice will be in that family of answer choices. The "odd man out" or answer choice that doesn't seem to fit the parallel construction of the other answer choices is more likely to be incorrect.

# Special Report: How to Overcome Test Anxiety

The very nature of tests caters to some level of anxiety, nervousness, or tension, just as we feel for any important event that occurs in our lives. A little bit of anxiety or nervousness can be a good thing. It helps us with motivation, and makes achievement just that much sweeter. However, too much anxiety can be a problem, especially if it hinders our ability to function and perform.

"Test anxiety," is the term that refers to the emotional reactions that some test-takers experience when faced with a test or exam. Having a fear of testing and exams is based upon a rational fear, since the test-taker's performance can shape the course of an academic career. Nevertheless, experiencing excessive fear of examinations will only interfere with the test-taker's ability to perform and chance to be successful.

There are a large variety of causes that can contribute to the development and sensation of test anxiety. These include, but are not limited to, lack of preparation and worrying about issues surrounding the test.

## Lack of Preparation

Lack of preparation can be identified by the following behaviors or situations:

Not scheduling enough time to study, and therefore cramming the night before the test or exam
Managing time poorly, to create the sensation that there is not enough time to do everything
Failing to organize the text information in advance, so that the study material consists of the entire text and not simply the pertinent information
Poor overall studying habits

Worrying, on the other hand, can be related to both the test taker, or many other factors around him/her that will be affected by the results of the test. These include worrying about:

Previous performances on similar exams, or exams in general
How friends and other students are achieving
The negative consequences that will result from a poor grade or failure

There are three primary elements to test anxiety. Physical components, which involve the same typical bodily reactions as those to acute anxiety (to be discussed below). Emotional factors have to do with fear or panic. Mental or cognitive issues concerning attention spans and memory abilities.

## Physical Signals

There are many different symptoms of test anxiety, and these are not limited to mental and emotional strain. Frequently there are a range of physical signals that will let a test taker know that he/she is suffering from test anxiety. These bodily changes can include the following:

Perspiring
Sweaty palms

Wet, trembling hands
Nausea
Dry mouth
A knot in the stomach
Headache
Faintness
Muscle tension
Aching shoulders, back and neck
Rapid heart beat
Feeling too hot/cold

To recognize the sensation of test anxiety, a test-taker should monitor him/herself for the following sensations:

The physical distress symptoms as listed above
Emotional sensitivity, expressing emotional feelings such as the need to cry or laugh too much, or a sensation of anger or helplessness
A decreased ability to think, causing the test-taker to blank out or have racing thoughts that are hard to organize or control.

Though most students will feel some level of anxiety when faced with a test or exam, the majority can cope with that anxiety and maintain it at a manageable level. However, those who cannot are faced with a very real and very serious condition, which can and should be controlled for the immeasurable benefit of this sufferer.

Naturally, these sensations lead to negative results for the testing experience. The most common effects of test anxiety have to do with nervousness and mental blocking.

## Nervousness

Nervousness can appear in several different levels:

The test-taker's difficulty, or even inability to read and understand the questions on the test
The difficulty or inability to organize thoughts to a coherent form
The difficulty or inability to recall key words and concepts relating to the testing questions (especially essays)
The receipt of poor grades on a test, though the test material was well known by the test taker

Conversely, a person may also experience mental blocking, which involves:

Blanking out on test questions
Only remembering the correct answers to the questions when the test has already finished.

Fortunately for test anxiety sufferers, beating these feelings, to a large degree, has to do with proper preparation. When a test taker has a feeling of preparedness, then anxiety will be dramatically lessened.

The first step to resolving anxiety issues is to distinguish which of the two types of anxiety are being suffered. If the anxiety is a direct result of a lack of preparation, this should be considered a normal reaction, and the anxiety level (as opposed to the test results) shouldn't be anything to worry about. However, if, when adequately prepared, the test-taker still panics, blanks out, or seems to overreact, this is not a fully rational reaction. While this can be considered normal too, there are many ways to combat and overcome these effects.

Remember that anxiety cannot be entirely eliminated, however, there are ways to minimize it, to make the anxiety easier to manage. Preparation is one of the best ways to minimize test anxiety. Therefore the following techniques are wise in order to best fight off any anxiety that may want to build.

To begin with, try to avoid cramming before a test, whenever it is possible. By trying to memorize an entire term's worth of information in one day, you'll be shocking your system, and not giving yourself a very good chance to absorb the information. This is an easy path to anxiety, so for those who suffer from test anxiety, cramming should not even be considered an option.

Instead of cramming, work throughout the semester to combine all of the material which is presented throughout the semester, and work on it gradually as the course goes by, making sure to master the main concepts first, leaving minor details for a week or so before the test.

To study for the upcoming exam, be sure to pose questions that may be on the examination, to gauge the ability to answer them by integrating the ideas from your texts, notes and lectures, as well as any supplementary readings.

If it is truly impossible to cover all of the information that was covered in that particular term, concentrate on the most important portions, that can be covered very well. Learn these concepts as best as possible, so that when the test comes, a goal can be made to use these concepts as presentations of your knowledge.

In addition to study habits, changes in attitude are critical to beating a struggle with test anxiety. In fact, an improvement of the perspective over the entire test-taking experience can actually help a test taker to enjoy studying and therefore improve the overall experience. Be certain not to overemphasize the significance of the grade - know that the result of the test is neither a reflection of self worth, nor is it a measure of intelligence; one grade will not predict a person's future success.

To improve an overall testing outlook, the following steps should be tried:

Keeping in mind that the most reasonable expectation for taking a test is to expect to try to demonstrate as much of what you know as you possibly can.
Reminding ourselves that a test is only one test; this is not the only one, and there will be others.
The thought of thinking of oneself in an irrational, all-or-nothing term should be avoided at all costs.
A reward should be designated for after the test, so there's something to look forward to. Whether it be going to a movie, going out to eat, or simply visiting friends, schedule it in advance, and do it no matter what result is expected on the exam.

Test-takers should also keep in mind that the basics are some of the most important things, even beyond anti-anxiety techniques and studying. Never neglect the basic social, emotional and biological needs, in order to try to absorb information. In order to best achieve, these three factors must be held as just as important as the studying itself.

# Study Steps

Remember the following important steps for studying:

Maintain healthy nutrition and exercise habits. Continue both your recreational activities and social pass times. These both contribute to your physical and emotional well being.
Be certain to get a good amount of sleep, especially the night before the test, because when you're overtired you are not able to perform to the best of your best ability.
Keep the studying pace to a moderate level by taking breaks when they are needed, and varying the work whenever possible, to keep the mind fresh instead of getting bored.
When enough studying has been done that all the material that can be learned has been learned, and the test taker is prepared for the test, stop studying and do something relaxing such as listening to music, watching a movie, or taking a warm bubble bath.

There are also many other techniques to minimize the uneasiness or apprehension that is experienced along with test anxiety before, during, or even after the examination. In fact, there are a great deal of things that can be done to stop anxiety from interfering with lifestyle and performance. Again, remember that anxiety will not be eliminated entirely, and it shouldn't be. Otherwise that "up" feeling for exams would not exist, and most of us depend on that sensation to perform better than usual. However, this anxiety has to be at a level that is manageable.

Of course, as we have just discussed, being prepared for the exam is half the battle right away. Attending all classes, finding out what knowledge will be expected on the exam, and knowing the exam schedules are easy steps to lowering anxiety. Keeping up with work will remove the need to cram, and efficient study habits will eliminate wasted time. Studying should be done in an ideal location for concentration, so that it is simple to become interested in the material and give it complete attention. A method such as SQ3R (Survey, Question, Read, Recite, Review) is a wonderful key to follow to make sure that the study habits are as effective as possible, especially in the case of learning from a textbook. Flashcards are great techniques for memorization. Learning to take good notes will mean that notes will be full of useful information, so that less sifting will need to be done to seek out what is pertinent for studying. Reviewing notes after class and then again on occasion will keep the information fresh in the mind. From notes that have been taken summary sheets and outlines can be made for simpler reviewing.

A study group can also be a very motivational and helpful place to study, as there will be a sharing of ideas, all of the minds can work together, to make sure that everyone understands, and the studying will be made more interesting because it will be a social occasion.

Basically, though, as long as the test-taker remains organized and self confident, with efficient study habits, less time will need to be spent studying, and higher grades will be achieved.

To become self confident, there are many useful steps. The first of these is "self talk." It has been shown through extensive research, that self-talk for students who suffer from test anxiety, should be well monitored, in order to make sure that it contributes to self confidence as opposed to sinking the student. Frequently the self talk of test-anxious students is negative or self-defeating, thinking that everyone else is smarter and faster, that they always mess up, and that if they don't do well, they'll fail the entire course. It is important to decreasing anxiety that awareness is made of self talk. Try writing any negative self thoughts and then disputing them with a positive statement instead. Begin self-encouragement as though it was a friend speaking. Repeat positive statements to help reprogram the mind to believing in successes instead of failures.

# Helpful Techniques

Other extremely helpful techniques include:

Self-visualization of doing well and reaching goals
While aiming for an "A" level of understanding, don't try to "overprotect" by setting your expectations lower. This will only convince the mind to stop studying in order to meet the lower expectations. Don't make comparisons with the results or habits of other students. These are individual factors, and different things work for different people, causing different results.
Strive to become an expert in learning what works well, and what can be done in order to improve. Consider collecting this data in a journal.
Create rewards for after studying instead of doing things before studying that will only turn into avoidance behaviors.
Make a practice of relaxing - by using methods such as progressive relaxation, self-hypnosis, guided imagery, etc - in order to make relaxation an automatic sensation.
Work on creating a state of relaxed concentration so that concentrating will take on the focus of the mind, so that none will be wasted on worrying.
Take good care of the physical self by eating well and getting enough sleep.
Plan in time for exercise and stick to this plan.

Beyond these techniques, there are other methods to be used before, during and after the test that will help the test-taker perform well in addition to overcoming anxiety.

Before the exam comes the academic preparation. This involves establishing a study schedule and beginning at least one week before the actual date of the test. By doing this, the anxiety of not having enough time to study for the test will be automatically eliminated. Moreover, this will make the studying a much more effective experience, ensuring that the learning will be an easier process. This relieves much undue pressure on the test-taker.

Summary sheets, note cards, and flash cards with the main concepts and examples of these main concepts should be prepared in advance of the actual studying time. A topic should never be eliminated from this process. By omitting a topic because it isn't expected to be on the test is only setting up the test-taker for anxiety should it actually appear on the exam. Utilize the course syllabus for laying out the topics that should be studied. Carefully go over the notes that were made in class, paying special attention to any of the issues that the professor took special care to emphasize while lecturing in class. In the textbooks, use the chapter review, or if possible, the chapter tests, to begin your review.

It may even be possible to ask the instructor what information will be covered on the exam, or what the format of the exam will be (for example, multiple choice, essay, free form, true-false). Additionally, see if it is possible to find out how many questions will be on the test. If a review sheet or sample test has been offered by the professor, make good use of it, above anything else, for the preparation for the test. Another great resource for getting to know the examination is reviewing tests from previous semesters. Use these tests to review, and aim to achieve a 100% score on each of the possible topics. With a few exceptions, the goal that you set for yourself is the highest one that you will reach.

Take all of the questions that were assigned as homework, and rework them to any other possible course material. The more problems reworked, the more skill and confidence will form as a result. When forming the solution to a problem, write out each of the steps. Don't simply do head work. By doing as many steps on paper as possible, much clarification and therefore confidence will be formed. Do this with as many homework problems as possible, before checking the answers. By checking the answer after each problem, a reinforcement will exist, that will not be on the exam. Study situations should be as exam-like as possible, to prime the test-taker's system for the experience. By waiting to check the answers at the end, a psychological advantage will be formed, to decrease the stress factor.

Another fantastic reason for not cramming is the avoidance of confusion in concepts, especially when it comes to mathematics. 8-10 hours of study will become one hundred percent more effective if it is spread out over a week or at least several days, instead of doing it all in one sitting. Recognize that the human brain requires time in order to assimilate new material, so frequent breaks and a span of study time over several days will be much more beneficial.

Additionally, don't study right up until the point of the exam. Studying should stop a minimum of one hour before the exam begins. This allows the brain to rest and put things in their proper order. This will also provide the time to become as relaxed as possible when going into the examination room. The test-taker will also have time to eat well and eat sensibly. Know that the brain needs food as much as the rest of the body. With enough food and enough sleep, as well as a relaxed attitude, the body and the mind are primed for success.

Avoid any anxious classmates who are talking about the exam. These students only spread anxiety, and are not worth sharing the anxious sentimentalities.

Before the test also involves creating a positive attitude, so mental preparation should also be a point of concentration. There are many keys to creating a positive attitude. Should fears become rushing in, make a visualization of taking the exam, doing well, and seeing an A written on the paper. Write out a list of affirmations that will bring a feeling of confidence, such as "I am doing well in my English class," "I studied well and know my material," "I enjoy this class." Even if the affirmations aren't believed at first, it sends a positive message to the subconscious which will result in an alteration of the overall belief system, which is the system that creates reality.

If a sensation of panic begins, work with the fear and imagine the very worst! Work through the entire scenario of not passing the test, failing the entire course, and dropping out of school, followed by not getting a job, and pushing a shopping cart through the dark alley where you'll live. This will place things into perspective! Then, practice deep breathing and create a visualization of the opposite situation - achieving an "A" on the exam, passing the entire course, receiving the degree at a graduation ceremony.

On the day of the test, there are many things to be done to ensure the best results, as well as the most calm outlook. The following stages are suggested in order to maximize test-taking potential:

Begin the examination day with a moderate breakfast, and avoid any coffee or beverages with caffeine if the test taker is prone to jitters. Even people who are used to managing caffeine can feel jittery or light-headed when it is taken on a test day.
Attempt to do something that is relaxing before the examination begins. As last minute cramming clouds the mastering of overall concepts, it is better to use this time to create a calming outlook.
Be certain to arrive at the test location well in advance, in order to provide time to select a location that is away from doors, windows and other distractions, as well as giving enough time to relax before the test begins.
Keep away from anxiety generating classmates who will upset the sensation of stability and relaxation that is being attempted before the exam.

Should the waiting period before the exam begins cause anxiety, create a self-distraction by reading a light magazine or something else that is relaxing and simple.

During the exam itself, read the entire exam from beginning to end, and find out how much time should be allotted to each individual problem. Once writing the exam, should more time be taken for a problem, it should be abandoned, in order to begin another problem. If there is time at the end, the unfinished problem can always be returned to and completed.

Read the instructions very carefully - twice - so that unpleasant surprises won't follow during or after the exam has ended.

When writing the exam, pretend that the situation is actually simply the completion of homework within a library, or at home. This will assist in forming a relaxed atmosphere, and will allow the brain extra focus for the complex thinking function.

Begin the exam with all of the questions with which the most confidence is felt. This will build the confidence level regarding the entire exam and will begin a quality momentum. This will also create encouragement for trying the problems where uncertainty resides.

Going with the "gut instinct" is always the way to go when solving a problem. Second guessing should be avoided at all costs. Have confidence in the ability to do well.

For essay questions, create an outline in advance that will keep the mind organized and make certain that all of the points are remembered. For multiple choice, read every answer, even if the correct one has been spotted - a better one may exist.

Continue at a pace that is reasonable and not rushed, in order to be able to work carefully. Provide enough time to go over the answers at the end, to check for small errors that can be corrected.

Should a feeling of panic begin, breathe deeply, and think of the feeling of the body releasing sand through its pores. Visualize a calm, peaceful place, and include all of the sights, sounds and sensations of this image. Continue the deep breathing, and take a few minutes to continue this with closed eyes. When all is well again, return to the test.

If a "blanking" occurs for a certain question, skip it and move on to the next question. There will be time to return to the other question later. Get everything done that can be done, first, to guarantee all the grades that can be compiled, and to build all of the confidence possible. Then return to the weaker questions to build the marks from there.

Remember, one's own reality can be created, so as long as the belief is there, success will follow. And remember: anxiety can happen later, right now, there's an exam to be written!

After the examination is complete, whether there is a feeling for a good grade or a bad grade, don't dwell on the exam, and be certain to follow through on the reward that was promised...and enjoy it! Don't dwell on any mistakes that have been made, as there is nothing that can be done at this point anyway.

Additionally, don't begin to study for the next test right away. Do something relaxing for a while, and let the mind relax and prepare itself to begin absorbing information again.

From the results of the exam - both the grade and the entire experience, be certain to learn from what has gone on. Perfect studying habits and work some more on confidence in order to make the next examination experience even better than the last one.

Learn to avoid places where openings occurred for laziness, procrastination and day dreaming.

Use the time between this exam and the next one to better learn to relax, even learning to relax on cue, so that any anxiety can be controlled during the next exam. Learn how to relax the body. Slouch in your chair if that helps. Tighten and then relax all of the different muscle groups, one group at a time, beginning with the feet and then working all the way up to the neck and face. This will ultimately relax the muscles more than they were to begin with. Learn how to breathe deeply and comfortably, and focus on this breathing going in and out as a relaxing thought. With every exhale, repeat the word "relax."

As common as test anxiety is, it is very possible to overcome it. Make yourself one of the test-takers who overcome this frustrating hindrance.

# Additional Bonus Material

Due to our efforts to try to keep this book to a manageable length, we've created a link that will give you access to all of your additional bonus material.

Please visit http://www.mometrix.com/bonus948/mttclearndis to access the information.